En*cycle*opedia

The international guide to alternatives in cycling

On a bicycle we approach perfection; we travel swiftly, silently and efficiently, enjoying our surroundings without endangering them, on a machine that can be enjoyed by young and old, rich or poor. The machine can be made in huge factories by multinational companies or in small workshops, by inspired enthusiasts and craftsmen, on automated productions lines or handbuilt to order. Such varied conditions produce an enormous choice for the individual cyclist.

Encycleopedia celebrates this choice. Our aim is to delight you with machines that you might have never seen outside these pages, but which are commercially available. Use Encycleopedia to acquire the vehicle which is perfect for you, your family or your business and to equip your cycle to meet your individual needs. Conformity and narrow vision are holding back the development of cycling worldwide. We hope that there are ideas in this book which will help make a difference.

The Overlook Press
Woodstock & New York

Encycleopedia

©1999 Alan Davidson and Jim McGurn. This is the fifth edition.
Encycleopedia was first published in Great Britain in October 1993 by
Open Road Ltd, The Danesmead Wing, 33 Fulford Cross, York, YO10 4PB
Tel: +44 1904 654654 Fax: +44 1904 654684
Email: peter@bcqedit.demon.co.uk Website: http://bikeculture.com/

Published in the UK, in English and German versions, by Open Road Ltd, and distributed
by subscription and through cycle stores worldwide by them and their agents.

First published in the USA in 1998 by
The Overlook Press, Peter Mayer Publishers Inc,
Lewis Hollow Road, Woodstock, New York, 12498
Encyclopedia is distributed by the Overlook Press and
their agents through bookstores worldwide

A CIP Cataloging-in-Publication Data for this book is available from
The Library of Congress.

Open Road Edition ISBN: 1898457 04 2
Overlook Press Edition ISBN: 0 87951 884-7

Open Road, publishers of Encycleopedia, also publish Bike Culture Quarterly
and Bycycle magazine. Encycleopedia and Bike Culture Quarterly are also published
in the German language. Open Road is a small company, dedicated to promoting
cycling worldwide, and is supported by over 200 cyclist shareholders.
Address for worldwide (including UK) subscriptions/ordering enquiries,
except from countries mentioned separately below:

United Kingdom (non-bookshop orders)
Open Road Mail Order, Unit 1, East Riding Business Centre,
Annie Reed Road, Beverley, East Yorkshire, HU17 0LF, UK
Tel: +44 1482 88 03 99 Email: openroad@nite-direct.demon.co.uk

North America and Canada
To order additional copies of this book, contact
The Overlook Press, 2568 Route 212, Woodstock, New York, 12498
Tel: (914) 679-6838 Fax: (914) 679-8571

For back numbers and other merchandise, and for bike stores orders, contact
George Otto Jnr, Open Road USA, 104 S. Michigan Avenue,
Suite 1500, Chicago, IL 60603, USA.
Tel: +1 312 201 0101 Fax: +1 312 201 0214 Email: lai@lai.org

Germany, Austria, Switzerland
Kalle Kalkhoff, KGB, Donnerschweerstr. 45, 26123 Oldenburg
Tel: +49 441 8850389 Fax: +49 441 8850388

Australia
Ian Sims, Greenspeed, 69 Mountain Gate Drive, Ferntree Gully, VIC 3156
Tel: +61 3 9758 5541 Fax: +61 3 9752 4115 Email: ian@greenspeed.com.au

New Zealand
Cycle Works, PO Box 33051, Christchurch
Tel: +64 3 338 6803 Fax: +64 3 338 6231 Email: bikes@tpnet.co.nz

Netherlands
Luud Steenbergen, Trapperkracht, Soerabayastr. 4, 3531 EB, Utrecht
Tel/Fax: +31 30 296 1015

Conceived, compiled, edited and produced by
Alan Davidson and Jim McGurn

Editor in Chief: Jim McGurn
Editorial Director: Peter Eland
Editorial team: Jim McGurn, Peter Eland, Edgar Newton, Steve McKay, Tim Kirk
Commercial Direction: Alan Davidson
Art Director: Brian Holt
Additional Design: Jeffreys Design, S+L Designs,
Alison Brownbridge, Alan Scaife.
Product care and assembly: Mike West
Studio Photography: Paul Batty, 6 Derwent Park, Wheldrake, York, YO4 6AT, UK
Tel/Fax: +44 1904 448 663.
Additional Photography: Jason Patient and Sue Darlow

Video
Camera Work: Amy Davidson, Alan Davidson
Editor: Amy Davidson
Producer: Alan Davidson

Encycleopedia was printed by William Gibbons & Sons Ltd, PO Box 103,
26 Planetary Road, Willenhall, West Midlands, WV13 3XT

Translated into German by Annette Marti, Miriam Steinmann and
Angelika Schneider. German to English translations by Peter Eland

Encycleopedia 99: The Guide to Alternatives in Cycling

RRP: UK £12, USA $19.95, Germany DM 35

How to use
Encycleopedia

Welcome to Encycleopedia

This is a rather unusual book, so please take a few
moments to read these pages before going any
further. We hope it'll put the book in context, and
give you some idea about why we went to all this
trouble.

What's it all about?

Encycleopedia is a platform for imaginative
inventors, designers and engineers who are trying
to change the world for the better by offering
real practical transport alternatives. By bringing
them all together in one book we provide them
and their ideas with credibility and status. We also
hope it's a fascinating read for everyone out there
who cares, and who might one day need one of
these marvellous products in their own lives.

Behind it all is our conviction that pedal-power
has an enormous contribution to make in bringing
this planet back from the brink towards a more
human-scale, sustainable future. Cycling harms
no-one and benefits everyone. Human-powered
transport is more than getting from A to B: it's a
way of life and a state of mind.

Who's behind Encycleopedia?

Our firm is called Open Road. We're a bunch of bike
fans based in York, England, although our agents
and correspondents are scattered around the world.
We're supported by a broad base of reader-
shareholders. Encycleopedia is also published in a
full German-language edition.

Do manufacturers pay for space in Encycleopedia?

Yes, although neither we nor they see it as
advertising. They take part by invitation only. We
write the text for each entry, in consultation with
the manufacturer, and we design the pages. The
fee (which we keep deliberately low to give
smaller manufacturers the chance to take part)
just covers our costs: as well as the editorial work
there is photography, video filming, translation and
co-ordinating the manufacturers' sales information
to hundreds of Encycleopedia-affiliated cycle shops
around the world.

Getting hold of the products

Your first port of call should be one of the affiliated bike shops listed towards the end of this Encycleopedia. We believe strongly that a good network of specialised, local bike shops is vitally important for the future of cycling. Please do support your local bike shop, even if it does sometimes cost a little bit more than mail-order.

You may strike it lucky and find that they have the product you're looking for in stock, but it's more likely that the dealer will have to source it for you. We provide all of our affiliated shops with ordering information about each of the products in Encycleopedia. It may be, though, that for a variety of reasons they're unable or unwilling to get hold of the product without a firm order. In such cases you should approach the manufacturer directly.

In some cases the manufacturer only ever sells direct. We explain things on the page itself and give you, where relevant, the details of the company. If they have agents or distributors in other countries, we've indicated that as well – and contact addresses for these countries are listed on page 145. It's a good idea, when you contact manufacturers or shops, to let them know that you saw their product in Encycleopedia.

Incidentally, some of the more specialised shops may run hire services, so that you can try out some of the bikes before you decide to buy. Ask the shops directly.

What will the products cost?

It's very difficult to give an idea of the price of a product beyond its country of origin. Not only is it expensive to send bicycles around the world, but insurance, import duties, local taxes and the overheads involved all mean that you can expect to pay significantly more outside the country of origin – often twice as much if the product comes from another continent.

For this reason, we've given the price of products in the country of origin, in the currency of that country (with some rare exceptions). Encycleopedia is read in so many countries that no other approach makes sense.

The Encycleopedia website

The Open Road Website http://bikeculture.com/ is viewed by thousands of people each month. We feel that while the technology is not yet ready to support full, paperless editions of our products, it does provide a valuable communications tool, and has the potential to allow considerable reductions in the consumption and transport of raw materials and paper around the world.

We are aware, though, that very many readers have no access to the Internet, nor would they necessarily want it. We retain our commitment to full paper editions, and believe strongly that there is something special about a well-produced book. We hope that Encycleopedia qualifies.

The Encycleopedia Video

You can order, to accompany this book, an hour-long video showing more than half of the featured products in action and in close-up, and covering other topical cycling themes. You can see how folders fold, how trailers hitch and fold, how the riding position on recumbents looks, and so on. Each featured product is described in a minute-long section, with a useful English commentary. This video benefits from a considerable new investment programme from the publishers, Open Road. It is provided in either NTSC (N. America) or PAL (W. Europe) formats and is available in the UK for £8.00 including postage, with equivalent prices from our agents in other countries. Ordering details are on page 138.

Bike Culture Quarterly

If you enjoy Encycleopedia, you'll also enjoy Bike Culture Quarterly, our magazine for the open-minded cyclist. It's a colourful, ads-free celebration of the diversity of cycling, and amongst other things, it's a 'breeding ground' for products which could appear in future Encycleopedias, but which are not yet commercially available or are just prototypes. There's much more too – history, art, campaigning, and, as with Encycleopedia, there's a German edition too. Many people take out a combined subscription to both Encycleopedia and Bike Culture: details are on page 138.

Bycycle

Sharp reporting and features with bite define Bycycle, our bi-monthly magazine primarily aimed at the UK reader – though readers anywhere will find much of interest. Bycycle takes ads, but they're carefully controlled and we maintain a strict 'ed-ad' ratio of three to one. Although it is a UK magazine, Bycycle is available worldwide.

SUE DARLOW

The Scene Changes. The standard diamond frame bike has been with us for over a century. It's a superb machine and is the sole means of personal transport for millions around the world. But as we approach the Millennium, a new culture of cycling is developing, characterised by a refreshing new inventiveness in the design and manufacture of cycles and accessories. The diamond frame may still be king of the road but leads a whole procession of exciting new designs.

Sometimes new thinking results in a classic bicycle design being taken to an exciting level of refinement. At other times a completely different configuration appears. Many lines of development are set out in Encycleopedia. New bicycles are being designed to meet a wide range of modern needs – for going faster than a conventional bike, or being more portable than a conventional bike, or transporting huge loads, or carrying children efficiently. These are entirely practical aims and have little to do with wanting to be different. They extend what pedal power can do, so that we are enabled to take control of our own transport decisions.

Almost every cyclist has room for at least one more specialist cycle in his or her life. Like most things involving physical effort, using the right tools can help turn what were once chores into truly enjoyable experiences. The market for specialised bikes will grow as pedal-power reaches into parts of our lives where it has not gone before – at least not in recent history.

We have been here before. In the 1880s, pedal power was seen as having huge advantages over horsepower for providing swift personal transport and carrying small loads. It was not clear that the high wheeler would be replaced by the compact safety, so a wonderful surge of ingenuity was applied to developing different varieties of the new machine.

The diamond frame won through. It worked fine for most people's practical purposes and its victory was consolidated in the 1930s when the International Cyclists Union banned from international sport any machine deviating from very restrictive 'diamond' frame design parameters. With the application of new materials such as carbon fibre and a better appreciation of factors such as aerodynamics, these parameters are seen as a severe limitation by racing designers. Fortunately manufacturers of leisure and utility bicycles have no such restrictions. They are producing a stunning range of modern machines, and you will see a fine selection in the following pages.

Contents

Two wheels and some sticks

It was for mankind a long and eventful journey of the intellect, from rolling boulders and tree trunks around, to gliding about, feet off the ground, on a couple of wheels held together by a neat little collection of sticks in triangles. We look back down the highway of cycle technology, and find that ideas and inventions of the past are still with us today.

Developing the balancing act. For thousands of years we transported ourselves and our few tools using the most efficient and adaptive machine of all: our bodies, and a pair of shoes is still one of our most empowering artifacts. But the dynamics of other objects in daily life must have suggested that more might be possible. There was the equilibrium of a child's play hoop, the in-line balance of skaters crossing lakes on sharpened deer antlers. The idea of balance on two wheels probably came from many sources, and who knows how many times in history a two-wheeler was invented for a bit of fun, ridden round the village, and then consigned to oblivion.

Subdivisions of human-powered technology were later to intertwine. The concept of balls in bearings, so cleverly set out by da Vinci, was to be perfected centuries later in the development of the bicycle, and applied to the wheels of roller skates.

From Servant-Power to Serious Play.
It was by harnessing other animals that we began to benefit from external power sources for our land transport. Very early attempts to replace horse-power with human-power resulted in heavy four-wheeled carriages powered by servants pressing on treadles, while their lord and master sat up front steering the monster around his country estate. Who knows, it may have been a great amusement for all concerned, as well as being simply another enquiry into the potential for human power.

These days there is still a playful amateur interest in applying pedal-power to four wheels, with self-made multi-seat pedal-vehicles turning up at public events, often as a parody of our obsession with motor cars.

Two Wheels Good. The industrial revolution made mankind organise

for bigness. Machines such as trains needed national co-ordination and infrastructure.

However, another aspect of the human spirit flourished almost unnoticed in the far-off forests of southern Germany, a country almost untouched by the industrial revolution which was reshaping our mental and physical landscapes elsewhere. In 1814 Baron von Drais, social misfit and inventor extraordinaire, took a bicycle to work. He was Master of the Forests, and used his 'running machine' for tours of inspection and for fast journeys from town to town. His breakthrough lay in recognising that a single steerable front wheel made balance possible. Pedals were not on his agenda: the rider pressed feet against the ground. Drais tried to commercialise his invention, had only limited success, and died in poverty.

Held up at Newbold-on-Stour

Ready for take-off. Along came the pedal, and feet left the ground. Cycle technology helped shape society, and was shaped by it. Nothing seemed impossible, as the might and cleverness of industrial processes were applied to machines which might revolutionise the leisure and work of millions. The idea of running a chain to the rear wheel allowed gearing to happen, which, in turn, brought about the end of the enormous front wheel. Pneumatic tyres meant real comfort, and a rollercoaster of inventiveness brought ideas of such useful and charming variety that they are almost all with us still, in modern guises.

New areas of leisure were opened up: for the middle

classes, and then the masses. This new mechanical marvel increased 'marriage distances': cyclists could court partners in distant villages and towns, and the bicycle is said to have been the most potent factor in increasing the gene pool of humanity.

The bicycle allowed millions to travel to work cheaply and at the same time it independently added greatly to the mobility of labour.

It gave a degree of self-determination to women becoming a symbol for, and a useful tool in, the emancipation movement.

The bicycle, and the tricycle, became effective tools of commerce, carrying letters, parcels, shop deliveries, and industrial goods.

For millions the bicycle could transform fatness into fitness, sluggishness into exciting speed.

As with many other tools of the industrial revolution, the bicycle was put to military use. Elaborate parade-ground cycle drills kept the armies in Europe and the US busy in peace time, but the bicycle played little part in the world wars.

All the while inventors were busy taking pedal-power into new realms. Some took to the waters, and then to the skies. Some went for minimalism, some for complex multi-cycles.

The bicycle gave birth to a multitude of exciting sports, from long-distance road-races to fast and furious track events.

It allowed us to travel afar,

THE FIRST HUMAN-POWERED FLIGHT TO THE MOON!

discovering and appreciating the world at a sociable pace, passing through crowded cities, distant communities and new-found wildernesses. Harming no-one, damaging nothing.

The bicycle is a human-scale, infinitely-adaptable, astonishingly efficient, community-friendly, life-enhancing miracle machine. While unthinking citizens are charmed by laughable images of carefree lifestyles and promises of independence, the bicycle brings a message of measured hope and real freedom of choice, as opposed to the worldwide destruction derby of transport madness.

Cyclists are the pioneers of a new mentality, and the adventure of pedal power has only just begun.

The Other Island

For three days the people of the island had watched the limousines arrive, black droppings from fat helicopters.

This was the summit conference, which would think up the big idea to snatch the western world out of economic crisis. For seven days the limousines were to roll back and forth, along the half mile of motorway from airport hotel to conference centre. Anchored off-shore were the luxury yachts of private corporations, their hospitality suites and shuttle boats constantly busy.

The crisis was everywhere. A world order built around the motor car economy was running on empty. Global commerce was in turmoil, with international warfare only a riot away. The world's oil was running out, and what little was left found its way into the tanks of the powerful, the privileged and the military. The island itself, once a paradigm of tiger economics under a popular dictator, was paralysed by devaluation, unemployment and bewildered indignation. They had done their loyal best. They'd helped the national economy by maximising their car use, till gridlock had smothered their cities and the acrid air had wrecked their children's lungs.

The sun rose and set on the third day without the answer being found. There was no big energy source waiting to take the place of oil. Nuclear-powered personal transport was possible, but deemed, by a narrow margin, too dangerous. Gas, alcohol, hydrogen: they'd all been tried, and found wanting. And solar power, said the scientists, was a joke when it came to shifting the 100 ton lorries on which much of the world's food supply depended.

Over the previous ten years unusually violent weather and tidal waves had kicked and punched the island till the concrete cracked. It was on the morning of the fourth day that one particular hurricane abruptly changed course and headed for the island. Out in the bay a group of politicians and their advisors were caught unawares, as their luxury yacht was blown out to sea. They cowered below deck, while the crew fought for control.

It was well into the night that the storm finished its game by spitting the vessel against the rocky coast of a small island. That morning a curious flotsam of grey suit and yellow life jacket lay alive but exhausted on the beach of a sheltered cove, and in the warming light of dawn his sore limbs began to stir. The politician's eyes looked up to the skyline, resting on silent silhouettes of human figures, each rolling on pairs of wheels. He could make out couples riding close together, families with young children on wheels, and the occasional single cyclist gliding past them all at speed.

Memories of boyhood and student days floated randomly through the politician's mind. He remembered the red and steel of his first bicycle, and his first ride without his mother's guiding hand on the saddle. He remembered cycle rides through forests, with college friends, and a particular girl who cycled close to him, in a bubble of beauty. He remembered old photographs he had seen, of his grandparents, standing proudly with bicycles, their main form of transport. Then he remembered the summit conference a decade or so ago, where the leaders of the world had wobbled a hundred metres on bicycles, and how he had shrank from joining them, mindful of his status.

In the following days the horrors of his ordeal were tamed by the hospitality and calm of the people living on the island. He was taken in and befriended. He experienced new ways of thinking and of living which seemed at once shockingly bizarre and absolutely natural. During long cycle rides with the elders he learned of how the people had found for themselves a fine and ever-changing balance between private needs and community values. High technology was there to be found, in the advanced communication systems which allowed people and businesses to interchange without mass travel. It was there in the hospital for the few who needed it, and in the schools for anyone who cared to drop in. Advanced technology was also at work here and there across the island, quietly measuring the effects of human industry on water, land and air.

Super-light bicycles were the dominant form of transport. They were everywhere, and belonged to the community. In fact they were so common that there was always one at hand when an islander needed it, and cycle theft was pointless. Some cycles carried tiny electric motors which could be refreshed in minutes at any of the thousands of recharging stations to be found alongside the windmill parks at the edge of each village.

Not all cycles were the same. They appeared in all configurations for every task imaginable. There were pedal-powered bike-buses, load-carrying recumbents, and superb folders for those who needed them. Some bicycles had special styling, extra gadgets, and lascivious names to match. They were the heavy, high-status playthings of the business community. Here and there across the island craftsmen in workshops made fine racing machines, which were ridden by athletes in competitions during public holidays, cheered on by enthusiastic spectators, each of whom knew at least one of the riders personally.

There was a fiercely proud and highly respected cadre of taxi drivers, employed by the islanders to carry people and goods about in electric vehicles. They were trusted by parents to take their children safely to school, and they could overtake a cyclist only when the cyclist gave a wave of permission. There were trains on the island, visiting stations with enormous cycle parks, and with bays for electric taxis on the other side of every platform. The railway also visited factories and quarries, and transported rocks and cement for the construction of the massive tidal defensive walls which were to withstand the coming onslaughts, at the same time sucking power from the waves for the generation of electricity.

How, asked the politician, had all this been financed? The elders had a simple answer. The people were happy and healthy. They had no great need for costly institutions of state designed to put things right after they had gone wrong – the hospital was small, the police force was negligible, and the prison had been converted into an enterprise centre for the disadvantaged.

On the seventh day of the summit ten billion people sat nervously around their televisions for the announcement from the summit. The summit chairman sat before a hundred cameras, looking remarkably fitter, leaner and more relaxed than ever before. In his hand he held the communiqué, the sheet of paper which might determine the destiny of humankind. He smiled, turned the paper round, and a billion television screens were filled from edge to edge with a thickly drawn picture of a bicycle.

Jim McGurn

Portables

Bikes are great when they're carrying you along, but when the roles are reversed they can be nothing but trouble. Whether you're trying to get on a train or just into your cramped flat, their famous efficiency can seem small compensation for the trouble they can give, especially when short-sighted architects and train operators join in the conspiracy. Which is a great shame, as the bike is the undisputed king of the short-distance journey, and so should be ideal for people living in densely-populated areas. And what more efficient way of long-distance travelling can there be than combining rail and bike? But sadly, it is rarely easy getting a standard bike on a train, especially at peak times.

So, how about a bike you can fold up and put in a bag? Sounds ideal, but what's it like when you put it together again and ride off into the traffic? The first modern folders were clunky heavyweights designed to be plonked into the boots of cars rather than carried any distance to public transport. They were folding utility machines, shopper bikes which could be built cheaply, used occasionally and dumped in the shed when their performance quickly sapped the initial enthusiasm of the owner. It was the desire to design bicycles which could be carried some distance and over a station platform bridge without rendering the owner incapable of cycling which led to some extraordinary advances. Some models fold small enough to be taken on planes as hand-luggage.

There is usually an area of compromise, between foldability and rideability, and so the best folders are, of course, those which do both well. There is huge variety. Some models need a minute or two to fold down, others fold in seconds. Some are great for round-town, others you could race on. Some have small wheels combined with suspension, others are just standard bikes which fold in the middle. You have to set your own priorities, which might include comfort, handling, weight, ease and speed of folding, size when folded, and of course, cost. The challenge of meeting these needs has fascinated many an experienced designer.

Many folders are bought by practically-minded people who would run away from the notion of 'cycling as lifestyle'. At the other extreme are folder enthusiasts who have developed their own sub-culture, clubs and events. Owners' motivations may vary, but there's little can beat the sheer practicality of jumping off a train and onto your unfolded bike, as fellow travellers queue for taxis and buses.

Enthusiasts can find out more by contacting:
A to B, 19 West Park, Castle Cary, Somerset BA7 7DB, UK.
Tel/Fax: +44 1963 351 649
Email: post@a2bmagazine.demon.co.uk
Website: www.a2bmagazine.demon.co.uk

CMK

It's a top-end ATB, with carbon-fibre frame, disk brakes, and a weight of just 11.5kg. So why is it in the 'portables' section?

Because this is a folding bike, and a very fine one. With clever design and cutting-edge materials, 'tm-design' have made their CMK exotic, visually stunning, yet above all eminently practical. With full-sized 26"(559) mountain-bike size wheels, there's no compromise on performance: depending on your choice of tyres and components, it's equally happy in the city, on a 100-mile road ride, or on the roughest mountain-bike racecourse.

The CMK is built around a carbon fibre monocoque frame, with a single-bladed front fork and a single-sided rear triangle. There's no need to remove a

wheel for puncture repair. The specially-designed rear axle takes standard transmission components: top-end parts from Shimano or Sachs are usually fitted.

The folding mechanism at the centre of the frame is patented: in just 15 seconds and without any tools, the bike folds into a package measuring around 995 x 680 x 440mm (39" x 26" x 17"). The carbon construction and tri-spoke wheels are all wipe-clean surfaces – important for a folder which may travel with other luggage.

For more comfort, especially off-road, 'tm-design' have developed a one-sided 'Roto-C' suspension fork, also in carbon fibre, with 50-110mm of travel, and weighing just 1250g. Available to retro-fit or as original equipment on the CMK,

there is also a version available to fit other mountain-bikes – both versions are designed for use with disk brakes. While the CMK wheels are design-specific, similar tri-spoke 'Shreddair' 26" wheels to fit standard MTB dropouts and rim brakes are also available separately.

tm-design

Like most great inventions, the CMK was born of the originator's frustration. Thomas Müller was simply fed up with trying to get full-size bikes on trains. A keen cyclist himself, he was forever finding that combining cycle-touring with train journeys was more trouble than it was worth. He couldn't find anything on the market that combined full-size wheels with easy foldability. Thomas Müller, along with Reiner Stüllenberg and Thomas Lerch, work as a team at 'tm-design', a small, independent company based in Solingen near Cologne. 'tm-design' work primarily on contract to larger, manufacturing companies, mainly designing bikes, but also in other areas. Although they design in steel and aluminium, their special expertise is in carbon fibre, and it was just a matter of time before this expertise was applied to create the ultimate folder. Working in cooperation with Matthias Gölitz from designers 'Phase 2', the CMK was born, with the first production machines becoming available in early 1999.

tm-design GmbH, Itterstr. 35, 42719 Solingen, GERMANY. Tel +49 212 2331447 Fax +49 212 2331448

The CMK costs from around DM7500 in Germany, but please check with tm-design. The 'shreddair' wheels cost around DM1549. Prices will vary worldwide.

Roland Plastics Ltd

Invented by Mark Sanders, the first Strida was produced for five years up to 1992, and around 25,000 were made. After production ceased Mark looked for a partner to produce the Strida 2, which would take advantage of both design experience and advances in materials technology since the first model.

In 1995, precision moulding company Roland Plastics approached Mark. They were looking for a prestige product to display their moulding expertise. It was an ideal match, and detailed design work began in February 1996. Developing the complex and exacting moulds for the Strida 2 took almost two years. The bottom bracket mount, for example, was aluminium in the previous version, but is now produced from Dupont's advanced Verton polymer. The result is a lighter, more cost-effective product without any performance compromise.

Roland Plastics, Wickham Market, Suffolk, IP12 0QZ, UK.
Tel +44 1728 747777 Fax +44 1728 748222
Email strida@rolandplastics.co.uk
Website http://www.rolandplastics.co.uk/
plastics/strida.htm

In the UK, the Strida costs around £335.
Prices will vary worldwide.

STRIDA 2

You can enjoy some bikes for their intricacies and design complexities. Others can charm by their elegant simplicity. The Strida's simplicity is its strength.

It's designed for short trips up to five miles (8km), and to be instantly available whenever you need extra mobility. That means minimising the disincentives to taking a folding bike with you, and making the folding and unfolding process as fast and easy as possible.

The Strida 2 achieves these design goals with calculated elegance. The frame is minimalist: just three rustproof aluminium tubes connected by three plastic joints. Folding or unfolding is extremely quick, taking just four or five seconds with practice. The two wheels clip together and the bike can then be easily pulled or pushed along by the stem, so there's usually no need to lift it. If you do have to, it weighs just 22lb (under 10kg).

A toothed belt drive avoids the dirt and maintenance problems of a chain, and twin hub brakes give reliable low-maintenance braking in all weathers. For short distances, there's no need for gears, and the Strida's 54" gear is comfortable up to a speed of around 10mph (16km/h).

The steering is a very direct, with the short wheelbase, but this also makes the bike very manoeuvrable. Within a few minutes the Strida 2 becomes as simple to ride as it is to fold. The saddle is easily moved up and down the rear tube to adjust for leg-length. High-pressure 16" (305) Vredestein tyres with reflective side-walls give low rolling resistance. The wheels are mounted from one side only, so puncture repair is simple.

The Strida 2 comes with a rear rack which can carry up to 30lb (13.4kg), and a range of accessories are available, including mudguards in a variety of colours, lights, a special saddle bag, and a large stowage bag to cover the folded bike.

BROMPTON

Rides like a real bike, folds like magic. Many Brompton owners delight in collapsing their bike to the astonishment of onlookers – though the less keen-eyed may miss the whole folding performance: it's all over in under 20 seconds. The folded package measures just 565mm (22.2") high, 545mm (21.4") wide and 250mm (9.8") deep, with all the oily guts packed safely away on the inside to keep you clean. Castors on the rear carrier let you pull the package on most surfaces, rather than lift the whole weight.

Unfolded, the Brompton offers a reassuring ride, smoothed by a rubber suspension unit just behind the seatpost. It's a nippy bike, with 16" (349) wheels and a variety of gearing options: the L3 and L5 come with 3 and 5 speed hub gears respectively, while the 'T' models are additionally fitted with racks and dynamo lighting, neither of which interfere with the fold. The full set of accessories add about 10% to the weight, bringing it to around 12.2kg – comparable to a conventional touring bike.

A quick release front bag is available, attached to the frame rather than the forks, so as not to affect the handling. A foldable basket is also offered, and the Brompton itself is available in red or black. The standard seat post adjusts to suit most riders, and for particularly tall riders, extra-long posts can be ordered.

The Brompton fits in the luggage rack of a bus, in the back of a taxi, in the cupboard under the stairs and behind your seat on the train. One bike fits all!

Brompton

The Brompton has been painstakingly refined over more than 20 years, and is, by general agreement, a design classic. Inventor and manufacturer Andrew Ritchie struggled in the early days with his extraordinary product, but growing awareness of the potential of folders, and the Brompton's own reputation, have

brought considerable success. A recent move to a new factory has taken some of the pressure off, but Brompton are still working flat out, with orders from across the world.

Brompton Bicycle Ltd., Kew Bridge Distribution Centre, Lionel Road, Brentford, Middlesex TW8 9QR, UK.
Tel +44 181 232 8484 Fax +44 181 232 8181
Agents in other countries: see page 144

In the UK, prices range from £407 to £573, and will vary worldwide.

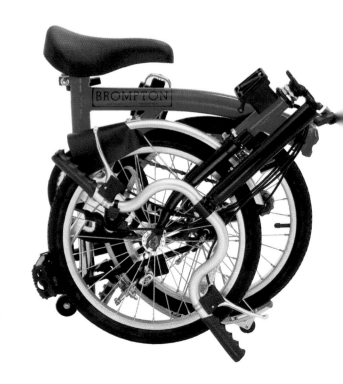

BIRDY

'Killing two birds with one stone' may be an unfortunate metaphor, but it perfectly describes one of the Birdy's most ingenious aspects. By making the pivot-points for the suspension – front and rear – also work as part of the folding sequence, the Birdy engineers have created a folding bike with an unusually stiff main frame, light yet solid. The suspension also evens out the ride from the 18" wheels, which are shod with specially-developed high-pressure Birdy tyres for on and off-road use.

The riding position is identical to that of a conventional 700c touring bike, and the Birdy is hands-off stable. It's a tribute to painstaking development work that the geometry has been refined to this degree, on a bike which also folds in less than 20 seconds to a 76 x 58 x 28cm bundle. That's small enough for hassle-free use on public transport: naturally, a carrier-bag is available if you'd rather be unobtrusive.

Birdys come in four flavours: Red (Shimano STX-RC/Nexave and Gripshift), Blue (Sachs 3x7 system, giving 21 gears between 25" and 108" (2.03 to 8.78 metres development), Elox (Shimano XT and Gripshift) or Green (Shimano Nexus 7-speed hub gear).

All feature the same frame of powder-coated 7005T6 aluminium and suspension, and have a wide range of accessories available – from rack, lights and mudguards to a carrier bag which converts into a rucksack. The elastomer suspension elements can be changed in seconds to tailor the ride to the rider's weight and preference. A 'comfort' stem is also available for those who prefer a more upright riding position. Weight ranges from 9.7kg for the Birdy Elox to 11kg for the Nexus-equipped Birdy Green.

riese & müller

In last year's Encycleopedia, we asked for Birdy stories even more wonderful than, for example, the paragliding fanatic in Germany who cycles his Birdy up mountains, then jumps off with the bike on his back, or the Birdy rider who took part in (and finished) a 186km race through the Italian Dolomite mountains. The stories keep coming in. One couple took their Birdys touring over the mountains of South Wales, and sightings of Birdys participating in triathlons have even been reported. It seems that Birdy owners particularly appreciate having a folder with the performance to put in a proper, enjoyable day-ride. As a tourer, it has the additional advantage that it folds quickly and easily for travel on public transport. And with over 5000 now on the road, there must be more stories out there...

riese & müller, Erbacher Str. 123, D-64287 Darmstadt, Germany. Tel +49 6151 424034 Fax +49 6151 424036 Email team@r-m.de Website www.r-m.de

In Germany, prices range from DM 1899 (Red) to DM3199 (Elox) and will vary greatly worldwide.

Voss Spezial-Rad GmbH

Father and son team Hans and Henning Voss have long been fascinated by the potential of folding bikes, and their business has for several years been an important name in this critically important sector of the cycling market in Germany: amongst other things, Voss Spezial-Rad are the German distributors of the Brompton from the UK. They also distribute the remarkable Montague TriFrame, a high-performance folding tandem imported from the United States, and this was featured in Encycleopedia 96.

Voss Spezial-Rad GmbH, Tulpenweg 2, G-25524 Itzehoe, Germany.
Tel +49 4821 78023 Fax +49 4821 79693

In Germany, the Turnaround costs between DM1885 and DM2379. The Bevo-Bike costs around DM2680. Prices will vary worldwide.

TURNAROUND

Many cyclists are attracted to the idea of owning a folder, but are reluctant to give up the handling characteristics of a standard bike. The Turnaround, with its full-sized frame and 26" (559) wheels, offers solid, predictable handling and genuine foldability. The 52cm CroMo frame –which Voss have had independentally tested and certificated for strength – hinges on the down tube; the top tube then folds down, allowing the bike to shrink to a suitcase-sized 89.5 x 30 x 68cm. This means it can be taken on public transport as hand luggage with no problem. Cyclist smile everytime they do this, because they know how much money and aggravation a folding bike can save them. They also know that folding bikes can be stored indoors, avoiding exposure to the weather and the greedy gaze of passing thieves. Fold-time for the Turnaround is about one minute, and a special cover is an optional extra.

The Turnaround comes in four variants: There is a pared-down 'Off-road' model, and a 'Touring' model, fitted with mudguards, lights and a rack. Both are available in either black or red, with either Nexus 7-speed or STX RC 24-speed gears. The Nexus version has a back-pedal brake, with a cantilever system at the front; the derailleur model features STX RC V-brakes front and rear. Total weight is between 13 and 15kg.

Also produced by Voss, and featured in last year's Encycleopedia, is the Bevo-Bike, with its unique front-wheel-drive. This medium-wheelbase machine combines user-friendly over-seat steering with a relatively high rider position and forgiving handling. Seating and steering positions are wonderfully adjustable, and the machine will fit riders up to 1.95m tall. The transmission mechanism is patented under the name 'Top-Drive', and neatly avoids the long chain runs found on similar bikes. It also allows you to carry luggage between the wheels, improving ride quality when loaded. The Bevo is available with the

Sachs or Shimano seven-speed hubs, and the manufacturers are currently testing the Sachs 3x7 system on the machine. The front wheel is usually also fitted with a V-brake or a Magura hydraulic brake; lighting and mudguards come as standard. Options include a Zzipper fairing and an under-seat rack.

BERNDS

Any experienced cyclist will tell you that saddle-height is crucial, for both pedalling efficiency and knee health. Particularly with folders, it's all too easy to set the saddle height a few millimetres out. Ride the Bernds, however, and you know that everything's just right. The folding mechanism of the seat post returns your saddle to precisely the right spot, facing forwards, every time.

The Bernds is a sophisticated design, evolved over a period of years. The cruciform CroMo frame gives a stiff and stable ride, and elastomer rear suspension takes any harshness from the high pressure 20" (406) tyres. With a handlebar stem adjustable for height and length, and a wide range of saddle adjustment, the Bernds fits riders from about 1.65 to 1.95cm (5'5" to 6'5") tall. It's a lightweight machine too: total weight is from 12.2 to 13.8kg, depending on specification.

Folding the Bernds is simple: the rear wheel swings underneath, stem and handlebars fold down, and the seatpost pulls out and hinges forwards. The 90 x 60/75 x 15cm folded package sits securely on the rear rack. If you leave the saddle in position, it makes a fine handle by which to roll the Bernds along, running on the rear rack caster wheels.

Zwei plus zwei

Thomas Bernds, inventor of the Bernds folder, has been thinking bikes almost as long as he can remember. He built himself a recumbent at school, and then built another during his metalwork apprenticeship. He knew that bike design was his destiny, and started producing the folding bike that bears his name in 1992.

Thomas recently entered into a partnership with Zwei plus zwei, who have made their name sourcing and distributing cycle trailers and other niche products. They have taken over responsibility for manufacture and distribution of the Bernds Faltrad, leaving Thomas free to focus on further development of the design.

Zwei plus zwei, Bismarckstr. 56-62, 50672 Köln, GERMANY. Tel +49 221 9514700 Fax +49 221 95147020 Email zweiplus@aol.com

In Germany, the Bernds costs from DM 1689 to DM 2390. Prices will vary worldwide.

The Bernd is now available with the Sachs 3x7 hub/derailleur gearing system. An oil-free belt-drive is also possible: Duomatic 2-speed, Shimano Nexus 4-speed or 7-speed hubs can be used. Options include a lighting system, the rear rack and stand, front low-riders (perhaps unique on a folding bike), a front basket with Klick-Fix mount, a carry-bag and a lighter protective cover.

Not many bikes will excel whether you're commuting daily by public transport, going on holiday, or just out riding for the weekend. The Bernds is that rare find: a folder with the no-compromise performance of a full-sized bike.

TACTIC PANACHE

The new Tactic Panache is a folding bike with big ambitions. It is designed to be a complete travel system, and lives up to that promise in style.

With a long wheelbase and refined geometry, the Panache has excellent handling. The frame is aluminium, and the Panache weighs just 12kg fully-equipped. The design places special emphasis on adjustability and comfort: seat and handlebar posts are made from lightweight heat-treated, cromoly steel, with a natural 'spring' for comfort, and both use a reversible, swan-neck telescopic design to give a wide range of independent reach and height adjustment. Even the brake levers have adjustable reach, and the standard bike fits everyone in the household from 147 to 198cm (4' 10" to 6' 6"). The five-speed model comes with a new quick-release stem to smoothly adjust the handlebar reach as the height is changed.

You can fold the Panache into a compact package in less than 20 seconds, and, fully-folded, it's strong and stable enough to act as a seat. Reverse the process, and saddle and

handlebar are returned precisely to their correct positions. As we go to press, new clamps are under development, which will lock into position with a quick rotary action, and will self-adjust to ensure that the correct closing torque is applied.

Leave the handlebars unfolded, and the Panache is transformed into a luggage trolley: your load remains undisturbed on the rear carrier, and

you steer with the handlebars, so both brakes and bell remain within easy reach. You can pull even heavy loads up and down stairs without undue effort.

Three and a five-speed versions are available, and both use Sturmey-Archer hub gears, with or without back-pedal rear brakes. Close attention has been paid to equipping the Tactic with quality components, including twist-

grip gears, dual-pivot brakes, and cartridge bearings. The five-speed version comes with a Selle Royal suspended saddle and 16" (305) Primo tyres. Dynamo lights are standard, and the five-speed uses a Lumotec halogen front light and a Busch & Müller Toplight with a 'standlight' facility – it stays on when you stop. High-quality durable paintwork comes in burgundy red, turquoise or titanium.

Tactic Bike Company

Born in 1998, and significantly redesigned for 1999, the Tactic Panache was developed in London by a team of designers specialising in structural analysis techniques from the aerospace industry. The Panache soon became the focus of intense development. Much work was required for the many patent applications which sprung from the design process, and more patents are expected as the team develops a new luggage system and a seven-speed version. The Panache is built in the UK by George Longstaff Cycles, and is available through a wide range of outlets – ring Tactic for details. Distribution details for Holland, Germany and other countries were being finalised as we went to press, so please contact Tactic, also if you're interested in becoming an agent.

Tactic Bike Company Ltd, 263 Goldhurst Terrace, London NW6 3EP, UK. Tel +44 171 624 6268 Fax +44 171 813 2890 Website www.tacticbike.com

In the UK, the 3-speed costs around £479, the 5-speed around £589. Prices will vary worldwide.

Dahon

In 1975 Dr David Hon was looking for inspiration. He had tired of working on laser technology and wanted to turn his energies towards peace not war. At the same time, the oil crisis was causing huge queues for petrol – a sad spectacle which inspired him to consider more efficient methods of transport.

It took seven years for Dr Hon to develop his design, which he unveiled in 1982. Despite winning several design awards and competitions, no major manufacturer showed any interest. Determined to go it alone, he quit his job, gathered funds from friends and family, and set up his own factory in Taiwan. By 1983 Dahon folding bicycles were in full production. Dahon work hard from their headquarters in California to promote cycling and to bring the practical, economic, folding bike to the masses.

Dahon have dealers in many countries. In case of difficulty, contact headquarters in Los Angeles: Tel +1 818 305 5264 Fax +1 818 305 9153 Website: www.dahon.com Email dahon@ficnet.net

In the USA, the Speed costs around $700 to $800. Prices will vary worldwide.

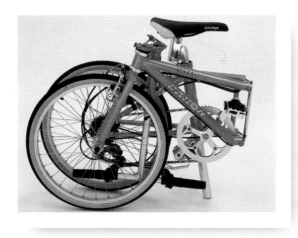

SPEED

A million bikes and seventeen years: that's the level of experience that's behind the Dahon Speed, a folding bike which makes no compromises when it comes to performance. Dahon are expert in making affordable folding bikes: but with the Speed, fast riding pleasure was top priority.

High-pressure Primo tyres on 20" (406) Alex hollow-section alloy rims give a fast, zippy ride. The Sachs 3x7 transmission provides 21 gears without the clutter of a front derailleur. A three-speed hub-gear option is also available for those who prefer pure hub gearing. Gripshift gear changers and V-brakes provide fingertip control. The Pro-max seat-post suspension soaks up bumps, with 41mm of travel. With a lightweight 4130 cromoly frame, the Speed weighs only 12.5kg. Eyelets are provided for a rear rack and full mudguards, and Dahon produce a full range of accessories.

Folding takes just 10-15 seconds, and uses Dahon's patented 'Lite-Touch' system. Large levers open or close easily with little hand force – yet lock absolutely solid and play-free. The folding procedure is simple: fold the pedal, saddle down, stem up, fold down the handlebars, then fold the main frame. Both frame and handlebar latches are secured with safety catches when the bike is being ridden. The Speed makes a compact package of around 28 x 56 x 81cm (11" x 22" x 31"), with the chain neatly inside. The main frame clamp linkage-bar even makes a comfortable carry-handle.

The Speed is Dahon's flagship folder: it joins a range of over 80 models, all of them folding. Every style of machine is available, from full-size aluminium mountain bikes with suspension forks to conventional city shopping bikes. There's also a stainless-steel folder, the Quest, with 16" (349) or 20" (406) wheels.

SWIFT

Most folding bikes put portability high on the agenda, with the ability to ride far and fast taking second place. Animal Bikes have taken the opposite approach. With their 'Swift' they've aimed to design a bike that rides like a high-quality road bike, yet folds quickly for transport.

The frame is crafted from 7005 aluminium tubing, a high quality aircraft-grade alloy with exceptional fatigue characteristics. The 24" wheels (bead seat diameter 520mm on the Swift, 507mm on the off-road version) are an unusual choice, but, say the designers, "combine the superior gyroscopic effect of big wheels – hands-free riding stability – with the light weight and responsiveness of small wheels". There are a number of high-performance tyres made in these sizes. The 'unified rear triangle' suspension brings comfort with no 'biopacing' and minimal rider-induced vibration. Frame, wheels, suspension, and carefully-designed steering geometry combine to make an unusually fast machine with a smooth and stable ride, even on demanding road surfaces.

The Animal has a 'three-level' fold. The fastest and easiest makes the machine small enough to fit two of the bikes into the boot of a small car. The second stage, which requires the removal of both wheels, fits the entire bike into a case measuring 23" x 26" (58cm x 66cm). Finally, without the wheels, the Animal can be folded so compactly that it will fit into an aircraft hand-luggage case (56cm x 36cm x 20cm). This means that the frame can be kept with you, and it's just the robust wheels and touring accessories which you'll have to entrust to the baggage-handlers.

With an 18-speed Shimano 105 groupset, the Swift weighs around 10kg. There's also a 27-speed (Shimano LX) touring/offroad model. A full range of accessories is being developed to suit both models.

Animal Bikes

While Yap Fook Fah was studying Engineering at Cambridge University he met Richard Loke, a keen ultra distance rider and co-editor of the British recumbent magazine, Recumbent UK, and soon became fascinated by many aspects of cycling. With his engineering background, that fascination quickly developed into a desire to improve and develop aspects of bicycle design, and the two spent several years experimenting with ideas and prototypes to form the design philosophy behind Animal Bikes. Fellow cycling enthusiast and CAD specialist Ong Jyh Jian soon joined the team, and they worked together to bring their vision of high performance, easily-transportable cycles to production. The first Animal Bikes were born in 1998.

Animal Bikes: Tel +44 1954 261557
Email richard.loke@analysys.co.uk
Website http://www.animalbikes.com
Recumbent UK: Website http://btinternet.com/~ laidback/recumbentuk

Prices not finalised as we go to press.
Please contact Animal Bikes for latest details.

Paris Maderna Scooter

It's very simple: you scoot to the station, you jump on the train, you jump off the train, and you scoot to work. The Maderna City Scooter is designed to be a simple, practical, and fun complement to any public transport network. It's light, inexpensive, low-maintenance, and it gets you around. And there should be no parking problems: it's designed to be taken inside wherever you're going. The handlebar stem pivots at the fork crown, allowing the machine to be carried or pushed along on one wheel. Don't look at it as a bike with no saddle, it's a scooter with pedals.

The Scooters' steel frame is fitted with 16" (305) wheels and a front brake, and the overall weight is around 10kg. Basket and lights are optional extras, and the recommended price in Austria is 4300 Schillings. From March '99, a new limited edition will be available direct from the manufacturers, with a saddle. The price should be around ATS5400. Prices will vary worldwide.

Paris Maderna
Paris Maderna, Zeltgasse 12, A-1080 Vienna, AUSTRIA.
Tel +43 1403 0158 Fax +43 1403 01584
Email maderna-city-scooter@netway.at

Ciro

The year was 1993. The Berlin Wall had fallen, and the city was suddenly choking with traffic. Dipl. Ing. Sieghart Straka had a vision: a short-distance vehicle, half the weight of a bike and easily stowable. So the 'Ciro Compact Roller' was born, an advanced high-tech vehicle for convenient city travel at up to bicycle speeds. The appeal of the concept centres around excellent cornering ability, and foldability within seconds.

The all-purpose model is the Ciro Magic. There is also the Ciro Terrific range: hot slalom scooters with a wide choice of wheel types: High-Speed, fat Tractor Wheels or Super Slicks.

Ciros are produced in Germany. The manufacturers also make finely-engineered accessories for the Windcheetah recumbent trike, which they import from England (and which is featured in this Encycleopedia). On demand they will also adapt Windcheetahs for riders with special needs.

sTRAKa sPORTs
sTRAKa sPORTs, Dipl. Ing. S. Straka, Niebuhrstrasse 62, D-10629 Berlin, GERMANY.
Tel +49 30 3270 1616 Fax +49 30 3270 1617
Website http://ourworld.compuserve.com/homepages/ciro_roller

In Germany, Ciros cost from around DM 399. Prices will vary worldwide.

Family Cycling

Child-seats, tandems, trailer bikes, adult tricycles: the range of cycle designs for parents to carry their children has never been so good in terms of options and quality. And the choice of good quality solo bikes for children is improving rapidly.

Such solutions are needed urgently, because, in most countries, children have been largely kept off public roads due to the perceived danger of road traffic. A vicious circle sets in: the more some parents transport their families everywhere by car, the worse conditions are for those looking for alternative transport and leisure. But well-designed and constructed cycling products aimed at the needs of young families can be an integral part of a compromise between protection and stimulating the child's sense of independence. You can take children with you on trailer-bikes and tandems to encourage them to develop their cycling skills, while the youngest can enjoy the fun from a child seat or trailer. Such combinations can give children a thrilling sense of speed and ease at an age when they would be struggling to keep up on an individual child's bike.

You need to think carefully about your children's needs, which will change with age. Do you really want a double-trailer, when one of your charges is almost capable of sitting on the back of a trailer-bike? You also need to look at what it is you want to do: buzzing round town, day-trips, or maybe combining cycling with driving or public transport. The more your children begin to enjoy cycling, the more worthwhile it will become to invest in special machines such as tandems. But child trailers and tandems are worth acquiring even for a few years of intensive use by a growing family, for they have a good resale value if they've been well maintained

Whether it's a means of getting to school, or a way of accessing the countryside, getting children out of cars is a way of giving them a new quality of life. Also, the demand for an environment safe enough for children to cycle in will lead to an improvement for all age groups. Streets with reduced traffic volumes, lower traffic speeds and traffic-free sections will create breathing space for the whole community.

Banana Trike

What's bright yellow, has three wheels and will raise a smile whereever it goes? The Banana Trike from the tropical island of Tåsing off Denmark, with its voodoo wheels to mesmerise any kid who sees them. It grows in two sizes: there's the Mini Banana to catch them young from three to five years old, and the Maxi Banana for five to seven year-olds.

Young Banana-pilots will want to take it to the edge, so it is fitted with puncture free tyres on nylon wheels and is almost maintenance free. It's been durability-tested in the playgrounds of Denmark, and survived the real-life rough-and-tumble without a whimper. The trike is fitted with a back-pedal brake on the front wheel, so there's no need for vulnerable cables, and the seat is a tough polyester-reinforced nylon net. A tubular prow protects the chain wheel

and also serves as a handle to pull the trike around or tilt it onto its rear end for storage.

The steering is sure to hone the rider's sense of balance and co-ordination. The sub frame bearing the seat, front wheel and transmission is attached through pivots to another frame bearing the back wheels and handlebars. To steer, tilt the front end by pushing on the handlebars. Because it's so low to the ground, even children with balance problems can enjoy the Banana.

Banana trikes are produced by Hjordt

Specialcyckler, where the top banana is Uffe Hjordt Brink. Uffe first appeared in the pages of Encycleopedia '96 as the manufacturer of the elegant Bjällby recumbents, which he still produces alongside his own machines. Uffe began working on an adult-size Banana trike in Spring 1998. Our six-foot tall (183cm) writer, who pedalled down the corridor chewing his knees in the junior version, can't wait.

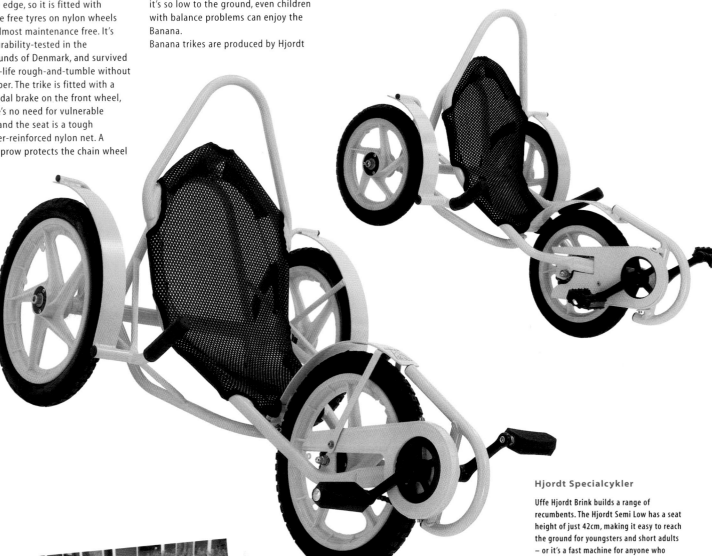

Hjordt Specialcykler

Uffe Hjordt Brink builds a range of recumbents. The Hjordt Semi Low has a seat height of just 42cm, making it easy to reach the ground for youngsters and short adults – or it's a fast machine for anyone who likes laid-back aerodynamics. The Hjordt Super Low is a pure racing machine, developed in cooperation with Anders Ettrup, the national HPV champion of Denmark in 1997, and made to order. The seat height is just 24cm.

Bjallby recumbents are well-known in Denmark. Designed by Curt Bjällby, they are made by Uffe Hjordt Brink. The Bjällby Easy & Tough (see Encyclopedia 4) are fine touring or commuting recumbents, with rear suspension on the Easy. The Bjällby Lux comes in a choice of tyres and has racing rims and high pressure tyres. It is fitted with a parking stand, lock and a luggage rack for which tailor-made bags are available.

Hjordt Specialcyckler, Uffe Hjordt Brink, Granstein 4, 5700 Svendborg, DENMARK. Tel +45 62 226231 Fax +45 62 226239

In Denmark, the Banana trike costs from dKr 4300 (Mini or Maxi). Prices will vary worldwide.

Brilliant Bicycles

Brilliant Bicycles is a division of Pashley Cycles, whose PDQ recumbent is featured elsewhere in this Encycleopedia. The Brilliant range is made up of cycles and trailers formerly produced by Cresswell Engineering, which Pashley acquired in 1997. Designer Richard Cresswell is now Director of Engineering at Pashley, and continues to improve the Brilliant range, which also includes the Foldit and Micro folding bikes (featured in Encycleopedia 4). Brilliant Bicycles is also a cycle shop, in the coastal town of Berwick-upon-Tweed. With a small frontage yet a cavernous interior, it has most of the Brilliant range, and many Pashley machines, on permanent display, and test-rides can be arranged by appointment. The Brilliant staff have particular expertise in supplying cycles for people with special needs.

Brilliant Bicycles, 17a Bridge Street, Berwick-upon-Tweed, Northumberland TD15 1ES, UK. Tel 01289 33 14 76 Fax +44 1289 302 345 Email enquiries@brilliantbicycles.co.uk Website www.brilliantbicycles.co.uk

In Europe prices start at DM2400 for a frameset, and vary greatly worldwide.

Two's Company

A tandem is something every family should have – and the Two's Company from Brilliant Bicycles is designed to make owning one as easy as possible. The 20" wheels allow the rear seat to go low enough for children, and most young riders will be hard-pressed to outgrow this bike: the seatposts are long enough to suit two riders of 183cm (6'). Oversized tubing makes the frame strong enough to carry adult weights, with drum brakes and a five-speed hub gear giving low maintenance and reliable operation in all weathers. With the front wheel folded sideways the tandem will fit across the back of a

car on a standard carrying rack.

The Two's Company is an ideal tandem for growing families, and is versatile enough for hire operations, where reliability is important, along with the ability to fit a huge variety of customers.

Brilliant Bicycles have also come to the rescue of families who need stable and robust trailers which can accommodate growing children. The U+1 tricycle trailer, hitched to an adult bicycle, is a superb way of introducing a youngster to cycling – or two children can ride the impressive U+2. Both trailers have 20" wheels with

alloy rims and six-speed indexed gears. An optional luggage rack can be fitted between the wheels to bring home the family shopping, or to carry touring luggage.

This sturdy trailer configuration is also ideal for adults who may never be able to ride independently, perhaps because of balance problems. The Add-1 has a larger frame, a low step-through height and an optional hub brake. All the trailers are linked to the towing bicycle through a universal joint with a safety wire and clip. If the towing bike falls over, the trailer will stay upright.

Me'n'u2

Is this the world's first production double-childback triplet? Designed to keep the family together when the children get too old (and heavy) to sit passively in a trailer, yet are too young to ride their own bikes, the St John Street Cycles Me'n'u2 triplet keeps adult pilot and two child stokers together on one bike. While the adult keeps complete control, the children feel part of the team, and simply by raising the saddles and adjusting the stoker bars for reach, many years of growth can be accommodated. The rear and mid riding positions are carefully-designed for smaller riders, with specially-machined 120 and 140mm double-drilled cranks.

If there's just one child to accommodate, a Voyager childback tandem may be the solution. This model has been carefully designed to bring the price of tandeming down, without affecting safety or riding pleasure. It uses low-cost components where this is appropriate – the transmission – and top-quality parts where safety is involved: brakes, rims and headset. The frame is butted cro-moly steel. The Voyager range is available from stock in three sizes for adults, as well as in two childback sizes. There is also a higher-

specification 'Enduro' version, with drop bars, carriers, mudguards and lighter rims.

Outgrow the Voyager, and SJSC will part-exchange it for a Discovery, their top-of-the range touring tandem. Several are known to have circumcycled the world, and an even lighter, stiffer and more resilient version is also available in Reynolds 853 tubing. Soon to be introduced are three new tandems, including an off-road tandem with 'the fattest tyres available'!

All of SJSC's tandems and triplets can be supplied with S+S Bicycle Torque Couplings. Using this system, a tandem frame can be split and fitted into a 66 x 66 x 25cm (26 x 26 x 10") suitcase, making regular use of public transport a practical proposition, and taking your tandem away from the not-so-tender care of baggage handlers.

St. John Street Cycles

St John Street Cycles has been trading for 15 years, specialising in Audax bikes, touring bikes and tandems. Under the leadership of Robin Thorn, the business has grown steadily, and now employs 32 staff. According to their website, their 'no-bullshit' approach to advising customers can sometimes offend, but is more often appreciated by customers as a refreshing change. They also operate a no-quibble 'refund service' of particular interest to customers ordering at a distance.

SJSC have particular expertise in small, diamond-framed ladies cycles, and also build a wide range of solo bikes for touring. An affiliated non-smoking, vegetarian cycle café-bar, the 'Cycle Inn' has recently opened just next door to the shop.

SJSC, 91-93 St. John Street, Bridgwater, Somerset, TA6 5HX, UK.
Tel +44 1278 441 502 Fax +44 1278 431107
Email sjscycles@dial.pipex.com
Website http://www.sjscycles.com

In the UK, the Me'n'u2 triplet costs £999, Voyager prices range from £699, and all prices will vary worldwide.

Kemper Fahrradtechnik
Michael Kemper has seen his load-carriers put to a wonderful range of uses. One of the most ingenious, perhaps, is the Bike Doctor service, which sends Filibuses to the rescue of stranded cyclists across Germany – as described in Bike Culture Quarterly 15. A skilled mechanic is just a phone call away, with 25kg of tools and spares on the front rack . Bicycles can't quite match the load-carrying capacity of trikes and quads, but when the priority is getting through heavy traffic, the agility of the two-wheeler makes it a more practical proposition.
Kemper would be interested to hear from prospective agents in Germany or beyond.

Kemper Fahrradtechnik, Rheinweg 70a,
41812 Erkelenz, GERMANY.
Tel +49 2431 77017
Fax +49 2431 980 672
Netherlands: see page 144

In Germany, the Filibus costs from DM 2000, the Lorri from DM 1800, and Pedersens from DM 2800 (complete). Prices will vary greatly worldwide.

FILIBUS

It's astonishing what you can carry on a bicycle, and it's also amazing how much easier and safer the process can be when you use a machine that's been designed for the job. When it comes to carrying children, the extra reassurance of a special-purpose load-carrier can be especially valuable. Two children travel in comfort on the Filibus, but this is a vehicle that can do much more than just child-carrying.

The Filibus is a true multi-function machine, with payloads of 50kg on the front and 25kg on the rear carrier. Magura hydraulics are usually fitted at the front, and a back-pedal brake at the rear. The ultra-solid stand not only eases loading and unloading, but also provides a neat pivot for quick 180° turns. The wheels are 20" (406) front and 26" (559) rear, the frame size is 53cm, and the gearing involves a Sachs Pentasport 5-speed hub. Options include aluminium load-boxes, custom colours and a second hydraulic brake, or a V-brake. A front child-seat can be mounted on a suspended sub-frame, with the child facing you for good eye

contact, or facing forward to see the world.

The Lorri is the Filibus's little brother. Shorter, and lighter, the 15.5kg Lorri is still a very capable load-carrier. It has strong 20" wheels front and back, V-brakes, and proven Sachs hub gearing. Both Lorri and Filibus use large-section tubing to achieve lightweight frames strong enough for everyday, robust use.

The Classic Pedersen takes another approach, employing the principle of triangulation devised by Mikael Pedersen before the turn of the century. Kemper's incarnation of the Pedersen design aims for maximum performance through lightweight, precise construction, while remaining true to the spirit of the original. Each frame is made to measure: customers have ranged from 1.5m to over 2m in height. The customer has complete choice over every detail of the frame construction – from custom braze-ons to initials engraved on the steerer tube.

BABYBIKE

Safety by design – it's the new buzzword in child safety circles. It means that all possible hazards – such as neck damage when cycling with a sleeping toddler, or the danger of limbs falling into spokes – should be avoided from the start, rather than corrected later by adding seperate safeguards such as wheelguards which can be removed or fall off, or footstraps, which can work loose or be incorrectly fastened. If safety is built-in, there's also no need to rely on the user remembering safety instructions from the manual – which may go unread, or not be handed on to a new owner if the unit is sold.

Babies of just a few months old are not only safe (by design) but also comfortable in the Babybike, able to lie down snugly in a cleverly-mounted car seat, securely restrained with a three-point harness plus a belt. The seat can not only be mounted with the child facing forwards, but also backwards to offer protection for the eyes against cold or wind-borne irritants. Complete protection from cold, rain and sunburn can be provided with the 'tent' cover – although transparent windows let you keep an eye on the young occupant. The seat's reclined position has further

benefits: it's easy for a child to fall asleep, and the head and neck are well-supported.

The seat clicks into a stainless-steel frame which attaches to your carrier rack via shock-absorbing springs. The quick-release system makes Babybike a truly multi-functional child-carrying system: the seat can be quickly transferred to a baby buggy or trailer, or used as a car seat (while the child continues dreaming about the cycling tour).

If you buy the system before birth, you won't need to buy a separate car baby seat, as the Babybike seat is approved for use in cars (up to a child weight of 10kg), according to the most recent version of the relevant testing protocol (ECE-R44-03). This doesn't apply for use on bicycles, and according to the manufacturer, the Babybike accommodates children up to 15kg (3 years), a limit imposed more by the strength of the average carrier rack than the size or stiffness of the Babybike unit itself.

Babybike Nederland bv

After a very positive experience carrying his young baby in the Babybike, Hans Postma decided to test the Babybike for toddlers between 10 and 15kg as well. Last summer, on holiday, his youngest son (aged 3) fell asleep as they approached a crowded riverside café. All heads turned to watch the young family park their bikes and remove the seat from the carrier rack, while their child continued dreaming undisturbed. The onlookers were even more amazed when the family rode off with the child still asleep.

Hans is now a member of the European working group to update current safety standards for bike seats. The group's mission is to formulate minimum safety standards. Hans hopes that provisions for sleeping toddlers will be accepted as minimum safety requirements. The stricter the standard, the better, he says: "Bicycle 'arm chairs' are in several respects safer by design than ordinary bike seats. The Babybike is the most extensively tested bicycle arm chair in the world (tests by TNO, ANWB, ENFB: customer satisfaction rating 98%, CE and ECE R44 03)." Babybike would like to hear from prospective agents or dealers. Meanwhile customers all over the world are served directly from Holland.

Babybike Nederland bv, Postbus 372, 1400 AJ Bussum, NETHERLANDS.
Tel/Fax +31 35 695 1908 Email babybike@tip.nl

In the Netherlands, the Babybike costs around 250 Euros, including the seat, sprung frame, blue shelter, and an additional safety belt.

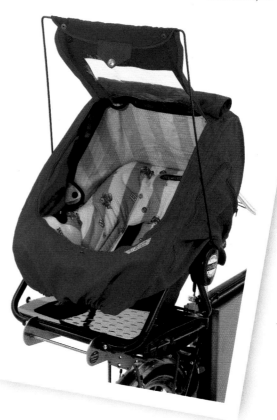

STROLLER PACK

The Stroller Pack is an inspired combination. A two-wheeled backpack, with a tee-bar stand for when you come to a stop, it doubles as a stroller which can take you places that most child-carriers cannot venture: down a rocky path into a steep gorge, or up and down platforms as you change trains. If you're enjoying the wilderness in the sun, so will your child: a sun bonnet provides shade for a cool ride.

The aluminium frame, including wheels, weighs just 10.7lb (4.8kg), yet has a load capacity of 75lb (35kg). Converting between stroller and pack is quick and easy, and the whole unit can fold up small enough to fit into an aircraft overhead luggage-rack.

The Stroller Pack is not a compromise product. When used as a back pack it lets you tackle any terrain easily – and it's also perfect when used as a stroller. The large 12" wheels roll smoothly whether you're going up or down steps, walking on sidewalks, over grass, across sand or on a rough track, or jogging. The child sits back and enjoys the ride. Parents want an active lifestyle these days. The Stroller Pack lets their children have a piece of the action, too!

There are six all-terrain jogging Strollers machines in the Kool-Stride line up. The Junior weighs just 16lb (7.1kg) and carries a human payload of 75lb (33.5kg). The Senior carries up to 85lb (38kg). there's also a deluxe version, the Paramount, and the two-child version the Lil' Deuce.

All Stroller frames are manufactured from sturdy, lightweight, specially-extruded oval aluminium tubing. All models have stainless-steel spokes and hardware, and all plated components are subjected to a 48-hour salt spray test. All Strollers have two mesh storage areas, one behind and a larger one underneath the seat. Five-point safety harnesses are fitted with a single buckle for ease of use and the Zipper Seat allows the child to sit upright or recline. The stroller will fold down easily and quickly, with quick-release wheels, and all machines are fitted with two brakes.

New for this year is the 'Special Use' Stroller. This is, in many cases, a viable alternative to a wheelchair. Based on existing Stroller technology, the Special Use has a larger seat and a solid foot-bar. This machine can take children and adults up to 150lb (68kg).

Kool-Stop International Inc

The Stroller Pack idea goes back to the late 1960s, when geologist John Ingalls was working in the Northern Territories of Alaska, and wanted a way to transport his daughter over rough terrain. Twenty-five years and three children later John had brought the Stroller Pack to an advanced state of development. At this point, Kool-Stop International stepped in and offered to take the project further. Seeing the Stroller Pack as a valuable extension of their range, they have used their expertise in mass production methods to bring these life-changing machines to a wide audience at affordable prices. Kool-Stop's child-carrying bike trailers are featured in the 'Trailers' section of this Encyclopedia.

KOOL-STOP International Inc, PO Box 3480, La Habra, CA 90632, USA.
Tel +1 714 738 4973 Fax +1 714 992 6191
Website www.koolstop.com

In the USA the Stroller Pack costs from $199.95. Prices will vary worldwide.

Trailers

Trailers let you do things with bikes which other options simply can't match. Try carrying a cello on a bike, or the contents of a flat, or a sack of flour. Panniers front and back are great for many tasks, but when the volume and weight of your cargo rise above a certain limit, trailers are the thing.

They can be attached to your favourite bicycle or shared with the family or friends. Some are designed to be pushed as trolleys so you can wheel them into buildings or through pedestrian areas. Some are substantial enough to carry children or to be used for business deliveries.

Trailers come in many shapes and sizes – indeed, the variety and number of trailers on the market can be bewildering. However, in much of Europe, a remarkable business has cut through the confusion and has done much to raise the profile of cycle trailers, both for the cycle trade and in the eyes of the general public.

Zwei plus zwei ('Two plus Two') was set up in 1992 by Andreas Gehlen and his business partner Walter Röpling, both from Cologne, Germany. They act as a sort of clearing-house for bike shops or individuals who wish to order trailers. Although based in Germany, they have a distribution structure across Western Europe. The beauty of their operation is that by acting as wholesaler for all of their trailers (which are made in various countries) they can handle the intricacies of sourcing and importing. It's simple for a bike dealer, faced with a customer interested in a trailer, to order through their national Zwei plus zwei agent, rather than trying to deal with the individual trailer manufacturers.

The Zwei plus zwei catalogue, distributed to dealers, displays a wide range of trailers with helpful advice for the buyer. A British agent, Stuart Morris of Bike-Hod, has recently joined the network, and the catalogue is now available in English as well as German.

What should you consider when choosing a trailer? According to Andreas Gehlen, the main distinctions are between one and two wheels, and between those trailers which attach at the seatpost and those which attach at hub level.

Single-wheel trailers can usually carry no more than about 30kg, but their advantage lies in their low weight and good 'tracking' behind the bike – running in the path of the towing bike's own tyres. These are often useful off-road, where other types become unwieldy.

Two wheeled trailers can carry much more – the practical limit seems to be 100kg or so. Although some trailers can carry more than this, it's debatable whether human power and standard bicycle brakes are really up to the job, especially in hilly areas.

A drawbar which attaches at the seatpost often makes an excellent handle for using the trailer as a handcart, and it's at a convenient height. With heavy loads, though, a low hitch is less likely to affect the handling of the bike.

There are specialist trailers these days for carrying anything from canoes to pets. Many intensively-developed designs make safe and comfortable carriers for children. It's surprising what can be managed safely and without resorting to petrol power. Hitch one to your bike and see how easy it can be.

Zwei plus zwei, Bismarkstr. 56-62, 50672 Köln, Germany. Tel +49 221 951 4700 Fax +49 221 9514 7020
Two plus two UK, Bike-Hod, 2 Middle Way, Lewes, Sussex, BN7 1NH, UK. Tel/Fax +44 1273 480 479

BYKABOOSE

Trailers that can carry large or heavy loads can be correspondingly difficult to store. The Bykaboose is an exception: the nylon-coated body folds down in seconds to form a thin package measuring just 34" x 21" x 3.5" (86 x 54 x 9cm). The frame is made of powder-coated aluminium, and the struts which support the edge of the body have automatic spring tension adjustment. Two 16" nylon wheels with a track of 60cm give excellent stability. The hitch tongue and pin are stainless steel for reliability, with a reinforced rubber tongue providing articulation. The hitch attaches to the rear axle of almost any towing bike, and it's both recumbent and tandem-friendly.

Bykaboose trailers have a recommended load capacity of 110lb (50kg), with 4.5 cubic feet (200 litres) of cargo space. The strong lightweight base and frame structure allow many different types of cargo to be transported very efficiently, and each trailer has a fitted cover to keep your cargo dry. The cargo space rises from a 17" x 28" (43 x 71cm) base to an 33" x 20" (85 x 50cm) rim. The trailer weighs less then 16.5lb (7.2kg) when fully-assembled and can be collapsed completely when not in use. An alternative is the Bykaboose Stubby, which is about six inches (15cm) shorter and correspondingly lighter, making it ideal for touring.

Bykaboose trailers have a unique stainless universal hitching system that is simple, strong and easy to use on any type of bicycle, with no special adaptors or fittings needed. It's also recumbent and tandem-friendly – it'll fit pretty much anything with a left-hand dropout.

BYKaboose International Ltd

The Bykaboose trailer design was originated by Russell Robinson, a graduate of the Massachusetts Institute of Technology. After considerable research and development it went into large-scale production, thanks to the business skills of Chip Zellet, the son of a close acquaintance of Russell Robinson. Sadly Russell Robinson passed away recently, but both Chip and his Operations Manager Jeff Gabbard see the success of the Bykaboose as a working testimony to Mr Robinson's vision and experience.

The people at Bykaboose enjoy hearing about how their trailers are used out in the big wide world. Everything from a cello to the body parts of a hunted elk have been carried by Bykaboose owners. One owner even transports his dog, a 190lb Great Dane. US cycle race teams use their Bykabooses to set up race courses, and trail advocates often use them to carry tools when out maintaining the paths. Bykaboose recently donated a batch of trailers to aid programmes in Africa.

BYKaboose: 466 Central Ave. #37, PO Box 8235, Northfield, IL 60093, USA.
Tel +1 847 441 9163 or +1 800 441 9163
Fax +1 847 441 9167
Email info@bykaboose.com
Website www.bykaboose.com

In the USA, the Bykaboose costs around $249, and the Stubby around $234. Prices will vary worldwide.

Chariot trailers

Chariot trailers are made in Calgary, Canada. The company was set up in 1992, and developed their range of trailers from the ground up. Today, they're proud to be the market leaders in Canada, and have big plans for the rest of the world. They say they're serving a growing number of young, active families who are turning their back on the car and television in their leisure time and would rather be out in the open air: cycling, walking or jogging. In a very real sense, Chariot are contributing to the mental and physical health of the next generation.

Distribution in Europe: Zwei plus zwei, see page 39.
Manufacturer: Chariot Carriers Inc, Bay F, 6810-6th St. SE, Calgary, Alberta t2H, Canada.
Tel +1 403 640 0822 Fax +1 403 640 0749
Website www.chariotcarriers.com

In Europe, the Chauffeur costs from DM 899, the Cabriolet from DM 649, and the Cheetah from DM 599. Prices will vary worldwide.

CHARIOT CHILD TRANSPORT SYSTEM

Child rearing can be a notoriously expensive pursuit, so it's always best to buy a quality product that will do a lot of other things, too. The Canadian firm Chariot has come up with a versatile carrier which meets all your child transportation needs in one unit – a bike trailer which converts to a jogger, to a more leisurely stroller, or to a pull-along hiker, excellent on rougher tracks or nature trails. With simple conversion kits, the transformation to another mode is achieved, without tools, in a matter of seconds. The child carrier can also be folded for easy transportation. The trailer attaches to the bike by a clever quick-release moulded hitch, with a ball and socket joint to allow the trailer a full range of motion. Two 8″ pivoting front wheels, adjustable height handlebars and a parking brake convert the trailer into a stroller. You can leave these on the trailer when it's behind the bike, by simply turning the front wheels upside-down out of the way.

The jogging kit includes a 20″ front wheel, handlebars with brake, and a storage bag. The hiking kit comes with two attachment bars with gripped handles and a comfortable shoulder harness system.

All Chariot trailers feature secure five-point fixing child harnesses, built-in reflective surfaces, a safety flag, and there's always plenty of storage space behind the seat. There are three models: the Chariot Chauffeur and Cabriolet both carry two children while the Cheetah carries one. Some of the range sport rugged 20″ moulded wheels, whilst the Chauffeur has quick-release 20″ (406) alloy spoked wheels. The Chauffeur also has an aluminium outer wheel frame, side vents and tinted windows.

One of the pleasures of a system like the Chariot is that owners have one less thing to worry about: as Chariot say: "On family time, the agenda is always flexible". The Chariot has the versatility to cope, fuss-free, with every eventuality.

KOOLITE TRAILER

The Kool-Stop Original Trailer has been a boon to cycling families for some time now. The makers have pulled off the difficult trick of producing a trailer which suits the very different needs of the parent in front and the young occupant(s) behind. But how do you improve on a classic? When Kool-Stop decided to produce a new trailer, the Koolite, they started by examining every single design point, looking for improvements on each.

The child-carrying package was deemed to be already very good. The children, or child plus a lot of luggage, are secured in a five-point harness with single buckle fitting. The patent-pending zipper seats can be fitted individually to face forwards or backwards. The high-visibility body is of a tough and durable nylon fabric, and the roll-down front and rear windows protect children from the vagaries of the weather. When the front window is rolled up there is still a mesh screen for protection from insects and road debris. Load capacity is 100lb (45kg).

With the child so well catered for, Kool-Stop looked at what they could do to make the rider's job easier. They came up with the centre-pull tongue, a 'U' shaped arm which fits quickly to both lower chainstays with snapper pins. This, in turn, hitches to the trailer via a universal joint which moves freely in all directions giving the rider a much easier 'pull'. The chassis is now made of super-lightweight aluminium and cromoly tubing, bringing the weight down to just 23.5lb (10.4kg), making the whole experience more of a pleasure for the rider as well as the child.

The classic Original carries on in production: both this and the Koolite share the patented quick-release wheel system that allow the trailers to be folded flat in less than two minutes. Folded, the Koolite measures 31" x 28" x10" (79 x 71 x 25cm).

Sister models in the range are the Papoose Caboose and the Li'l Trooper, both of which have rear stowage compartments. A full range of accessories are available for all models.

Kool-Stop International Inc

The Kool-Stop company, most famous for their Kool-Stop brake pads, also produce three completely different types of load-carrying trailers, as well as the Stroller Pack and joggers featured in the 'Family' section of this Encycleopedia.
The Kargo Van is a nylon-sided trailer built onto a chassis similar to the 'original' Trailer and has a 300 litre, 190lb (85kg) capacity. The Wilderbeast is a mono-wheeled trailer with a central, folding space-framed stowage area – towing capacity is 70lbs (31kg) – and the third is the amazing Kool Mule, another one-wheeled device which carries up to six pannier bags in two rows of three, giving a towing capacity of 100lbs (45kg). The Kool Mule was featured in the previous edition of Encycleopedia.
KOOL-STOP International, 1061 S. Cypress Street, La Habra, CA 90632, USA Tel: +1 714 738 4971 Fax: +1 714 992 6191

In the USA, the Koolite costs around $450. Prices will vary worldwide.

Burley Design Cooperative

Burley have been making trailers for more than two decades, combining the best of democratic workplace practices with ecological manufacturing. They minimise waste even before they start building: tubing, for example, is ordered in the exact lengths required, rather than in bulk. They call this precise use of material 'precycling'. The business is co-owned by the workers, and all are paid equally, with business decisions tackled by 'task teams'. All participate in product development and testing, using Burley products for their own cycling activities.

Burley Design Cooperative, 4020 Steward Rd, Eugene, OR 97402, USA. Tel +1 541 687 1644 Fax +1 541 687 0436 Email burley@burley.com Website http://www.burley.com
Agents in other countries: see page 144

In the USA, the Cub costs around $320, and prices will vary worldwide.

BURLEY-CUB

Child-carrying usually involves more than just carrying children: there's extra clothing, food, toys, and you might even want room for your shopping. The Burley-Cub obliges, with ample space for two children and for extra loads – the interior width is a generous 27" (68.5cm). The monocoque polyethylene shell provides a strong base, and the 16" (305) wheels are supported by an elastomer suspension system. The wheels can be quickly retracted under the trailer for storage or easy transport – no tools required, and no loose parts to get lost. The rest of the trailer can be folded down in less that 30 seconds. Overall weight is 30.5lb (13.6kg) and maximum load (with a generous safety margin) is 100lb (45kg).

Options include alloy wheels (shown on the main picture), a '2-in-1' cover for all-weather cycling, and a 'Walk 'n Roller' kit, which converts the Cub, or any of Burley's other trailers, into a walking/jogging 'stroller', in under a minute. It includes a detachable push handle, parking brake and a front wheel that flips up out of the way for when you're back on the bike.

Family cycling is Burley's strength: their products include two further trailers, the d'Lite and the Solo, and a range of tandems.

The Piccolo trailer bike was featured in Encycleopedia 4. This trailercycle hitches to Burley's 'Moose Rack': a rigid, cro-moly platform with a clever coupling device for quick and secure attachment. The coupling's location directly over the rear axle of the lead bike provides snug in-line handling around bends, eliminating potentially-dangerous 'curb clipping' on corners.

The Piccolo is designed for children between the ages of four and ten. It comes with alloy handlebars, a 20" wheel and a six-speed, freewheeling rear cluster so the child can help the pilot pedal along, or simply coast when tired. The Moose Rack accepts panniers even when the Piccolo is mounted, and both rack and Piccolo come with a lifetime warranty.

BOB Yak 16 & Coz

There's only one trailer you can take down a fast singletrack, and it's got only one wheel. Yes, the BOB Yak is the trailer the mountain-bikers take seriously – it's simple, it's light and it goes almost anywhere. But the BOB Yak has a lot to offer on-road, too. When you're not using it for a camping tour you can take it out on a shopping trip: its narrow profile gives easy passage through congested traffic, and when you're out in the open you benefit from the Yak's excellent aerodynamics, and from the low rolling resistance of the durable 16" high pressure tyre. Even better, the low fixing point and centre of gravity minimise any effect on the lead bike's handling. At 5.6kg the Yak is one of the lightest trailers on the market, but can carry up to 32kg, thanks to its rigid cro-moly steel frame. A water-resistant 'Yak Sak' made of rip-stop nylon keeps your load dry and clean, and can improve the aerodynamics of awkward loads.

The 8.6kg Coz trailer has the same excellent handling as the Yak, but it packs away into its own 52 x 39 x 26cm waterproof box. With a 23kg load capacity, this is a great trailer for the traveller.

Both Yak and Coz attach via a specially-modified quick-release skewer (extras are available for your second bike). You simply take out your existing rear axle and put in the new skewer, which can stay there permanently. This simple technique means that virtually any bike – ATB, tandem or recumbent – can be converted with ease to pull a Yak. Special 'BOB NUTZ' are available for solid-axle hubs, tandem hubs or hub gears, and all BOB trailers come with a safety flag, mudguard (fender) and reflectors.

BOB Trailers

The originator of the Yak is Phil Novotny. His widespread touring experience and his years of commuting convinced him that pannier systems could go only so far, and that another solution was needed. As a company BOB is dedicated to reducing dependence on automobiles by extending the range of bicycle use for recreation and transportation.

BOB trailer addicts take part each year in a very unusual event; the BOB Nationals, which take place during the San Luis Obispo Criterium in the USA. The race is contested by over 75 participants on 60 bikes-trailer combinations, cheered on by spectators lining the course in downtown San Luis Obispo. These Nationals also incorporate a trailer parade. The 1998 theme was 'Creative Cargo', with BOB trailers decorated in imaginative ways.

They regularly receive emails from Yak owners across the globe. Two German world-tourers reported how they took Yaks through Mongolia, each carrying a 45kg load: water for four days crossing the Gobi desert.

Distribution in Europe: Zwei plus zwei, see page 39.
Manufacturer: BOB Trailers, 3641 Sacramento Dr. #3, San Luis Obispo, CA 93401, USA.
Tel +1 805 541 2554 Fax +1 805 543 8464
Email bob@bobtrailers.com
Website http://www.bobtrailers.com/
Agents in other countries: see page 144

In Europe, the Yak costs around DM 499, the Coz around DM 399.
Prices will vary worldwide.

VITELLI CAMPING

Bumping through Mongolia heavily-laden for four months is a hard test for any cycle tourist, and it's certainly a tough test for a trailer. Luckily, the Vitelli 'Camping' trailer which Olaf Meinhardt chose to carry his gear has proven its worth many times in just such trying circumstances. It's a lightweight metal basket design, which can carry sixty kilos but itself weighs just six.

As the name suggests, it is perfect for campers, or those with limited pannier space, such as tandem riders, or solo riders with childseats. Everything is built for reliability: the alloy wheels run on sealed bearings, and the drawbar is compatible with the proven Weber coupling. There's an optional waterproof bag to fit the 85 x 40cm load area. The Camping is also cleverly designed to make life easy when it's off the bike: the drawbar can be arranged vertically to make a practical handle, and the whole trailer packs into the basket in minutes.

Vitelli Velobedarf
Distribution in Europe: Zwei plus zwei.
See page 39 for full details.
Manufacturer: Vitelli Velobedarf, Dornacherstr. 101,
CH-4053 Basel, SWITZERLAND.
Tel +41 61 361 7070 Fax +41 61 361 5770

In Europe, the Camping costs from around DM 739.
Prices will vary worldwide.

KOMFORT & COCOON

Almost any parent buying a child trailer will need to wheel it around off the bike – and the Kid Car Komfort and Cocoon trailers are cleverly designed to fill both roles perfectly. A third jockey wheel comes as standard on the Komfort, and the cross-beam of the frame makes an excellent push-bar.

In trailer mode, the Komfort lives up to its name: the passenger compartment is well-padded and offers good protection from the elements. Two children from ages one to seven and together weighing up to 45kg can be accommodated, each with a three-point safety harness, or a single seat can be arranged in the middle of the trailer.

The Cocoon is slightly smaller, but there's still plenty of room for two six-year-olds. Naturally, the aluminium frame of both models folds down small for storage or transport.

De Vogel
Distribution in Europe: Zwei plus zwei, see page 39.
Manufacturer: de Vogel, Postbus 567, Drachten 9200 AN,
NETHERLANDS. Tel +31 561 441615 Fax +31 561 441 731

In Europe, the Cocoon costs around DM 599,
the Komfort around DM 999.
Prices will vary worldwide.

Leggero Classico

Solid aluminium walls make a reassuringly stable base for the Leggero Classico. Two children up to five years old (weighing up to 50kg) are a respectable load by any standard, and a rigid trailer chassis is a must for safe, predictable handling. The children inside are held gently but firmly in place with a three-point harness designed to fit all sizes. There's plenty of room for two full-size toddlers: at shoulder-height, the passenger compartment measures 60cm across.

When the children do outgrow the Leggero, or if you just manage to escape for a few days, the Leggero converts to a fine camping trailer, with a neat canvas enclosure for your belongings. It can be ordered initially in this touring guise, or as a conversion kit for the child trailer. Both versions use the 'Becco' coupling: a light yet secure device which leaves a minimum of clutter on the bike when you're not towing the trailer.

If you've dropped the children off at school, you might choose to do some shopping. Once again, the Classico shows its versatility. In seconds the seat can be folded away against the back wall of the trailer, leaving a huge load area free. If, instead, you need to travel by public transport, the Leggero packs down small: the sides fold inwards, with wheels and other parts neatly tucked away in the base.

Stainless steel mudguards and a tow-handle are available as options. There's also a polypropylene roof, which offers extra stiffness and roll-over protection.

The Twist

Brüggli

Going back to basics with trailer design, Swiss trailer manufacturers Brüggli announced in 1998 the fruits of a long research program: the Twist. With an elegantly simple design, the Twist is both strong, light and affordable. The large moulded bucket seat is a solid base for a welded aluminium safety frame, which offers all-round protection, and mountings for a neat rain-cover. A removeable bag hangs on the back.
A height-adjustable three-point harness adapts to all sizes of child, and the disk wheels ensure that limbs won't get tangled in spokes. Brüggli have been making trailers for over ten years, and in the design of the Twist, that experience has been put to good use.

Distribution in Germany: Zwei plus zwei, see page 39. Manufacturer: Brüggli, Hofstr. 3+5, CH-8590 Romanshorn 1, SWITZERLAND. Tel +41 71 466 9494 Fax +41 71 466 9495 Email info@brueggli.ch Website www.brueggli.ch

In Europe, the Classico costs from DM 899, The Twist from DM 599. Prices will vary worldwide.

WEBER RITSCHIE

Weber Werkzeugbau

"Why", asks Herbert Weber, inventor of the Ritschie, "do so many taxi drivers go around in expensive cars?" It's not that they earn huge money. The answer, he feels, is that if they're going to sit in the car for eight hours, they might as least get one that's comfortable.

That anecdote is about as far as Herbert Weber's interest in cars goes. He does believe, though, that for parents who use trailers intensively it's impossible to invest too much in a vehicle with the maximum performance, safety and comfort – and this applies both to the trailer and to the bicycle which tows it. Choose a reliable and comfortable machine with strong brakes, on which you feel comfortable. That way the whole family will enjoy the ride.

Distribution in Europe: Zwei plus zwei, see page 39
Manufacturer: Weber Werkzeugbau, Königstr. 25, D-83254 Breitbrunn, GERMANY.
Tel +49 8054 7544 Fax +49 8054 1234

In Europe prices start at DM 1499, and vary worldwide.

In a splendid synthesis of high-tech materials and child-centred design, Weber's Ritschie trailer is a truly sophisticated transport solution. Whether carrying two children (up to the age of 6, weighing up to 50kg) or a load of touring luggage, the Ritschie follows faithfully, its ride cushioned by swing-arm suspension. And when you stop, there's a foot-operated parking brake to stop the trailer rolling away.

The 14.5kg Ritschie combines light weight with remarkable performance and safety thanks largely to the materials used in its construction. The chassis is made from a honeycomb composite: aluminium walls pressed and bonded to a honeycomb polycarbonate core. The result is a light, very stiff bodyshell which forms the base of the trailer.

The Ritschie is unique, to our knowledge, in that it has a seat that adjusts in depth and angle to suit the child. This seat , and the removeable roof-piece above, are made from foamed polypropylene: the same material used in modern cycle helmets. The children are held in place with a five-point harness, multi-adjustable, and they have plenty of room: the Ritschie measures a generous 64cm wide at shoulder height, and cushions over the wheel-arches act as arm-rests. The roll-over top combines sun, insect and rain protection.

There are plenty of useful options to extend the use of the Ritschie. A lockable touring top is available, to make an effective, waterproof load-carrier, or there's a jogger conversion kit for child-carrying off the bike. A set of woollen cushions offer extra luxury – especially when it's cold – and there's also a very practical hold-all which attaches to the back of the trailer. It's an excellent way to carry all of the extra necessities of family life, and comes with a shoulder strap and mounting for an LED rear light.

When it's not in use, the Ritschie folds down to a compact 78 x 58 x 26cm package, and there's an optional cover for extra protection in transit.

CYCLONE TRAILER

Catching a train with a Cyclone trailer is a surprisingly hassle-free operation. Detach towbar and wheels, stow them inside, and climb on board with nothing more outrageous than a large duffel bag alongside your bike. It's even pleasant to carry, with two strong and comfortable handles.

On the road the 5.2kg Cyclone carries up to 50kg or 100 litres, rolling smoothly on high-pressure tyres with reflective side-bands. The 16" (305) wheels have sealed industrial bearings. The hitch is made from stainless steel and Delrin (an engineering plastic), and is designed for easy one-handed operation. It fits to the rear axle of just about any bike.

Radical Design also make a fine range of cycle luggage, many models recumbent-specific, which are featured in the 'Accessories' section of this Encycleopedia

Radical Design
Radical Design, Hoofdstraat 8, 9514 BE Gasselternijveen, HOLLAND. Tel/Fax +31 599 513 482
Agents in UK and Germany: see page 144

In Holland, prices range from f 800, and will vary worldwide.

DEUXJON

A bike trailer is a very practical thing to own, but it can be quite an encumbrance when it comes to putting it away, or transporting it by car or train. The Deuxjon offers an excellent compromise, without sacrificing durability or strength for the sake of a complex fold: the frame packs down flat, but the load compartment is a very solid plastic container that can be lifted from the trailer and used elsewhere. There are two types of boxes, rigid and folding, in a range of sizes. They also stack together, allowing you to carry several different sizes at once. The trailer is towed via a ball and socket seat-pin hitch and a range of sizes is available. The wheels are 16" (305), overall weight is 7.5kg, and with its low centre of gravity, the Deuxjon comfortably carries up to 50kg. The largest box has a 60 litre capacity. A fully rigid frame is also available, for heavy-duty use.

Deuxjon Trailers
Deuxjon Trailers, 78 Craven Avenue, Plymouth, PL4 8SW, UK. Tel +44 1752 253638

In the UK, prices range from £249. Prices will vary worldwide.

BIKE-HOD

Tesco, one of Britain's largest supermarkets, now runs a fleet of Bike-Hods at one of its stores – lending them to shoppers wanting to take a full week's shopping home on a bike. Many first-time users are amazed at how easy it is to tow quite considerable loads. "You don't know it's there" is a common reaction. The basic Bike-Hod weighs just 5.5kg, and follows your bike faithfully while carrying up to 50kg. It will pass comfortably through any standard doorway, and attaches to your bike in an instant – simply push the pin through the patented hose-hitch. It's also a manoeuverable hand-cart off the bike. The tow-arm can be swivelled round for compact storage or for journeys on public transport. The bag shown, made by Carradice, is one of a range of bags and baskets available.

Distribution in Europe: Zwei plus zwei, see page 39.
Manufacturer and UK distributor: Bike Hod Trailers, PO Box 2607, Lewes, East Sussex BN7 1DH, UK.
Tel/Fax +44 1273 480479 Mobile +44 403 649 408
Email bike-hod@pavilion.co.uk

In the UK, prices start from £169, bags from £34.95. Prices will vary worldwide.

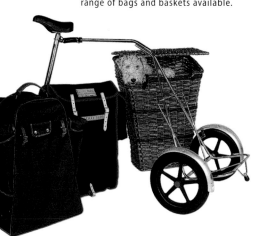

BLACKY

If you need a simple and effective trailer for everyday load-carrying, you can't go wrong with the Blacky. With a strong steel chassis and an impact-resistant 90 litre plastic box, it can take anything you can throw in it up to a capacity of 90kg. The loading area (72/62cm long, 41/34cm wide and 31cm deep) will cope with a full load of shopping, a worthy batch of paper for recycling or any variety of other loads for business or home.

The drawbar and frame can be dismantled for storage, and the box can be quickly detached, which is useful for carrying loads indoors at the end of your journey. Supplied complete with a ball-joint coupling, the Blacky is a very affordable way to extend the carrying capacity of your bicycle well into the small van league.

Distribution in Europe: Zwei plus zwei, see page 39.

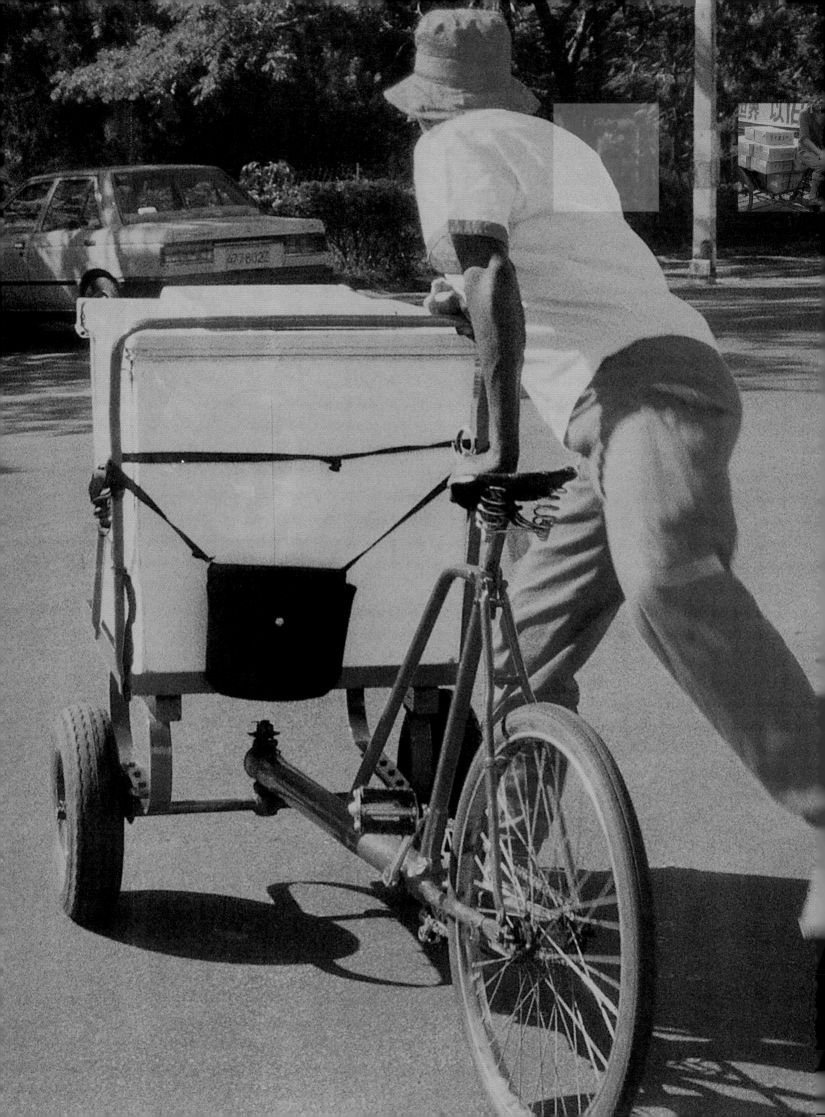

Load-Carrying

There has been a trend over the last few years for fashionable shops in bijou areas to plant a transporter bike outside the front, with their name on it. It never goes anywhere, it never carries much more than a couple of plant-pots, but creates a nice image. People like transporter bikes. They serve as a challenge to car culture and characterless, dehumanising shopping malls which depend so intimately on the surrounding car park.

Have the days when using a bike for carrying heavy loads was a practical option gone forever? Apparently not. There has been a distinct counter-trend to the creation of new shopping centres, as cities wake up to the fact that they can compete, if they make the effort. While most shoppers still love cars, they don't like them in the streets they actually shop in. So city-centres are gradually freezing out the motor-vehicle. Sometimes planners have shown a tendency to throw the baby out with the bath water, to restrict the bicycle along with the motor car. But with the car removed, access can be improved for both cyclists and pedestrians. Locals on bicycles can again enjoy rapid access to their city centres, while day trippers can wander around without risk of being mown down by a truck. But there is still a need to move goods around,

whether it's a big load of mail to the post office, or just a pile of shopping to a car park on the edge of town.

Fortunately, parallel to this renewed demand for low-impact, versatile carrying machines have come exciting new developments in bike technology, producing strength without crippling weight, a wide choice of gears and brakes capable of arresting the largest load. A huge range of options are available now, ranging from trailers with a 30kg payload to quadricycles which will take a quarter of a tonne. There's no pretending that that 250kg load will pedal the vehicle up a hill for you, but these 'bicycle HGVs' can easily outclass their diesel equivalents in certain scenarios, when all the implications of motorised deliveries are taken into account: fuel costs, insurance, maintenance, capital, parking and access restrictions.

Pedal-powered deliveries also mean healthier, happier, more productive staff. And intrigued, admiring customers. Once again, human power wins out, when used in the right way, in the right place. Load-carrying cycles are popular with the public at large mainly because they're cute. They are popular with businesses because they are incredibly efficient at carrying out their specific roles. So let's flood our towns and cities with them and see how our environment improves.

CHRISTIANIA TRIKE

"Own a Christiania, and a whole range of tasks become easy. For businesses small and large, a Christiania comes as a great liberator. Without the hassles and expense of owning, parking and fuelling motorised vehicles, you can use the instant mobility and load-carrying capacity of the Christiania to serve your clients better, solve problems swiftly and accomplish tasks that would otherwise be near-impossible."

Andrea Casalotti runs a load-carrying business in London, and Christiania trikes are the mainstays of his fleet. Delivering everything from organic wholefoods to medical supplies, the trikes have proved both versatile and reliable. Andrea has become something of a convert, especially when it comes to explaining how suitable a trike can be for a small business such as his. Small entrepreneurs needing business transport can have an effective vehicle, for loads up to 100kg, at a fraction of the 'cost of entry' of motorised vehicles.

Big business can benefit, too. The PR benefits of delivery by trike can be immense, and among the latest to realise this are Carlsberg, the brewers, who recently chose the Christiania as a mobile vending platform, complete with refrigerated box. Other types of container are also available, from the standard box of 9mm marine plywood to fully-waterproof containers, as used, for example, by the Danish Post Office. Even a child in a wheelchair can be accommodated in a specially-adapted version. Many parents find the Christiania ideal for transporting children: they're in full view, protected by the box, which can be fitted out with bench seat and a waterproof cover complete with windows.

The Christiania Trike itself has been refined over many years. It is available with either hub or derailleur gearing, and has effective hub brakes in each front wheel, with a parking brake provided as standard. Unloaded, the trike weighs about 40kg.

Christiania Bikes

Christiania Trikes are made in Denmark, and they take their name from Christiania, a car-free suburb of Copenhagen where the business was started many years ago by Lars Engstrøm. Lars and his wife Annie have a host of stories about the ingenious uses their customers find for their trikes: from families whose trike is a complete 'car replacement', to disabled riders for whom the Christiania's stability is essential. Their photo-album also shows businesses who have sent pictures of their trikes in action, from farmers (who can even carry pigs and other livestock in the front box) to ice-cream companies. There are Christiania agents in many European countries, and the trikes are also available though many Danish bike shops.

Christiania Bikes, Dammegardsvej 22,
DK-3782 Klemensker, DENMARK.
Tel +45 56966700 Fax +45 56966708
Agents in Germany, the Netherlands, Sweden and UK:
see page 144

Agents in Germany, the Netherlands, Sweden and UK: see page 144

In Denmark, prices range from around DK 7149, and will vary worldwide.

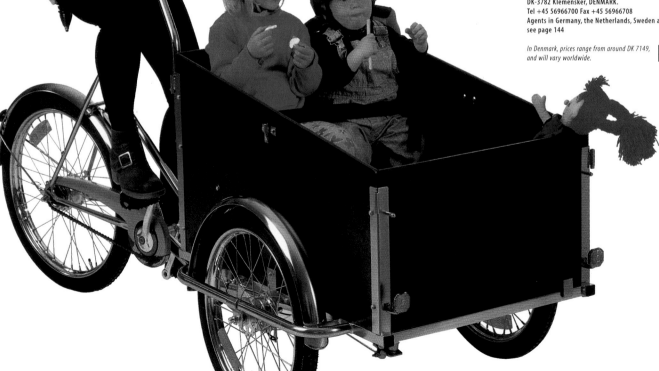

PICKUP

In cities across Europe entrepreneurs are putting Pickups into action. In its people-carrier mode the Pickup is a high-tech modern alternative to the traditional rickshaw; in load-carrying form it shifts up to 180kg safely and easily.

Pickups have been at the forefront of the revolution in transport thinking, pioneering new attitudes to urban mobility. In Britain, six machines transport customers to and from a supermarket in London – and shoppers are often fighting for places. In Belgium a Pickup Taxi fleet is particularly popular with old ladies on shopping trips who ask the fit young drivers to load and unload their shopping. The same fleet now has a contract with the delivery company TNT to deliver all parcels under 25kg to city-centre destinations: the lorries stop outside town.

The vehicle itself is a solid workhorse: the chassis is steel, and braking is provided by Sturmey-Archer drums. The use of standard components throughout – a design priority – is particularly important overseas. In fact, every wearing part, even those used in the roller-clutch system for the two-wheel drive, is available off the shelf worldwide. The transmission is usually via three, five or seven-speed hub gears and the articulating chassis keeps all four wheels on the ground on uneven terrain. At 35kg, it is still remarkably light for such a useful machine.

Experience has shown that a single rider propelling a heavy load, or several passengers, needs to engage the lowest, slowest gears when gradients are encountered. Starting off can also be strenuous, so Seat of the Pants have developed an electric-assist system to give a helping hand in just these situations. A 600W rare-earth pancake motor is combined with a unique lightweight rapid-charge battery, making the system ideal for taxi or courier operations. On each return to base the battery can be topped up in a matter of minutes, and because the system is so light (12kg all in) its weight has hardly any effect on pedalling performance. The maximum assisted speed is 18km/h (12 mph).

The Seat of the Pants Company

The Pickup is made entirely in-house at the Seat of the Pants Company near Manchester, UK. Special liveries are no problem, and various bodywork options are available, including the new Pickup Van. The load area provides 1.4 cubic metres capacity and is fully-enclosed, waterproof and lockable.

A useful accessory for the Pickup is a front fairing – not only for aerodynamics, but, more importantly, for weather protection. Taxi operators and couriers who use the Pickup day-in, day-out have found the fairing almost essential to help keep them dry – and it also gives even more visibility in traffic, as well as useful advertising space.

The Seat of the Pants Company, L&M Business Park, Norman Road, Altrincham, Cheshire, WA14 4ES, UK.
Tel +44 161 928 5575 Fax +44 161 928 5585
Email bobdixon@seatofpants.u-net.com
Website www.windcheetah.co.uk

In the UK, the Pickup costs from £1900 for the basic Truk, rising to £3250 for a fully-equipped Taxi. The electric-assist kit costs £1900. Prices will vary worldwide.

TRANSPORT BIKE

Reiko

Nobody likes to see a good idea go to waste. When consultant engineer Reiner Körtner saw Gerium Bründt and Peter Garus' prototype Transport Bike, built as the culmination of their degrees in design engineering, he knew that it had to go into production. But he had to move fast, to catch the 1998 trade fairs, which happen in late Autumn in Germany. The deal was made at the beginning of July 1998, and by September Reiko was born.

Reiko Fahrräder & Zubehör, Fröbelstr. 50, D-33330 Gütersloh, GERMANY.
Tel +49 5241 33 77 77 Fax +49 5241 33 77 99

In Germany, the Transport Bike costs from around DM 2758. Prices will vary worldwide.

Versatility is the name of the game when it comes to load-carrying. Companies that specialise in pedal-powered haulage often have to buy a range of different machines, to carry anything from a letter to lawnmower. The Reiko Transport Bike (Transportfahrrad in German) is primarily a large-capacity goods-bike, with a payload of 80kg. But if you buy a second one, you'll find that one plus one makes much more than two! With Reiko's linking kit, you can bolt two Transport Bikes together to make a tandem with a carrying capacity of 300kg. And you can use one or two riders, depending on the load, and how far it's going.

The Transport Bike is based around a powder-coated Cro-moly steel frame, available in a choice of five different colours. Custom-built frames are also offered. Cantilever brakes and the Nexus 7-speed hub are standard, but as each bike is assembled to order, options such as disk or hydraulic brakes are also available. The rear wheel is 26" (559), and at the front there's a choice of 18" or 20" (406). The smaller 18" size is best for when the bike will be ridden at slow speeds and for tight manoeuvring, while the easy-rolling 20" option is ideal for more open stretches of road.

Transport Bike is actually surprisingly easy to ride. The low centre of gravity means that even with a full 80kg payload, the handling is really quite straightforward. Notice, too, the built-in load straps, and the extra heavy-duty propstand. A heavy-duty rack on the back offers further loading possibilities.

The manufacturers stress that Transport Bike is not just a work bike. You can mount a child-seat in front of you, where many parents prefer to put their child, and it's also great for touring with a full load of outdoor gear.

Rikscha

Just as rickshaws are outlawed in many third-world countries in the name of 'progress', so the crowded, polluted streets of Europe's cities are again turning to pedal power as a transport solution. Specialist manufacturers such as Bürkle in Germany are now mixing the old and the new, applying the latest technology to produce machines offering new levels of performance and productivity.

Bürkle's Rikscha is built to last, with a stainless steel frame, double-clamp forks and robust moped wheels with 3.5mm spokes. The frame can be fitted with a choice of rear units, including a double seat, a load bed, or a wheelchair passenger unit. Custom-built options are also available, including a mobile sales counter.

Any machine carrying a human load needs big reserves of stopping power, and the Rikscha is fitted with hydraulic disk brakes on all three wheels, with, of course, a parking brake. The aluminium and steel seat-unit contains a lockable boot, and the waterproof Airtex canopy

folds neatly away when not required.

Transmission is via a Sachs 7-speed hub, allowing you to change gear while stationary, and is run through a differential to the two separate rear axles. All cables are neatly routed through the frame, keeping them well out of harm's way. The total weight is around 65kg, and optional extras include an advertising plate, a 'street-legal' kit (mudguards, seatbelts, lights etc), bar-bag, toolkit, larger canopy, and an electric booster-motor for the front wheel.

Experience has shown that European customers are reluctant to entrust themselves to a rickshaw unless the machine in question is clearly modern, well-designed and safe. It is clear even at first sight that the Rikscha qualifies superbly.

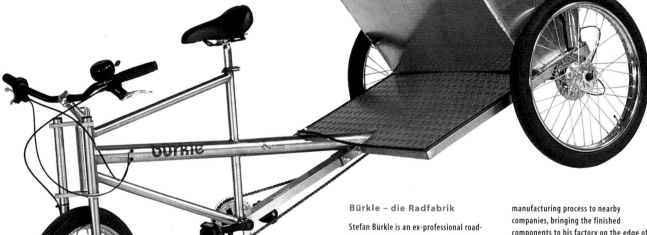

Bürkle – die Radfabrik

Stefan Bürkle is an ex-professional road-racer who, tired of his job as a technician, decided five years ago to set up as a bike manufacturer. Aware of the high level of competition in the mainstream sectors of the bike industry, he spotted a niche in the load-carrying market, and began by specialising in pizza-delivery bikes. It wasn't long before a client asked him if he could produce rickshaws too. His products are now in use in cities right across Germany, and as far afield as Réunion Island in the Indian Ocean.

With ever-increasing production levels, Stefan is starting to farm out much of the

manufacturing process to nearby companies, bringing the finished components to his factory on the edge of the Black Forest for final assembly and quality control. As Bürkle also rent out Rikschas, they usually also have a few second-hand examples in stock.

Bürkle, Die Radfabrik, Rösleinweg 10, D-75334 Straubenhardt, GERMANY.
Tel/Fax: +44 7082 50106
Email radfabrik@hotmail.com

In Germany, the Rikscha chassis costs around DM4900 – the passenger unit costs DM1600 and the load bed DM900. The electric-assist unit costs around DM2500, including battery and charger.
Prices will vary world-wide.

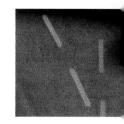

City Bikes

Cities are probably cycling's home territory, and as the renaissance in urban cycling gathers pace, bikes are being developed to match. With the vast majority of journeys being less than five miles (8km), the bicycle has to be the most efficient, cheap, flexible and sociable method of transport we have.

As the penny drops amongst the population as whole, newcomers begin the search for the bicycle which will help them change their lives. A major deterrent in many countries has been the type of bicycle available in the shops. The narrowly competitive nature of the cycle industry, coupled with consumer ignorance, has led to many people being sold bikes which are simply not good enough for the job. Many are barely capable of being maintained and kept on the road, and components such as mudguards and lights are presented as being 'optional extras'.

Even when people are prepared to spend above the average, they often end up with a modified mountain bike. It might be very well made, but will not be a bike designed in the first place for urban use.

If you're mainly interested in getting to work on time, all you want is something that is simple and reliable, whatever the season, whatever the weather. Fortunately, this situation has begun to change. Much new thinking has been encouraged by recent interest in hub gears, and even hub brakes, from the Japanese company Shimano, and the German company Sachs.

These new components, offering weather-proof, low maintenance reliability, are not particularly new ideas, but they are good ones, and are putting city bikes centre stage.

City bikes need to be as robust and light as possible, and subtly designed to give stability and comfort without sacrificing performance. After all, it is good acceleration, fast gear changes and sharp braking which help a cyclist integrate with urban traffic, and therefore remain safe. Another consideration is that the higher the quality of the bike the more likely it is that the rider will want to cycle further afield on it, at weekends and on holiday. On top of all this, the city bike must look good, leaving behind the image of the urban workhorse.

City cyclists need to be able to arrive at their destination in the same condition as if they had come by car, which means, in many countries, mudguards and chainguards. Lighting needs to be straightforward, and preferably built into the vehicle. How many motorists would be prepared to buy a car, and then go down to the auto-supplies shop to buy a set of lights to fit themselves? And how many would want to have to remember to take them with them each time they went out?

At last manufacturers are realising that city riding presents its own set of demands, and producing some superb bikes.

CULTURE, AVENUE, DELITE

riese & müller

Heiko Müller and Markus Riese launched their range of city bikes in 1997, but were already widely known for their Birdy, featured in the *Portables* section of this Encycleopedia. As designers, their skills are sought-after by manufacturers worldwide, and their influence can be seen in many of today's suspended bicycles. Meanwhile, they continually refine their range – and an important element of this process is the company bike ride. Every Wednesday, without fail, the entire staff leave the factory to test and evaluate new components or designs on the hills around Darmstadt.

riese und müller GmbH, Erbacher Str. 123, D-64287 Darmstadt, GERMANY.
Tel +49 6151 424034 Fax +49 6151424036
Email team@r-m.de Website www.r-m.de

In Germany, prices are approximately as follows: Culture Blue DM 1999, Culture Orange DM 2899, Avenue Red DM 1999, Delite Blue DM 2199, Delite Yellow DM 3299. Prices will vary worldwide.

The Culture is a do-anything bicycle. Clever design has brought together the best of mountain-bike technology and the practicality of a true city machine – and the result is a machine you could happily ride all day on tour.

Full suspension means that cobbles, potholes and ruts are no longer an obstacle. The suspension elements can be changed to suit the weight of the rider, and the rear suspension has damping adjustable to taste. The rear swing-arm pivot is designed for rigidity, so the suspension won't affect the stiffness of the aluminium frame.

The frame's spectacular 'V' design is practical, too: the low step-through height makes getting on and off a breeze. There are two sizes: 48 or 55cm. The frame can be fitted with a full range of well-designed accessories, including rear carrier adapters for Ortlieb pannier bags or a childseat.

On the front can be mounted an adapter for KLICKfix baskets or front bags, and a D-lock mount can be fitted to the 'seat tube'. Lighting and mudguards are standard.

The Culture comes in two models, Orange or Blue. The Orange uses Shimano's 24-gear Nexave groupset, offering a wide gearing range and all-weather roller-brakes. The Blue uses mid-range Shinano componentry, with V-brakes for excellent stopping power.

The Culture's sister model is the Avenue, equipped with the Shimano Nexus seven-speed system. Full suspension, a low step-through height and the integrated carrier make this a superb shopper and steed for the everyday.

Completing the range is the new Delite, a sporty hybrid. With light weight, full suspension and a frame-mounted carrier, it's capable of full touring, and the very adjustable riding position make it comfortable. The suspension, with an oversize industrial pivot, is designed to minimise pedal-induced bounce. The Delite Yellow is the lightest (10.9kg), with aero rims and spokes, and high-pressure tyres. The Delite Blue is a great general-purpose sportster, with affordable components. It's a delight to ride!

Schauff GmbH

Schauff is one of Germany's largest cycle manufacturers, yet it remains very much a family business. Hans and Ute Schauff took over from founder Hans Schauff Sr. in 1968. They inherited a business built up from the original Schauff cycle shop and frame-building workshop that started in 1932. Their son Axel specialises in computer-aided design and has won awards for the La Luna city bike and the Wall Street Duo Tandem (both featured in Encycleopedia 4). Thanks to this and other work Schauff is the only bicycle company listed in Germany's top ten 'Design Ranking'.

In 1997 Jan Schauff founded Soil, a new high-end product-line within the Schauff range. The range covers everything from mountain bikes (with various levels of suspension) to road racing machines, and in 1998 two titanium bikes have been added to the range, including a disc-braked, fully-suspended mountain bike weighing under 10kg.

Schauff products are available at cycle shops throughout Europe. In case of difficulty, contact Fahrradfabrik Schauff, Postfach 1669, Industriegebiet, D-53406 Remagen/Rhein, GERMANY.
Tel +49 2642 93640 Fax +49 2642 3358
Email schauff@aol.com
Website www.schauff.com

In Germany, the Andalusia Disc costs around DM 2499. Prices will vary worldwide.

ANDALUSIA DISC

The traditional general-purpose bike is still at the heart of cycling. Mountain bikes and lightweight racing machines are wonderful for mountains and races, but for reliable, enjoyable transport in urban or rural environments, you need a quality city bike. Taking appropriate technology from both MTB and road bike fields, Schauff have produced the Andalusia Disc, a bike that can take the rider far from the city as easily and as well as to the shops.

Magura Louise disc brakes front and rear will be a revelation for anyone who hasn't experienced the all-weather, long-lasting stopping power of disks. You can fly down hills knowing that brakes will stop with power and control no matter what the load. Even in the rain, there's no need to clench the levers painfully: a light touch is enough – particularly welcome for riders with weak hands.

Mudguards, rack and dynamo lights are fitted as standard to the lightweight cromoly frame. Gears are

Shimano LX 27-speed, with XT derailleurs. The Union Quattro dynamo runs Busch & Müller lights, the rear light with a 'standlight' that stays alight even when stationary. Both lights have reflectors built in. The Andalusia Disc comes with a unisex Selle San Marco Regal leather suspended saddle, while the hand sewn leather grips on the handlebars provide the finishing touch.

Another general-purpose bike with a difference is Schauff's Alexis Electric 700C: the world's first fully-suspended electric bike using 700C wheels. Front suspension is a spring elastomer, with hydraulic rear suspension, and both are adjustable for ride quality and rider weight. Schauff have been producing suspension cruising bikes since 1993, and these are especially popular for riders with back problems or rheumatism. This electric-assist version should, say Schauff, open up cycling to even more people. A low step-through frame and a weight of 26kg add to the

ease of use. The power is supplied by a Mitsubishi power pack, and the computer controlled Ni-Cd battery pack gives 40km (25 miles) range. A SRAM seven-speed hub gear offers a wide gear range and low maintenance, and the bike comes complete with rack, mudguards and dynamo lighting system.

Koninklijke Gazelle

Koninklijke Gazelle (Royal Gazelle) has been one of Holland's trendsetters in cycling for over a century. Founded in 1892, it is one of the oldest and largest cycle makers in Holland. Gazelle was acquired in 1987 by the Derby International Group, whose other brands include Raleigh (in Britain) and Brooks, as well as the German brands Kalkhoff, Rixe, Müsing, Focus and Winora. Gazelle's 550 employees produce around 300,000 bikes a year. The Company has over 1500 dealers in the Netherlands, and about 20% of production goes to countries such as Belgium, Germany and Denmark. They make everything from mountain bikes, hybrids, race bikes to children's cycles. Components designed in-house are exclusively fitted to all Gazelle bikes.

Koninklijke Gazelle BV, Postbus 1, 6950 AA Dieren, NETHERLANDS.
Tel +31 313 429 911 Fax +31 313 422 558
Email info@gazelle.nl Website www.gazelle.nl

In the Netherlands, the Furore costs around f 1799. Prices will vary worldwide.

FURORE

Comfort, performance, low weight, low maintenance: put them in any order you like, but they remain the cornerstones of good cycle design. The Gazelle Furore achieves this difficult combination in some style, bringing the best of modern design creativity to a genre of bicycle becoming known as the city hybrid.

The heart of the Furore is the oversized 6061 aluminium frame. Alongside the top-tube version is a 'Ladies' version, which is available either with a 'standard' low step-through frame (double downtube), or with a super-low easy-access frame (single, curved, oversize tube).

Rider comfort is cleverly built into many aspects of the Furore's design. Most noticeable is Gazelle's highly-adjustable Switch stem, which allows you to alter your handlebar position, pivoting from straight forward to straight up. This makes possible a variety of riding postures, and helps you choose a position which best distributes the amount of body weight you apply via your wrists and your bottom, easing soreness problems in both these sensitive areas. Once you have your optimum position there is nothing to stop you from adjusting it again to suit the kind of ride you happen to be on. The Switch is the first stem to be steplessly adjustable without tools, and was developed by Gazelle in partnership with industrial designers Peter van der Veer and Martijn Wegman.

Riding position is one thing, points of contact are another: Gazelle have seen to this with a fine gel-filled elastomer saddle, complemented by the Gazelle Aerowing Comfort handlebar grips.

The Furore is fitted with the low-maintenance Shimano Nexus seven-speed hub gear system, with simple operation via a Revo Shifter. Braking is powerful in all weathers, thanks to a Nexus rollerbrake in the rear hub, and a Sturmey-Archer Elite hub brake in the front. The lighting makes up a quality threesome: AXA HR+ dynamo, Gazelle PowerVision headlight, and AXA Optica Omega LED rear light, which automatically turns itself on when you ride in the dark.

Even the completely sealed chaincase and mudguards exhibit a flair for thoughtfulness and style not usually associated with such humble components. In fact, no design aspect is taken for granted by the Gazelle development team, led by Jo van Benthem: right down to the unique Gazelle Axis twist-operated bell!

NIRORAD

Customer satisfaction means, for Utopia, that the bike they supply must not only suit the customer down to the ground, it must also serve them well over decades rather than years. Utopia design bicycles specifically for the upright riding position. This style of cycling is, they believe, the most suitable for the everyday or touring cyclist for whom speed is not everything – the benefits include good visibility, an unstrained neck and lightly-loaded wrists. Because most of the weight is on the back of the machine, Utopia use single-butted Sapim spokes on every rear wheel, and insist that unsuspended saddles have no place in their range.

The latest Utopia cycle is the Nirorad, taking its name from the 'Nirosta' stainless steel from which it is constructed. Stainless steel is not an easy material to work with, but it guarantees complete corrosion-resistance and a fine appearance: the Nirorad is transparent powder-coated, enhancing the satinised finish of the thin-walled steel tubing. With a wheelbase of 116cm (more for taller frames), the Nirorad combining the

geometry of a classic touring bike with that of a West Coast cruiser.

The Nirorad is fitted as standard with Kangaroo suspension forks and an Airwings suspended seatpost – Utopia 'full suspension'. Every bike is made to the customer's precise specification. Utopia guide you through the options with their 'RadRatgeber', a comprehensive German-language guide to the components they recommend. At the end of it all, you have a bike that is truly your own. You can choose from nine different male or female saddles – or order the bike without and fit your own. Magura hydraulic brakes are a popular option, but cantilever, hub or back-pedal systems are effective alternatives. There's also a wide choice of transmissions – Utopia specialise in hub gears, but almost anything is possible. They were the first manufacturer to offer the Rohloff Speedhub for their bikes, and use a special version with solid axle and enlarged drillings to fit their single-butted spokes. Custom dropouts eliminate the need for a separate chain tensioner. On this, or on any other matter related to their cycles, Utopia are always delighted to advise.

Utopia

Utopia was built on the premise of sustainable development, and for this reason they source 90% of components from within Europe, reducing transport pollution. They select all of their production processes according to strict environmental criteria. The whole company recently moved to a new purpose-built factory constructed largely of wood, using the best principles of ecological architecture. The bikes are still craftsman-built, mostly by hand, using machines only where appropriate. Utopia have embraced the Internet, seeing it as a way to avoid the environmental cost of transporting paper catalogues around the world. Their German-language website allows their customers to design, specify, and price a bike on screen, or to browse the RadRatGeber (Cycle Guide), an informative and educational guide to the Utopia philosophy and to bikes in general.

Utopia, Kreisstr. 134F,
66128 Saarbrücken, GERMANY.
Tel +49 681 970360 Fax +49 681 9703611
Email utopia@saarmail.de
Website www.utopia-fahrrad.de

Prices depend on specification: a typical bike with Sachs Penta 5-speed gearing costs around DM1500, with Sachs 3x7 around DM1800, and with the Rohloff 14-speed hub around DM3500. The Nirorad costs from around DM2900. Prices will vary outside Germany.

Racing Bikes

It was much simpler in the old days. We didn't have all these different categories, a bike was just a bike. But nowadays it seems that there are as many types of bike as there are cyclists, and – particularly since the MTB explosion – the humble road bike has been sadly eclipsed. But the roadies live on, and cycle-touring is more popular than it has ever been.

Cycle racing is fast, addictive, and as old as bikes themselves. And it's hard. Hard on the riders, hard on their machines. Cycle sport involves a mixture of brain-work, endurance, exciting speeds, and danger. But there's also the technology. Races are often won or lost by the matter of a few seconds. Riders know this, so an integral part of the sport is the relentless quest for new and useful technological developments. Whether you are the manager of a pro team, or a young novice gazing through shop windows, having the best possible technology is an important aspect of your sport.

But racing can be on the receiving end of a spot of inverted snobbery nowadays. With the rebirth of cycling as a solution to all of humanity's ills, from congestion and pollution to alienation and crime, the whole 'Tour de France' side of things sometimes gets written off as a commercial sideshow. The cycle rights lobby has often had its work cut out to convince the powers that be that cycling is more than just a leisure pursuit. And the technological trickle-down from racing has not always benefited everyday cycling.

The great cycling events of the calendar have a colourful and heroic poetry of their own which takes them beyond the mundane and the showy. The Tour de France is one of the most testing of human endeavours. Finishing a single stage of the Tour demands the kind of physical fitness, stamina and psychological resilience to which most mere mortals can only aspire. Life in the peloton of riders is crowded and hectic with individuals riding as close as possible for aerodynamic benefit, with the constant danger of crashing at high speeds. And after 200 or more gruelling kilometres, they've got to do it all again the next day.

The effect on the rest of us is not always obvious. Heroic cycling feats mean more kids rushing out and emulating Greg Lemond and Chris Boardman instead of Michael Schumacher or Damon Hill. At the same time more and more people realise that there is something special about that unique combination of human power and relatively simple machinery – and because the higher levels of cycle technology are reasonably accessible to most of us, we can go out and buy the kind of bikes and equipment which the top professionals use. And if it's good for them, it's equally good for the rest of us – especially when we want the thrill of speed!

Cycling, on the edge of unaided travel, takes us as fast as it is possible to go, without leaving our spirit behind. Granted, we can whizz along in a train, a plane, or an automobile, but the experience lacks a certain something, that edge of reality which only self-powered travel provides. Whether the emphasis is on maximum human velocity, or simply pedalling steadily through the landscape, the road bike is still a machine which superbly combines the needs of the body and the spirit.

MAURIZIO TITANIUM

Eight kilograms isn't much. A few bags of sugar, a car bumper or, perhaps, a full-equipped Maurizio titanium racing bike on which to blast down the road to freedom. If you've never experienced the thrill of a really light, thoroughbred bike, you should – just try not to get addicted.

Titanium is for many competitive cyclists the dream frame material. Lighter than steel for the same strength, it also has excellent fatigue properties. Unfortunately, it's always been very expensive and came in one colour – titanium grey. It's these two drawbacks that the Maurizio range from Dutch company Blomson International have successfully overcome.

Built in Russia where titanium is most naturally abundant, Maurizio frames are transported to Holland, where, using a special pre-treatment of the metal surface, spectacular finishes are applied, fading the vibrant colours into the natural lustre of the titanium.

There won't be rust-spots where the metal is exposed: titanium is one of the most corrosion-resistant materials on the planet.

The Maurizio range covers road-racing, off-roading, cyclo-cross and triathlon. The road-race frame comes in three guises: the single-colour Classico, and the more dynamic Ventura and Fiori. Build-up options give a choice between Shimano 105, Ultegra and Dura Ace, and Campag Veloce, Chorus and Record goupsets. There's also a choice of either titanium or carbon fibre forks.

The frames are spectacularly light. The Fiori frame weighs just 1.28 kg, and you can have a complete bike at 7.8kg. Classico and Ventura frames weigh just 1,4 and 1.35kg respectively.

Two titanium off-roaders, a triathlon machine and a cyclocross bike complete the Maurizio range. Titanium forks, stems, seat posts and saddles are also available to complement the bikes.

Blomson International

The secret behind the Maurizio range is the new technology developed in Holland to apply spectacular finishes to the titanium frames. Each frame is X-rayed to check the quality of the welding, and is given a serial number, and is then sold with a five year guarantee. Blomson keep large stocks of all frame sizes, which means they can usually despatch orders within 48 hours.

Blomson International B.V., A. Hofmanweg 28, 2031 BL Haarlem, The NETHERLANDS. Tel +31 23 5422044 Fax +31 23 5422208.

In the Netherlands, prices range from f 4800, frames from f 2300. Prices will vary worldwide.

WATERFORD 2200

Road racing bicycles have received more design attention in the past century than any other type of two-wheeled machine. Waterford has distilled this knowledge into a purist's dream, down to the finest detail.

The Waterford 2200 uses a special oversize Reynolds 853 tubeset, with 1 1/8" top tube and 1 1/4" downtube. Waterford includes some unusual twists. Tapered chainstays flare to a diameter of 24mm at the bottom bracket, and the seatpost flares from 1 1/8" to 30mm. Together, these flares strengthen the bottom bracket area, allowing Waterford to lighten the tubing throughout the rest of the frame. The result combines stiffness, light weight, high reliability and great ride comfort.

Waterford remains a fan of lugged construction and continues to advance the art. Twenty years ago, virtually no quality racing bicycles were built without lugs. Today, lug builders are a rare species. Most lug builders have come to rely on off-the-shelf lugs which make even high-quality hand-built frames somewhat generic.

Waterford designs its own lugset to match its special tube dimensions. The current generation of lugs represents a pinnacle of design – with clean, low-profile lines without pretension. The Waterford lugset includes its own innovative details. Many lugs perform double duty, not only as structural supports but also as cable guides. This keeps the top tube free from braze-ons – the main hot-spots for corrosion. The lower head lug contains threaded guides into which plug the derailleur cables. The rider can adjust the cable tension on the fly. By integrating cable guides, Waterford also avoids the need to heat the main tubes any more than necessary.

Waterford uses beautiful Henry James investment-cast stainless-steel dropouts and fork crowns, specially-tapered Reynolds 531 fork blades and unique bridge reinforcements. The combination of stiffness at the crown and flexibility at the tips gives a superb ride.

From a distance, the Waterford has a clean if undistinctive look. Look more closely and you find careful attention from dropout to dropout, with painstaking precision in construction. The Waterford represents true fundamentalism in bicycle design.

Richard Schwinn (left) and Marc Muller

Waterford Precision Cycles

Waterford was set up in 1993 by Richard Schwinn and Marc Muller. Marc was among the pioneering framebuilders working with Henry James investment castings in the late 1970s. Marc took over the Paramount brand in 1980 and masterminded its rebirth, culminating in the development of the oversize design late in the decade. Marc's other innovations include vertical dropouts on mountain bikes, four-bar rear suspension linkages and 650C wheel designs. Richard's career includes work inside and outside the bicycle industry. Marc and Richard joined up at Schwinn in 1990, revamping Schwinn's engineering and technical services before buying the old Paramount factory in 1993 to form Waterford.

Waterford builds its standard and custom bicycles in southeast Wisconsin. Best-known for road race bicycles, they have a reputation encompassing touring bikes, cyclocross and mountain bikes. Waterford offers 21 stock road-racing geometries, among over 300 stock designs.

Waterford Precision Cycles, 816 W. Bakke Ave., Waterford, Wisconsin 53185, USA.
Tel +1 414 534 4190 Fax +1 414 534 4194
Website: www.waterfordbikes.com

Frame prices for the 2200 start at $1300. Complete (Ultegra) bikes based on the 2200 frame start at $2400. Waterford offers substantial custom flexibility.

New Series Moulton

In 1962, Alex Moulton injected fresh thinking into cycle design with his small wheeled 'F' frame bicycles and revolutionary front and rear wheel suspension system. Variations of this concept have been used to break HPV world and national cycling records. Twice, an AM has successfully completed the Race Across America. But, it is for every day riding and leisure touring that his concept was created and the New Series Moulton is a further advancement of that objective.

Central to this concept are the small wheels, strong, easy to accelerate and compact. The New Series uses 18.3" (ERTRO 406) wheels, with super-high pressure Continental tyres. Small wheels and high-pressure tyres demand suspension. At the front, four rubber torsion elements are linked in anti-dive geometry: this 'Flexitor' system eliminates 'stiction' (and so soaks up the smallest of bumps for a silky ride) needs no lubrication and no maintenance. A soft-lockout on the front forks allows the rider to limit the travel and to damp the front suspension for out-of-the-saddle sprints or climbs whilst on the move. The rear is an adjustable fluid-damped 'Hydrolastic' unit, a carry-over from Alex's innovative suspensions for the Mini and the MGF motor cars.

The New Series has a nine-speed transmission, with a wide range from 10t to 32t and closely-spaced ratios. The 'Wishbone' handlebar stem is fully adjustable with fingertip controls on the 'Mosquito' (narrow frontal area) handlebar. The low step-through frame separates into two for portability and into five parts for a really compact package. Available in polished aerospace 304 stainless steel or Reynolds 531 small diameter tubing, the complete bicycle weighs 22lbs.

The New Series Moulton is at the top end of the price scale, but one Moultoneer expressed the situation well. "To a music-lover, the cost of a top-notch stereo system is perfectly justified in terms of the pleasure it can bring. Money should be used to enhance your life – by buying the best"

Alex Moulton Ltd

There are now three ranges of Moultons in production. The New Series and the AM ranges are handmade on the Moulton family estate in Bradford on Avon. The APB is made under licence by Pashley in Stratford on Avon using Moulton jigs. There is also a version of the New Series available with the grease-free Thun belt-drive system, and the belt drive stainless steel model has been adopted as the 'Bentley bicycle'. Various accessories, including the AM-designed Lepper Voyager saddle with Reynolds 531 rails, and a range of custom made fairings, carriers and bags are available.

Alex Moulton Bicycles, Bradford on Avon, Wiltshire, BA15 1AH, UK.
Tel +44 1225 86 5895 Fax +44 1225 86 4742
Email ambikes@alexmoulton.co.uk
Website: www.alexmoulton.co.uk

Dwarf Safety

'Coming a cropper' was, to the young daredevils of the high-wheeler's heyday, all part of the fun of riding those magnificent machines. Other riders, who enjoyed the freedom and thrill of cycling, but not the danger, had to wait until the inventors came up with a safer sort of cycling.

The solution was the design which came to be known as the 'Dwarf Safety'. By making the front wheel smaller, and moving the rider back and down, weight was shifted to the rear wheel, significantly reducing the chance of the rider flying over the handlebars. To compensate for the smaller wheel, a chain drive was used to increase the distance travelled with each turn of the pedals.

It is this design which Mike West, a York engineer with twelve years' experience of building high-wheelers, has re-created. Modern technology ensures that the chains on Mike's

machines are much more reliable than those on nineteenth century originals. Mike also offers concealed modern ball-bearings for the axles, in place of the plain bearings often used on original machines.

The rims are made by another York craftsman, Len Clucas, to be built by Mike into wheels with the old-fashioned but very effective 'V' double spokes, with two ends at the rim. It takes three days to build a wheel: such long spokes need to 'settle in' overnight between truing sessions to allow the wire to stretch. 40" wheels are standard, but this can be reduced to 38" for shorter riders. The tyres are made of three-quarter inch thick rubber moulded around a 'helicoil' wire.

Ride this bicycle and you'll combine the exhilaration of high-wheeling without the terror: you'll also recapture a very special moment in history. The

most famous model with this layout, the 'Kangaroo' of 1884, enjoyed just a few years of success before being superseded by a new generation of bicycles with chain-drive to the rear wheel.

Mike stresses that the machine shown here is his prototype, and further machines will be equipped with more highly-refined handlebars with extra knee clearance. He has also made numerous detail improvements to tidy the appearance, including a radically-altered hub and fork layout.

Mike West

Mike West has been building high bicycles for twelve years. His original product, the 'Challenge' high bicycle, is built to a variety of specifications, and with choices of handlebar shape, handle grips style, crank and pedal type.

Wheel sizes are from 50" to 54". The bigger the wheel you can comfortably ride on, the faster you can go, since every turn of the pedals takes you the same distance as the circumference of the wheel. Yet the larger the wheel, the further there is to fall! A rider 6' (183 cm) tall can ride a 50" (127cm) wheel, but 53" (135cm) is recommended. Mike strongly recommends that if you are going to ride one of his bikes on a regular basis you should choose the modern and cheaper crank and pedal option; they make for a more enjoyable ride and don't look particularly out of place.

Mike West, Bishopthorpe Bikes, 35 Keble Park North, Bishopthorpe, York YO23 2SX, UK.
Tel +44 1904 703 413

In the UK, a cycle from Mike West costs £1500, although this will vary according to specification.

Fun Bikes

Pedal-power has always attracted inventive minds. When the major alternative to pedal power was still horse power, practical if odd-looking vehicles were designed to perform many civic functions. In Germany a firemen's quadricycle could be rushed to a blaze to deploy its pedal-powered pump. In America a Police Patrol Tricycle was used to transport criminals, secured hand and foot, to the lock up. There was a pedal-powered fish and chip shop in the UK, and knife-grinding bicycles, once common in Europe, are still found in India. The low running and purchase costs of pedal-powered vehicles have kept classics like the ice cream tricycle competitive against motorised equivalents.

Other specialised cycles have emphasised leisure and fun rather than utility – or the serious intent of their inventors was quickly subverted by entrepreneurs who spotted their entertainment potential. Arthur Hotchkiss, for example, devised a monorail at the end of the 19th Century for commuters to ride to an American factory. They powered themselves along a fence rail by means of a treadle mechanism driving a twenty-inch wheel. Such a comical contraption could be transformed into the perfect ride for amusement parks; which is where most monorails are now found.

The dream of bicycles on tracks persists: a Canadian firm has plans for a high tech system in which pedal-powered vehicles on rails would be boosted along tubes by air pumps. In complete contrast, enthusiastic mechanics around the world are designing their own bikes to ride along abandoned railways tracks; there are over 80,000 miles of abandoned rails in the United States alone. Dozens of patents have been granted for different designs.

Pedal-powered boats have been cruising lakes and rivers since the 1880s, driven by paddle wheels, or propellers. In the 1880s a Mr. Terry invented a tricycle which he rode to Dover, converted within minutes into a boat, and rowed over the Channel to France. Since then at least four waterbikes have crossed oceans. As part of their 'Pedal for the Planet' expedition, Jason Lewis and Steve Smith from Britain crossed the Atlantic from Portugal to Miami in 111 days.

The Americans were particularly inventive, especially during the great cycling boom of the late 1890s. That fascination for experimentation in cycling has returned in the USA, but there is also a great sense of fun. For the last twenty years, for example, an annual event has been held in Northern California in which a number of fantastic, locally concocted machines have taken to streets, beaches, rivers and bay for a three-day 'Kinetic Sculpture' race.

Everyone loves to go beyond the everyday experience of cycling, to create a spectacle, a splash or to turn cycling into a group experience. On the pages which follow we show pedal-powered vehicles which go that little bit further. Not only are they great fun for the riders, they are also an asset to any leisure facility worth its name. There is the Hydrobike which can tour canals and lakes, but which will attract the attention of entrepreneurs in the leisure industry. And the Octos: an astonishing 'friendship bike', one of which should be owned by every large community and leisure complex. And what a great way to conduct a business meeting, or catch up with a bit of gossip with your friends!

Staller Studios

Octos was conceived by artist/inventor Eric Staller, internationally recognised for his witty and humanistic mobile public artworks. He sees great potential for the Octos as a vehicle for hire or lease: it needs little imagination to see how an Octos can bring huge PR benefits to any event it attends, or to any organisation with which it is identified. It's also a great attraction in its own right: every theme park should have one circulating among the visitors, spreading goodwill and fun, and also providing fume-free, useful transport. The Octos is a moving experience for all: two people even met on a ride, fell in love and got married!

You can read more about Eric Staller and his work in Encycleopedia 4, page 126.

Staller Studio, Herengracht 100, 1015 BS Amsterdam, NETHERLANDS.
Tel/Fax +31 20 624 9198

The Octos costs around US$7500.00, excluding tax and shipping costs from Amsterdam. An Octos easily proves itself a solid investment at 40 rentals per year.

OCTOS

"I've been riding an Octos for a year now – I take it to festivals, civic events, corporate groups, schools and weddings. The Octos is a mobile party – every time I take it out I feel I am giving and receiving joy. All sorts of people climb on board, but the reaction is always the same: they are amazed and delighted. It's like an amusement park ride that has broken loose from its moorings and is rolling down the street. I love to watch the riders smiling, and the expressions of surprise on the faces of passers-by. It's a carefree ride for the passengers: they're pedalling, but someone else is steering. They feel secure and comfortable. They realise they are sharing something wonderful, and this starts some great conversations, even among strangers."

Hans Josso, Amsterdam

The Octos from Staller Studio is a futuristic tricycle for up to seven riders sitting in a circle. Since its introduction in Encycleopedia 4, artist and inventor Eric Staller has devoted a year to research and development. He has come up with a completely new transmission: a chain-drive system that has improved the efficiency many-fold.

The steering and handling have been drastically improved, simply by moving from four to three wheels. The Octos now can U-turn in its own length (240cm). The rider in charge of the steering is now at the back, rather than out in front as on the first Octos, excluded from the circle. This more inclusive arrangement strengthens the togetherness of the crew.

Made of steel tubing with an automotive finish, the Octos has motorcycle wheels and disc brakes. It weighs approximately 100 kilos.

EXPLORER

Why should the pleasures of pedal-power be restricted to dry land? On the Hydro-Bike Explorer a whole new experience opens up: quiet, pollution-free travel on the water.

Aquatic travel is never uphill, although you might have to fight against the current. On the Explorer that's no problem. With a cruising speed of 6-10km/h (4-6mph) and a maximum speed of around 15km/h (10mph), you can expect to overtake rowing boats and canoes with ease. The widely-spaced unsinkable floats make the craft extraordinarily stable, and the high riding position gives an excellent view of your surroundings. You can safely stand up and have a stretch from time to time – not something to be recommended on most small craft – and there's a handy 'glove compartment' for lunch and camera. You could even use the Explorer as a swimming or fishing platform.

A retractable rudder at the front controls the steering. The Explorer is highly manoeuverable even in reverse. It needs a minimum water depth of around 45cm (18"), depending on the weight of the rider, and the overall length is just over 3 metres. You can lift the propellor out of the water using the lever behind the saddle. Total weight is around 45kg, and you can mount a fully-assembled Explorer onto a car roof-rack, and it disassembles in minutes to fit into a small van.

The Explorer has been designed with the hire market in mind, so durability has been a design priority. Only seawater-resistant components are used, including an aluminium frame and stainless-steel gears. Maintenance requirements are minimal.

The whole family can share the Explorer experience. Conventional racks and child-seats can be fitted, or there's also the 'Explorer II': two 'bikes' and three floats coupled together to create a wonderful, waterborne sociable tandem with space for a child-seat between the riders.

Hydro-Bikes

The Hydro-Bike was developed over a period of four years in America. It's since been in action all over the world. Operators who use Hydro-Bikes in their fleets regularly report back: one told of how a hire manager saved the life of a canoeist in difficulty by jumping onto an Explorer and getting to the scene long before the official lifeguards. In America, two Hydro-Bikers rode 1800km (1200 miles) upstream along the Mississippi, taking just sixty days for the voyage. They reported no technical problems whatsoever. Indeed, a frequent comment from hire outfits is that it's impossible to tell a four-year-old Explorer from a brand-new vehicle, so corrosion-resistant are the materials used.

Manufacturer: Hydro-Bike, Inc., P.O.Box 889, Wyoming 55092, USA.
Tel +1 612 462 2212 Fax +1 612 462 1752
Website www.hydrobike.com
Agent in Germany: Victor GmbH, Halbmond 8, 21481 Lauenburg, GERMANY.
Tel 0049 4153 52 323 Fax 0049 4153 51048
Agents in other countries: see page 144.

*In Germany, the Explorer costs from around DM 3750.
Prices will vary worldwide.*

Power-Assist

Whether it's because of a minor disability, or just old age, not everyone can ride a bike. And in hilly or spread-out districts, all but the fittest people can feel daunted at the idea of relying on their own power to take them where they need to go.

The idea of putting a motor on a bike is almost as old as bikes themselves, but the idea of 'power-assist' has really come to the fore in just the last few years. Unlike mopeds, whose motors are their main means of propulsion, electric bikes are fitted with a small motor to help the rider when the going gets tough. The idea is not to make a faster, more powerful vehicle, but simply to flatten the hills and shorten the miles. The end product is essentially a fairly conventional bike, but one that lends a hand when required.

Electric bikes were pioneered during the 1980s, with various enthusiasts producing systems that were often based around a normal bike being retro-fitted with a motor. In 1990 the 'Velocity' was produced in Switzerland. This was a new development: instead of the motor connecting directly with the back wheel via a friction drive on the tyre or a separate chain and sprocket, its power was blended directly with that of the rider; the combined output was fed to the drivetrain. Since then, electronic 'couplers' have become common; they link the motor's output to the effort put in by the rider – so there's more assistance when you're working hard, for instance when climbing a hill. The motor only helps out when the rider is under pressure.

Consequently, some countries have enshrined couplers in legislation relating to power-assist bikes. If the transmission ensures that the machine behaves like a normal bicycle (albeit one with a rider whose legs get bigger on hills), then it is seen as such by the authorities. Other electric motors simply fit on to an existing bike and can be operated so that the power cuts in whenever the rider chooses.

Ten years ago, the electric-assisted bicycle was something of a novelty. But during the 1990s the idea really took off, and in the last few years sales have soared. Two-wheelers are less held back than electric cars by the difficulties in developing the next generation of rechargeable batteries. Less power is required, and it has been possible to produce machines that are of practical use. Consumer interest has also taken off – particularly in Japan, where sales have surged to over 150,000 electric bikes a year. The stage looks set for the rest of the world to follow suit. The electric bike will then come to be both a means of helping less energetic people back to mobility, and of drawing newcomers in to cycling. Fears have been raised that electric power will eclipse human power. But once healthy-bodied people get used to whizzing about on two wheels, they will probably come to learn that they can do the same under their own steam, without having to worry about charge levels. So their next bike might be a conventional mountain bike, and after that maybe even a city bike.

Z-BIKE

With cities across the world choking in exhaust, there's a special need for an electric bike affordable enough to tempt large numbers of motorists from their cars. For the less-athletic, elderly or for anyone who regularly faces long or hilly journeys, the ZAP Z-Bike could be the answer. The specially-made, low-stepthrough frame with 20" (406) wheels adjusts to fit a wide range of riders, and V-brakes provide powerful stopping from any speed. With 'Arc' handlebars and a dual-spring saddle, the riding poistion is comfortable and upright.

The heart of the Z-bike is the 22lb (9.1kg) ZAP Power System, which is also available separately to fit almost any bike or trike. It powers the rear wheel, and gives a maximum speed of 14mph (22.4km/h) and a range of up to 20 miles (32km), depending on terrain and how much you pedal. You can disengage the assist system at the flick of a switch. The charge time from the mains is five hours, or you can keep fit on the optional 'Exercise/Charging Stand' by recharging your batteries yourself, in as little as one hour. On some models, you can also switch the system to 'Regenerative Mode' to partially recharge your batteries as you roll downhill.

If that's not wild enough, how about the ZAPPY? This is an electric scooter with a fold-down steering column at the front, 'small enough to fit in a school locker, but fast enough to ZAP you across town'. To ride, you punt with your foot and/or engage the throttle for electric power up to 12mph (19km/h). The range is around 10 miles, and the machine comes complete with rear drum brake and integrated 110 volt charger. Recharging takes 4-5 hours, and the total weight is 16kg. Both Z-Bike and ZAPPY have the option of European-standard 220-volt charging.

ZAP Power Systems

ZAP, or 'Zero Air Pollution', is a company that bases itself on environmental credibility. Even when power-station emissions are taken into account, a ZAP-powered bike creates 90% less pollution than a petrol-driven car – and it could, of course, be powered from renewable energy.
ZAP was founded in 1994 by Jim McGreen and Gary Starr. In 1997, ZAP was one of the first companies to go public via the internet, and it now has over 1,500 shareholders. More than 20,000 ZAP bikes or power-packs have been sold to date in sixty countries. Clients include 130 different US law enforcement agencies ("We like the ZAP bikes because we can catch people faster!"). ZAP reports a recent surge of interest in Hollywood, where everyone from humble gofers to box-office stars are using ZAPPYs to get around the enormous film sets with ease and style.

ZAP Power Systems, 117 Morris St., Sebastopol,CA 95472, USA.
Tel +1 707 824 4150 Fax +1 707 824 4159
Email zap@zapbikes.com
Website www.zapbikes.com
ZAP Europe, XtraMOBIL AG, Schlössli im Laubi, CH-8193 Eglisau, SWITZERLAND.
Tel +41 1867 1525 Fax +41 1867 1406

In the USA, prices are around $675 for both the Z-Bike and for the ZAPPY. Prices will vary worldwide.

H POWER & SMARTWHEELS

Crossing the finish line in the 350-mile 1998 American Tour de Sol was a very remarkable vehicle. Powered by no less than four separate sources of energy, it was a demonstrator for one of today's most promising technologies. Third overall in the race, it was awarded the Engineering Excellence award. Alongside pedal power, a small solar panel and a bank of lead-acid batteries, it employed a 200-watt fuel cell from H Power Corporation.

A fuel cell converts chemical energy, stored as pure hydrogen and oxygen, to electrical energy, directly and silently. Other than water, the only by-product of this process is heat, which may be reclaimed to increase the already high efficiency of the process.

The gasses which power the cell, hydrogen and oxygen, can be produced efficiently and cleanly using electricity to break down water into its component elements. If the electricity comes from a renewable source, the whole cycle has remarkably low environmental impact. Wherever the energy comes from, there's no pollution at point of use. And unlike many battery systems, fuel cells don't require toxic heavy metals in their construction. Fuel cells have the

further advantage that they don't need lengthy recharging: so long as fuel is supplied, the fuel cell can produce electricity. Liquified hydrogen can be stored safely in robust canisters, with snap-on fittings for changing the tank.

Based on a Chaise 3 recumbent tricycle from Comfort Cycle of Cleveland, the vehicle which competed in the Tour de Sol is one of the first to be powered by fuel cell technology. The fuel cell used on the trike delivered the same power and energy as the battery system, in a package

about the same size, but half the weight. The potential for other vehicles, be they power-assisted bikes or velomobiles, lightweight cars or even buses, is huge.

The electric motor used on the Tour de Sol trike was no less remarkable than the power source. a 'SmartWheels' brushless DC motor built into the hub of the wheel providing 420 Watts of continuous power, with a peak of 750 Watts from a 24-30VDC power source. The control electronics, gearing and motor are all contained in the 6lbs (2.7kg) hub, protected by high quality seals from the weather. This simplicity makes it easy and economic to fit power-assist onto any bike, just by mounting a SmartWheel on the front fork.

Where more power is needed SmartWheels produce the Power Box, with 500W power and peak power of 900W: this is a more conventional brushless d.c. motor which drives the wheel though a chain and sprocket and is designed for load-carrying vehicles. The more powerful 750W Muscle Box uses neodynium magnets, and similar packaging, weighs only 7lbs (3.2kg) and comes in a 2" x 6" x 8" (5 x 15 x 20cm) aluminium case.

H Power Corp. & Smartwheels Corp.

Founded in 1989, H Power Corp. is a world leader in the design and development of fuel cell power systems. They have focused on "developing products with near-term payoff," starting with low-wattage portable applications, and working towards electric power generators for stationary and vehicular applications. The company has its headquarters and manufacturing facilities in Belleville, New Jersey. It also has facilities at its subsidiary in Montreal, Canada.
Smartwheels, Inc. was set up by Jim Dunn. Jim's primary work is as a manager of NASA's Regional Centre for Technology Commercialisation, where his job is to recognise new ideas that have a potential market. However, he also works developing other advanced technology in alternate energy and electric vehicle fields, and the Smartwheels project resulted from Jim's work designing and developing five award-winning entries in the American Tour de Sol races.

H Power Corp. 60 Montgomery Street Belleville, NJ 07109, USA. Tel +1 973 450 4400 Fax +1 973 450 9850 Email moreinfo@hpower.com Website www.hpower.com

Smartwheels Corp., 60 Prescott St., Worcester, MA. 01605, USA. Tel +1 508 7913200 Fax +1 508 791 6886 Email smartwheels@earthlink.net Website www.smartwheel.com

Comfort Cycle, 1422 Euclid Ave, Suite 872, Cleveland, OH 44115, USA. Tel 216 475 6100 Fax 216 475 1033 Website www.comfortcycle.com

In the USA, a Smartwheel costs from around $499, the Power Box from $449 and the Muscle Box from $549. Basic 10Ah 24V power packs inc throttle kit and charger $199, Hi-Power 20Ah version: $269. Comfort Cycle tricycles start at around $2295. H Power fuel cells cost from around $1950, but prices will vary greatly according to specification.

BK Tech AG

The Flyer was inspired by Reto Böhlen's and Philippe Kohlbrenner's long, hilly rides to work. They couldn't make the hills disappear, so began to wonder whether a little electric assistance could be arranged. They teamed up with Christian Häuselmann to develop a prototype and went on to form BKTech in 1995. The Flyer went into commercial production a year later, and within three months they had won the Vigier Young Entrepreneurs' award, and invested the Sfr100 000 prize money to good effect. A major input of venture capital followed, and the Flyer is now distributed through a network of around 50 retailers across Switzerland.

BKTech AG, Industrie Neuhof 9, 3422 Kirchberg, SWITZERLAND. Tel +41 34 448 60 60

Prices in Switzerland range from sfr4450 to sfr6000, and will vary greatly worldwide. If you are interested in the Flyer it would be wise to check the legal requirements in your country.

FLYER

Switzerland is a country famed for its enlightened attitude towards sustainable transport. Yet just a year ago, electric bikes were still seen – even by the Swiss – as a rather far-fetched idea. Now, companies like BKTech are introducing bikes whose practicality gives them popular appeal, especially in the areas where geography makes commuting by bike a trial for all but the fittest. The Flyer has even helped to bring about a new traffic category, the 'schnelle Klasse' (fast category) for electric bikes which are exempt from the previous restrictions requiring the power-assist to cut out at speeds above 20km/h.

The Flyer is based on a 53cm frame from Villiger, a major Swiss cycle-maker with a high reputation. The power unit fits neatly inside the 'diamond', with the power boost transmitted by a second chain onto an inner chainwheel. The motor measures how fast you are pedalling, and regulates its output to ensure that you don't have to strain at the pedals. It cuts out immediately if you

stop pedalling, so there's no danger of being 'carried away'.

The power unit contains a built-in, 'intelligent' charger: just plug it into a electrical wall socket. It's set up as standard to suit European (including UK) mains voltage, but other configurations are possible: check with BKTech. The lead-gel battery will charge up fully in three hours, has a built-in charge indicator, and also powers the front and rear lights. The 'cruising' speed is 30-35km/h, and the total range on a single charge is between 35 and 50km. Total weight, including battery and charger, is around 33kg.

There are four models available, in a range of colours: the Flyer 7 is fitted with a Nexus 7 speed transmission; the Flyer 3 x 7 has 21-speed Sachs gearing; the Flyer S also has Sachs gears, but with sharper geometry and upgraded components, and there's also a high-end 'Limited Edition' version available. You can order a Flyer S or 'Limited Edition' with a more powerful motor, and a solar-powered charger is available for all models.

DOLPHIN

Velocity Engineering

The Dolphin's power unit has an impressive pedigree. The variable transmission system is a spin-off from the Twike pedal-assist electric vehicle: Velocity's designer Michael Kutter was part of the original project team, and was working on a reverse-gear system. What he came up with didn't suit the Twike, but he noticed that it worked a treat on the two-wheeler he was using as a test-bed. He decided that it was too good to waste and kept developing it, and by 1996 Valerie Zumsteg and Jürg Birkenstock were able to win both the women's and men's categories at the World Solar Bicycle Championships on bikes fitted with Velocity power/transmission units.

Velocity Engineering AG, Burgweg 15, CH-4058 Basel, SWITZERLAND. Tel/Fax +41 61 6934358 Email velocity@swissonline.ch Website www.velocity.ch

In Switzerland, the Dolphin costs from Sfr 3500. Prices will vary worldwide.

As a dolphin swims through the sea, so a bicycle slips through congestion-choked cities. There are even more striking parallels to be drawn when it comes to the Velocity Dolphin electric-assist bicycle. Its marine namesake covers large distances through the ocean, using a minimum of energy, and without causing disruption to the natural rhythms of marine life as it passes. Just so does the Dolphin pass through the traffic, without pollution, and with maximum efficiency.

At the Dolphin's heart is its continually variable transmission, built into the rear hub. In combination with an electronic cadence sensor, its planetary gearing continuously varies the gear ratio between the chainwheel and the rear wheel. You keep pedalling at a comfortable, constant cadence, independent of your speed. You can accelerate from 0 to 33km/h (20 mph) without changing gear. Riding the Dolphin is very simple – just jump on and use it like any other bike, but with this one you can enjoy the sensation of travelling on what feels like an airport-style 'moving pavement'.

The Dolphin is fitted with an electronic security system incorporating an automatic immobiliser. Leave the bike unattended for four minutes, and the electric system locks up. To release it, you key in your personal code number. The frame's special dropouts prevent thieves from simply replacing the rear wheel and bypassing the electronic lock-out. Likewise, the battery is lockable in place.

The bike itself is built up on a specially-made aluminium frame, fitted with 26" (559) wheels and SRAM 3x7 gears. Stepover height is low, a feature especially appreciated by many women, and the built-in lights are powered from the main battery unit. With a cruising speed of 35km/h, the range is around 25km (15 miles) with the standard lightweight 7Ah battery pack, depending on terrain and use. An optional second battery pack fits under the carrier rack to extend the range to 50km (30 miles). You can quick-recharge at any household electrical socket: charge time from empty is just one hour.

Mobility

Everyone can enjoy cycling. There are no limitations, because pedal-power is infinitely adaptive. Its purpose is to enhance and extend the incredible power of the human body, so the machine is built around that body, with details of design responding to details of need. So if your body's not conventional, cycle technology can adapt. There are as many disabilities as there are disabled people. Consequently, the diversity of bikes for disabled people covers a vast range of needs. They are made all over the world by inspired designers and engineers, many of whom are disabled themselves.

The range goes from fairly standard bikes that are designed to be extra user-friendly, via easy-to-balance trikes and detachable wheelchair tandems, to ultra-light racing recumbent trikes with 84-gear hand-cranks.
Why do disabled people want to, or need to cycle? For the same reason as the able-bodied, and then some! The able-bodied have many activities which allow them to enjoy movement in the great outdoors: rambling, running, climbing, to name a few. But for the locomotor-disabled only the wheeled variety of recreation may be available, and the chance of a good bike ride can open up a whole new world.

The other reason is health. Most disabled people die not of their disability but of degenerative diseases associated with their inactive lifestyle. Swimming and 'wheeling' are limited in scope, but cycling combines exercise, pleasure, variety and practicality. In other words you can have a great time getting where you need to be, under your own steam, and keep fit in the process.

Cycling keeps you in touch with the sounds, smells and sensations of the real world. Sometimes the sky moves, the wind blows or the rain falls. Sometimes you stop to talk to people or to enjoy the view. Sometimes your muscles ache and you get fed up. That's what life's all about, whether you have a disability or not. Sitting passively in a car, cut off from nature and community alike, may be an unavoidable part of our lifestyle, but life-enhancing it is not.

Bikes for disabled people need to be extra-well designed and constructed. A problem which would be a minor irritation for most cyclists can become oppressive when even just getting on the machine is difficult. And of course, the implications of being stranded in the middle of nowhere, or crashing, are inevitably more serious.

The machines are often made in small production runs and may require considerable individual adaptation and the construction of special parts. So bikes for disabled people are often not cheap, although their cost can often be recovered from social security funds. But their potential for changing the quality of the owner's life makes a well-chosen machine more than good value for money.

ROLLFIETS, COPILOT, TRIO & T-BIKES 📼

Riding the Rollfiets is a shared pleasure. Bowling along a country lane or through busy city streets, able-bodied rider and disabled passenger alike are stimulated by the surroundings, by the motion and by the companionship of shared endeavour. Therapy at its best, invigorating the senses and the mind, while at the same time being perfectly practical.

The Rollfiets (known as the Duet in English-speaking countries) makes all this possible with a design of the highest quality, refined over more than 18 years. The latest 'Rollfiets NT' incorporates plenty of new technology – it is even more stable, more compact for transport and is adjustable to fit an even wider range of riders and passengers.

The wheelchair is based on an aluminium chassis, and is a fully-functional vehicle in its own right. The seat is 2cm lower than before, making transfers easier and improving stability. Headrests, arm supports and other specialised adaptations are available to suit almost any need, and the whole ABS seat-shell can be quickly removed, or swapped over for different passengers. The back support can be adjusted for angle, or folded forward as on a racing wheelchair. Two custom-made drum brakes ensure

powerful stopping, and a parking brake is fitted.

The 'bicycle' rear half attaches in seconds, and is normally equipped with a seven-speed Sachs hub gear. There are other options – a 'Mountain-Drive' two-speed bottom-bracket gearbox (see the 'Accessories' section in this Encycleopedia) and five-speed hub, or a power-assisted version with a small electric motor.

The cost of a Rollfiets is covered in many countries by various health insurance or social security provisions.

Support for applicants to such schemes, and much more, is offered by the 'Rollfiets Club' – an active association of thousands of enthusiastic users worldwide. Elderly, infirm or partly-disabled riders may be able to pedal for themselves, but find a two-wheeler uncomfortably wobbly. A tricycle may be the answer, and Robert Hoening offers a choice of two: the recumbent Trio and the upright T-Bikes.

The Trio will steer perfectly straight even at the lowest speeds, yet which

has the performance and braking to take full advantage of whatever amount of power the rider puts in. The relaxed seating position and rear suspension ensure comfort, even on longer journeys, and both handlebar and seat have a wide range of adjustment. A version is available for those with the use of only one hand. The Trio can be fitted with a range of special adaptations to suit other particular needs.

Standard equipment includes 21-speed Sachs gearing, full lighting, mudguards and a large carrier between the 26" (559) rear wheels. Braking is by Magura rim brakes on the front 20" (406) wheels, and two hydraulic discs at the rear. A parking brake makes mounting and dismounting steady and secure, and the handling is safe and predictable. The standard Trio weighs about 25kg, and a powerful motor version with a 500W engine and – according to the recent extra-energy test – a range of more than 150 km, is also available.

Another option for those wishing to resume their cycling on three wheels is a T-Bike (above). Well-known and widely respected for many years in the Netherlands, these tricycles are now being distributed worldwide (outside the Netherlands) by Robert Hoening. With two wheels at the front, obstacles can be negotiated with the widest part of the bike fully visible – and there are major benefits for stability, especially when braking. There are four sizes for all ages, and a host of possible modifications, including two motor-assisted versions (internal combustion and electric). The space between the front wheels can be filled with a capacious luggage basket.

Robert Hoening also distributes the delightful Copilot: a tandem which allows a disabled or partly-active child to take part in the steering process, giving them the therapeutically important sensation of being in control. The adult rider has wider handlebars, and so can override any mistakes or wilfulness on the part of the youngster.

Robert Hoening
Spezialfahrzeuge GmbH

The power of the pedal never ceases to amaze Robert Hoening. He feels that his is one of the best jobs in cycling – providing pedal-powered solutions to the mobility needs of thousands who might otherwise never know the pleasure of independent, self-propelled travel. His product range has been extending over many years – some machines originated elsewhere, but all are fully tested and further developed in the Hoening factory. The machines are distributed worldwide through agencies in individual countries, since he believes that special needs are best understood and fulfilled at a local level.

These products offer real therapeutic benefits for the rider, and the cost is often covered by health insurance or social security schemes. Robert Hoening is pleased to offer advice to those applying for such schemes.

Robert Hoening Spezialfahrzeuge GmbH, Ulmer Str. 16/2, D-71229 Leonberg, GERMANY. Tel +49 7152 979490 Fax +49 7152 979499 Email http:\\www.hoening.com For national agent details see page 145

The Rollfiets NT costs from DM 5.000. The cost is often covered by insurance. The Co-Pilot costs from DM 3.500. The Trio costs from DM 5.750, and the T-Bikes cost between DM 1.890 and DM 3.480. All prices will vary worldwide. The surcharge for any power assistance is about DM 3.000 to 4.000.

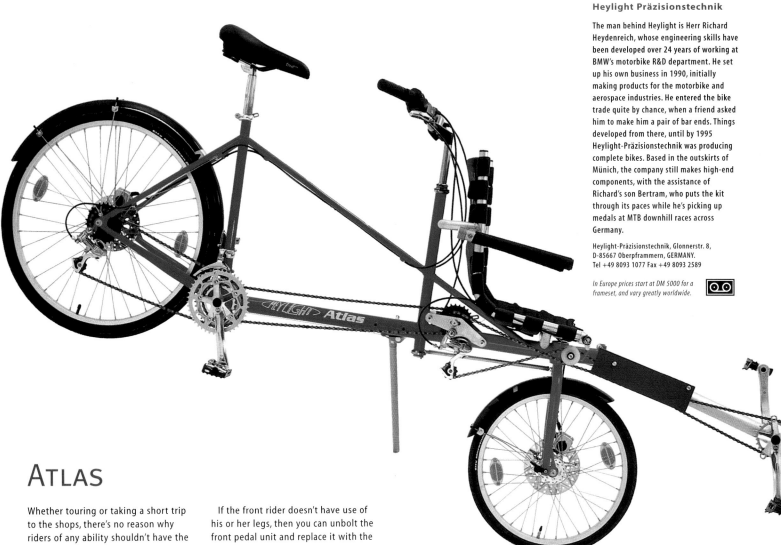

Heylight Präzisionstechnik

The man behind Heylight is Herr Richard Heydenreich, whose engineering skills have been developed over 24 years of working at BMW's motorbike R&D department. He set up his own business in 1990, initially making products for the motorbike and aerospace industries. He entered the bike trade quite by chance, when a friend asked him to make him a pair of bar ends. Things developed from there, until by 1995 Heylight-Präzisionstechnik was producing complete bikes. Based in the outskirts of Münich, the company still makes high-end components, with the assistance of Richard's son Bertram, who puts the kit through its paces while he's picking up medals at MTB downhill races across Germany.

Heylight-Präzisionstechnik, Glonnerstr. 8, D-85667 Oberpframmern, GERMANY. Tel +49 8093 1077 Fax +49 8093 2589

In Europe prices start at DM 5000 for a frameset, and vary greatly worldwide.

ATLAS

Whether touring or taking a short trip to the shops, there's no reason why riders of any ability shouldn't have the pleasure of using an absolutely top-class machine. The Heylight Atlas is designed to give just that pleasure to a very wide range of riders. Both riders get an excellent view of their surroundings and the road ahead, and their heads are close enough together to avoid the shouting match sometimes typical of conventional tandeming, particularly in noisy traffic. Experiences are easily shared, and the riding style is relaxed.

The Atlas Sprint, shown here, is for two pedalling riders. The stoker sits in the recumbent position, and can pedal as much or as little as desired: the front seat has a separate freewheel and gearing, and an adjustable pedal unit. The recumbent seat is a boon for anyone who can pedal, but has difficulty remaining perched on a conventional saddle. Balance problems are a thing of the past – the rear rider has full control – and the seat is hard to fall out of. If there is any 'stoker wobble', the low centre of gravity helps with control.

If the front rider doesn't have use of his or her legs, then you can unbolt the front pedal unit and replace it with the 'Handicap' leg-rest. A hand-crank system and a special wheelchair adaptor are under development.

A 'Kid' variant for child-carrying replaces the stoker with a childseat, which can face forwards or backwards. Alternatively, a load-carrying unit can be fitted.

The Atlas is very easy to handle. It has a tight turning circle, and with the leg-rest or pedal unit folded up it is only about 20cm longer than a regular bike, which makes for easier storage and transportation. Disc brakes from Sachs are mounted on 20" (406) and 26" (559) wheels for excellent stopping power. A two-legged stand is available as an option.

The magic of the machine has to be its versatility. One machine can carry infants, older children and adults of all abilities. It can take them metres or miles. And it fulfils each of these roles without compromise.

EXCELERATOR XLT

State-of-the-art performance in handcycles comes from the combination of racing wheelchair technology with high-performance bicycle engineering– and a sound understanding of the dynamics of hand-power. With the Excelerator XLT, Invacare Top End have put together a machine at the cutting edge of handcycle design, weighing under 30lb (13.4kg)

A single 6061 aluminium tube forms the backbone of the frame, and the geometry of the chrome-moly fork is carefully-chosen to give a stable ride at top speed. The low recumbent seating improves both aerodynamics and stability in fast corners. The seat is fully-adjustable for both angle and position, and front-mounted footrests can be adjusted back and forth for length. A 15° camber on the rear wheels gives impressive cornering stability, and the 72" (183cm) long cycle has a turning circle of just 18' (5.5m). Seat width is usually specified by the rider (it's generally the same as your wheelchair seat width), and the seat back is available in normal or narrow versions: the narrow back gives more room for arm and shoulder movement.

The standard ergonomic handles can be changed for either quad handles or for handles with attached quad gloves, depending on the strength of the rider's grip. There are many options for gearing: the Shimano Nexus seven-speed hub gear is standard, but a Sachs 12-speed hub and the Schlumpf Mountain-Drive bottom-bracket gearbox are available for greater gear range. For competitive use, a 24-speed close-ratio derailleur system can be fitted. All of the hub gears have built in coaster (back-pedal) brakes. The derailleur version requires a separate brake handle, so a hand must be taken off the pedals to brake.

There is a wide range of options. 24" wheels are standard, available in either racing, touring or off-road specification, and 26" Specialized carbon fibre wheels are an option for the dedicated racer. Rear view mirror, lights, safety flag and a cordless computer are all offered, whilst a custom water bottle and mount is highly recommended. Practical issues are not forgotten: a rack to carry crutches and a rear towbar for a conventional wheelchair can also be fitted.

Invacare Top End

Invacare Top End have been manufacturing handcycles since 1990, and are backed by the experience of Invacare Corporation, which traces its roots back to 1885, when the Worthington Company began producing vehicles designed for people with physical disabilities. Since a management buyout in 1978, Invacare has grown from a small US company employing 350 staff to a world-wide outfit employing nearly 5000 people. Top End, Inc. starting making racing chairs in 1986. Chris Peterson, one of the founders, designs all their products, several which are patented. He believes in listening to what a customer wants and building to meet their needs. This can be especially difficult with the physically challenged, as there are so many types of disablities and such a range of capabilities left after injury. Top End was acquired by Invacare Corp in 1993. Invacare Top End also produce the Excelerator and Li'l Excelerator. These are upright handcycles, more conventional in style and ideal for those who enjoy the freedom of a handcycle, without necessarily needing the performance of a racing machine. They are built with steel frames, but have the same high quality components and design. The Li'l Excelerator is a 20"-wheeled child's handcycle, and is fitted with a three-speed hub gear as standard.

Invacare Top End Sports and Recreation Products, 4501 63rd Circle North, Pinellas Park, Florida 33781, USA.
Tel +1 727 522 8677 Fax +1 727 522 1007
Email info@invacare.com
Website http://www.invacare.com
Agents in other countries: see page 144.

In the USA, the XLT costs from around $1995, and other Excelerators from around $1695. The Li'l Excelerator starts at around $1495. Prices will vary worldwide.

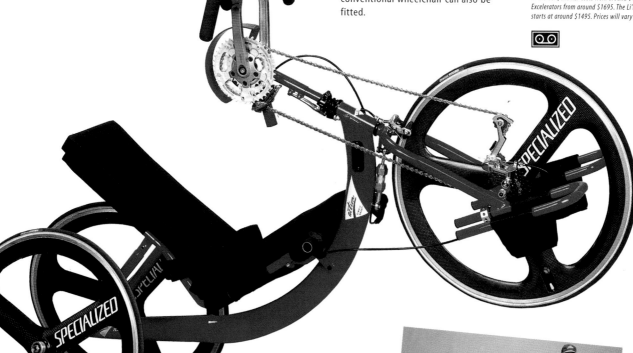

MOBILIS

A hand-cranked cycle does many things: it helps build upper-body strength, gives a cardiovascular workout, and gives independent mobility, too. Most customers of Mobilis handcycles from Rideable Bicycle Replicas are wheelchair users, but they have found that many able-bodied athletes also value the cross-training aspect of handcycling. Equally, many older riders find that the stability of a tricycle handcycle is ideal for gentle exercise.

The Mobilis is a quality machine with almost ten years of development behind it, and is designed for training or general mobility. Three sizes are available, from the child-size Lightning Bolt (with 20" wheels) to the full-size Armstrong (with 26" wheels). All have

powdercoated CroMo frames, and the front drive assembly has a patented stabilisation system. The design priority is ease of use, and straightforward handling: the steering is stable and precise.

The riding position is natural and comfortable, low for stability and offering excellent vision without straining neck or back. Both the crankarm and footrest are adjustable, and the seat backrests can be removed to suit. Weight is between 30 to 48lb (13 to 21kg) depending on model and specification. Standard derailleur gearing or hub gears can be fitted: usually a 21-speed derailleur on the Armstrong, and seven-speed on the smaller models.

Rideable Bicycle Replicas

The Mobilis range was originally developed by Thomas Valentino, who, after making several hundred custom handcycles in the early 1990s, formed the Mobilis Corporation to produce the machines in some numbers. Mobilis was acquired in 1998 by Rideable Bicycle Replicas of Alameda, California.

Rideable Bicycle Replicas was founded in 1974 by Mel Barron, producing replica cycles, mainly penny-farthings, for clients around the world. They are now the only commercial-scale manufacturer of antique-style bicycles in the world. Customers include Hollywood film studios such as Lucas and Universal, every Disney Park world-wide, the New York City Ballet, dozens of museums, and, of course, individual cycle enthusiasts everywhere, all sharing a demand for replicas that can actually be ridden. If you want something unique and antique, RBR can build it for you.

Together with his sons Greg and Adam, Mel still oversees the production of RBR bikes, which now include the multi-passenger Courting Cycle, high wheel unicycles, pedicab taxis, a lowrider bicycle, and of course penny-farthings galore. The latter come in sizes from 38" to 48", with special order sizes also available. RBR bikes are available in a choice of colours, or with a special high-polish metal plated finish.

Rideable Bicycle Replicas, 2329 Eagle Avenue, Alameda, CA 94501, USA.
Tel +1 510 769 0980 Fax +1 510 521 7145
Email mbarron@barrongroup.com
Website www.hiwheel.com

In the USA, handcycles cost from $950 to $1600. Rideable Replicas cost from $800 to $3600. Prices will vary worldwide.

STEP 'N GO CYCLES

Treadle Power Inc.

New technologies often end up being used in a very different way than the inventor intends or predicts. The Step 'n Go Cycle was originally developed by John Sandgren of North Dakota for use in factories and warehouses. However, until Stuart Lindsay of Treadle Power Inc. unveiled the first model to the public in 1992, John had no idea he would be creating a whole new world of mobility, freedom and joy for people of many different abilities. Treadle Power's vision is to match this unique cycle with people who will enjoy and benefit from its many functional features. This involves reaching riders with special needs and the professionals who work with them.

Made in Vermont, USA, the Step 'n Go can be shipped around the world by UPS. Treadle Power, Inc. is actively seeking representatives involved in special needs cycling or physical therapy.

Step 'n Go Cycles, Treadle Power Inc., 6 Linden Terrace, Burlington, Vermont 05401-4928, USA. Tel +1 800 648 7335 or +1 802 862 1870 Fax +1 802 864 6156 Email stepngo@together.net Website http://www.stepngo.com

In the USA, the 6-speed model is priced at $1249, with reasonably priced adaptations and accessories available. Prices will vary worldwide.

Why do pedals go round? Pedalling constrains the legs to move in an unchanging circle, which can be a difficult or impossible motion for many people. Happily, there is an alternative.

The Step 'n Go is completely different. The rider stands on two flat non-slip treadles, supported by the seat if necessary. To propel the vehicle, the rider shifts his or her weight from one foot to the other in a natural, stepping action. The treadles are linked so that as one falls in the power stroke, the other rises. The patented treadle transmission converts any movement into forward motion, no matter whether the strokes are short, long or uneven. It's a motion more akin to walking than cycling.

The upright position combines body weight with muscle strength, requiring very little effort to move the cycle. With two wheels in front, the rider is within the 'triangle of safety', and a companion or therapist can walk alongside the rider, unlike on a conventional tricycle. A wide range of speeds are possible, from barely-moving to fast enough to excite the adventurous rider. This makes it suitable for the cautious new rider in controlled settings, as well as great fun for the more skilled. Many adaptations are available, including range-of-motion adjusters, enhanced leverage treadles, lower gearing, and a selection of seating options. Custom adaptations are available on consultation.

The Step 'n Go is being successfully ridden by people of all ages and abilities, including those with cerebral palsy, arthrogryposis, strokes, spina bifida, arthritis, head injuries, hip, and knee or other joint replacements. Youngsters with Down's syndrome or developmental delay enjoy using the bike, improving their co-ordination, balance and motor skills. All riders can use the strength and abilities they have to gain freedom and mobility, and many find that their capabilities improve greatly over time.

The Step 'n Go cycle celebrates the best of universal design, breaking down the barriers between able-bodied and disabled riders. Many enlightened physiotherapists and rehabilitation specialists now recommend the Step 'n Go. It's also proved a great hit with able-bodied riders who prefer the treadle motion, and realise that for the same price as a decent stair-stepper, they can get a high-quality cycle to really go places!

Recumbents

You never forget your first time. After the initial bewilderment, the false starts and hysterical wobbling you catch the spirit, and with a heave that pushes you deep into your seat you glide into the world of recumbent riding: cycling's equivalent to the flying carpet. You're not on your bike, you're in it. The combination of sofa-like seat and head-up riding position make you feel like you're watching the country pass by in panoramic wide-screen.

You can't somersault over the handlebars, so you can fit (and use) the fiercest brakes available. You can't ground the pedals, so you can keep pushing round corners. Recumbents might look dangerously close to car-bumper level, but in fact on most city recumbents the seat is higher than that of a car. Instead of looking through you, cycle-blind drivers are more likely to give you a double-take.

It may take you some time to fully appreciate the qualities of a recumbent, for the riding style is quite different and both your brain and your body will need time to adapt. You certainly can't stand on the pedals and 'honk', and you use different muscles, all of which can make hill-climbing slower, especially for the novice rider. But the overall speed is still competitive, if you include the downhill stretches: recumbents are generally more aerodynamic than uprights. The other snag is that some recumbents can cost a fair bit more than a conventional bike, due to smaller production runs, custom-built componentry, and vigorous research and development activities.

Recumbents vary just as much as uprights: there are trikes, tandems, tandem-trikes, load-carriers, racers, tourers, city-bikes, and more. Alongside the usual variations of components, suspension, and frame materials comes the question of wheelbase. Recumbents with the wheels close together are often speedier and more manoeuvrable while the long wheelbase varieties are traditionally more popular for touring, and are easier for beginners to ride. The recent emergence of medium wheelbase recumbents is an attempt to reap the benefits of both styles.

Then there are cultural differences. North Europeans tend to prefer under-the-seat steering with relatively short wheelbases, where as Americans tend to go for longer wheelbases and above-seat 'easy-rider' steering. Then there are many countries where recumbents are as yet virtually unknown.

Get a recumbent, and you'll love it! Stealing along with the wind in your hair, not just down the back of your neck, on an exclusive machine designed by someone you may well be on first-name terms with, you're part of cycling's cutting edge. A great view, great comfort: just lie back and enjoy!

PRONE LOW-PROFILE

Graeme Obree, hour record holder and inventor of the 'Superman' riding position, likes to take things to extremes. After pushing the boundaries of the conventional riding position – and being banned each time – he's now turning his attention to human-powered speed attempts free from artificial design restrictions. The design he has chosen for this venture is the Prone Low-Profile.

Obree was particularly attracted by the aerodynamic advantages made possible by the prone riding position. With a minimal frontal area, and a smooth profile, these are very slippery machines indeed. Obree's going to take advantage of an aerodynamic fairing developed by the Prone's designer, Tim Elsdale. With this vehicle he will attempt the European hour record. The fairing, which has been extensively wind-tunnel tested, will be available to the public from mid-1999.

The Prone is made from thin-gauge Reynolds 853 tubing. The standard size fits riders over 5'8" (173cm) tall – smaller riders can have a bike made to order. Tim Elsdale has redesigned the bike slightly to take a 27" (700c) rear wheel. There's a choice of front wheel sizes: 20" (406) or 24" (507). With the 20" option, the back is flat and the position is as efficient as possible – while retaining a safe four to five inches of knee clearance for cornering. The 24" option gives a more open position which some find more comfortable. The rider is supported by

carefully-designed cushions, which slide along the frame for length adjustment.

Many people have had their preconceptions overturned by a test ride on the Prone. It's a surprisingly comfortable position, and the exhilaration of flying along, close to the ground and head out in front, is truly something to make your heart beat a little faster. What better cure could there be for the tedium of a day at the office?

The Seat of the Pants Company

Windcheetahs are made in Cheshire, UK, in a busy factory under the stewardship of Bob Dixon. Despite the bustle of production and development, he's happy to operate an 'open-door' policy: customers are welcome to visit and observe the manufacture of Windcheetahs and Pickups, the load-carrying four-wheeler featured elsewhere in this Encyclopedia.

Further Windcheetah accessories are made, with the full approval of the Seat of the Pants Company, by Sieghart Straka of Straka Sports in Germany, whose 'Ciro' scooter is featured in the 'City Bikes' section.

The Seat of the Pants Company, L&M Business Park, Norman Road, Altrincham, Cheshire, WA14 4ES, UK.
Tel +44 161 928 5575 Fax +44 161 928 5585
Email bobdixon@seatofpants.u-net.com
Website www.windcheetah.co.uk

In the UK, the Windcheetah costs from around £2800. Fairings cost around £350 each, and the lighting system around £250. Prices will vary worldwide.

WINDCHEETAH

An accidental classic, the Windcheetah recumbent trike was originally destined to be a training machine, put together by Mike Burrows for athletes attempting HPV speed records. It turned out to be so much fun that its training role is now secondary: it's a hedonistic machine for speed-lovers, which also turns out to be surprisingly practical.

Produced since 1993 by the Seat of the Pants Company in Manchester, the design has been evolving steadily. A significant change this year has been the move to 20" (406) front wheels, for which there is a huge range of high-performance tyres available. Fitted as standard are Continental Grand Prix slicks running at 9 bar (115psi). The kingpin castings have been subtly altered to reflect the new size, keeping the centre of gravity in the same optimal position as the original design.

Persistent demands from owners have led to the development of front and rear fairings, which fit any Windcheetah: both are crafted from carbon fibre, and the 1kg front fairing has a Lexan window. The 1.2kg rear fairing fits aerodynamically against the seat back, and the cowling behind the head is removable to reveal about 18 litres of waterproof carrying capacity – and there's plenty of room for A4 documents.

Complementing the fairings are restyled carbon mudguards and a carbon bottle/mirror holder.

Another long-awaited accessory is a custom lighting system: Seat of the Pants have obliged with a 750g twin-beam (25W and 5W) rechargeable system running on NiMh batteries, good for five hours on low beam. The 32mm diameter lamp units can be attached to the front derailleur post or to a custom carbon pod to match the front fairing. A remote console on the joystick controls all lighting functions.

Customers often ask about disc brakes. While not ruling them out in the future, the Seat of the Pants team believe that drum brakes are a lighter and just as effective system, and less affected by adverse weather conditions. Hydraulic-actuated drums are now available as an option: a single lever controls the drums in both front wheels for well-balanced stopping power.

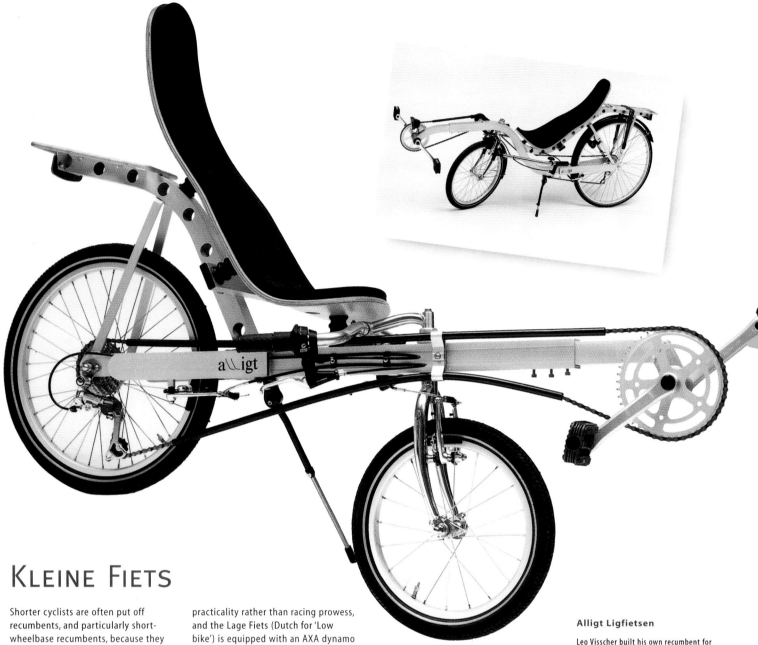

KLEINE FIETS

Shorter cyclists are often put off recumbents, and particularly short-wheelbase recumbents, because they can't find one that fits. The usual problems are seats which are too high for feet to reach the ground when stopping, and frames which are simply too long. No more!

Alligt's Kleine Fiets ('Small Bike') is designed specifically for riders of all ages between 145cm and 165cm tall (4'9" to 5'5"). The frame is of square section, TIG-welded anodised aluminium, and the chainset slides along for length adjustment. Seven-speed transmission is standard, with V-brakes providing ample stopping power for the 16" (349) front and 20" (406) rear wheels. Either 21 speed derailleur gearing or the Sachs 3 x 7 transmission is available to extend the gearing range. Complete with kickstand and sturdy integral carrier, the bike weighs around 14kg.

The Kleine Fiets is one of a range of recumbents from Alligt, and their 'Modern' SWB recumbent was featured in Encycleopedia 4 (then called the 'Classic'). Joining the range this year is a low-rider recumbent. Unlike many low riders, the emphasis is on

practicality rather than racing prowess, and the Lage Fiets (Dutch for 'Low bike') is equipped with an AXA dynamo lighting system, lock and kickstand, and weighs around 18kg, depending on equipment. It uses 20" (406) front and 28" (622) rear wheels. The frame, as on all Alligt machines, carries a full five year guarantee.

As well as recumbents, Alligt make a very practical cycle trailer, which can, as you'd expect, be fitted behind any of their bikes. With 20" alloy wheels and internal dimensions of 75 x 45 x 33cm, it can carry loads of up to 50kg.

Alligt Ligfietsen

Leo Visscher built his own recumbent for commuting while studying mechanical engineering in den Bosch, and set up the Alligt company with the backing of his family when he graduated. The varnished seats and mudguards have become something of an Alligt trademark – one which they reinforce at trade shows, with impressive stands of rough-hewn wood. Leo is positive about the reactions the bikes get at such events: "Last year people were asking 'What are recumbents?' Now we get asked questions about why our recumbents are special – recumbents are becoming much better-known and accepted." He stands by his belief that recumbents will make eventually up 5-20% of the overall bicycle market in the Netherlands.

Alligt Ligfietsen, Vogelplein 46, 5212 VK Den Bosch , NETHERLANDS.
Tel +31 73 6911 388 Fax +31 73 6911 387

Prices range from f1295,- to f2295,- in the Netherlands and will vary greatly worldwide.

Hornet II

'A two-wheeled symbiosis of fun and utility' is how Radius describe their recumbents – and who could disagree? The Hornet II is a sporty tourer, for the rider who wants a lively but comfortable machine with good luggage-carrying capacity. The elastomer suspension at the front is complemented by a hydraulic/pneumatic system at the rear, carefully designed to resist the 'pogo effect'. The bike emphasises rider comfort, with a patented seat design allowing easy, stepless adjustment. Similarly, the remote steering can be shifted forwards or backwards for a perfect fit.

The powder-coated cro-mo frame comes in four colours and three sizes, to fit riders between 1.60m and 1.96m. The wheels are 20" (406) front and 26" (559) rear. You can choose between LX and XT transmissions, and either V-brakes or Magura hydraulics. Other options include a dynamo lighting system, several rear rack systems (carrying up to four panniers), mudguards, and Ortlieb or Velocase luggage.

The medium-wheelbase C4 replaces the Red Pepper, which we featured in Encyclopedia 4, and the former Radius Viper. Two versions are available.

The C4 Allround features over-seat steering and Sachs Power-Grip shifters, while the C4 Touring has under-seat handlebars and Shimano bar-end shifters. The two models share a TIG-welded cro-mo medium wheelbase frame, V-brakes and Sachs 3x7 transmission. Rack, mudguards, and lighting are all fitted as standard, as is the anti-pogo rear suspension as used on the Hornet. There are two frame sizes, to fit riders between 1.62m and 1.98m, and the wheels are 20" (406) front and back.

Many riders prefer the low bars for longer journeys, but find above-seat steering more natural for town use. Luckily the C4 makes both possible: with a simple conversion kit and a few hour's work, the steering can be converted from above-seat to below, or vice versa.

Radius Spezialräder

Radius are one of the pioneers of recumbent cycling, having made their name in the mid-eighties with the Peer Gynt – the original long-wheelbase tourer, featured in the very first Encyclopedia, and still cherished by many riders today. It's been all change at Radius recently, but the marque continues under the care of new owners Nils Palm and Frank Tochtrop. As well as purchasing the rights to the Radius name and products, they have pledged to offer after-sales support to owners of previous models.

Liegerad Münster GmbH, Borkstrasse 20, D-48163 Münster, GERMANY. Tel +49 1805 723487 Fax +49 251 780358 Email mail@radius-liegeraeder.de Website www.radius-liegeraeder.de

In Germany, prices range from DM 3290 to DM 3690 (Hornet) or DM 2299 to DM 2699 (C4)

KETTWIESEL

"I don't want to get off!" said the twelve-year-old test-rider, refusing to budge from the seat of the KettWiesel. It's not hard to understand why. Riding the KettWiesel is sensational fun: with the seat low between the two 20" (406) rear wheels, you have tremendous stability for tight corners. The front wheel turns through a wide angle – so wide, that you can almost turn on the spot. V-brakes act so powerfully on each rear wheel that it's easy to get carried away: combine excessive braking and too much fun in the corners and you'll easily end up with worn-out tyres. Light weight means good acceleration: the KettWiesel weighs just 16kg.

Seven derailleur gears drive just the right-hand wheel: a differential would have added considerably to both weight and cost. The single-wheel drive works fine except in extreme cases: steep climbs on loose surfaces, or fast right-hand bends, when the weight is transferred over to the undriven wheel.

The KettWiesel is more than just fun – it's also a very practical vehicle. A large (30 litre) bag is available to fit behind the seat. The chain is protected by a teflon tube, and mudguards and lights complete the package.

The frame fits anyone from around 1.50m to 2.00m tall. It's just as much fun for those with balance problems or various disabilities – a wide range of special adaptations are available for the KettWiesel, as for the rest of Marec Hase's range. There's even an adaptor which lets you couple two KettWiesels together to form a tandem.

A more compact way to carry two is the Pino, the successor to the Periscop featured in Encycleopedia 96. The rear rider steers, and the recumbent front seat is versatile enough to accommodate anyone from children to full-sized adults, able or unable to pedal. With heads close together, communication is easy.

Hase Spezialräder

Hase Spezialräder have been building specialist cycles for over seven years, among them the Lepus, a suspended, folding trike which we featured in Encycleopedia 4. They work closely with organisations for the disabled, undertaking much custom-building, and provide a wide range of specialist equipment to adapt the machines for those with special needs. Marec Hase also works with the industrial testing company EFBe offering, in his Bochum factory, a laboratory testing service to manufacturers and importers of frames and forks. The team are: Alexander Krychtin (trainee), Marec Hase (design), Igor Pawitchenko (production), Ansgar Ammermann (assembly) and Kirsten Wilke (sales and marketing).

Hase Spezialräder, Karl-Friedrich-Str. 88, 44795 Bochum, GERMANY.
Tel +49 234 946 9050 Fax +49 234 946 9099
Email Hase.Bochum@t-online.de
Website http://www.t-online.de/home /Hase.Bochum

*In Germany, the KettWiesel costs around DM 3190, and prices will vary worldwide.
UK agents: see page 144.*

Fifty-Fifty

The Fifty-Fifty from Flevobike strikes an elegant balance. Somewhere between long and short wheelbase, between high- and low-rider, it's perfectly poised and seriously sporty, without losing sight of practicality. Weight distribution is perfect –a 50/50 split between front and rear wheels.

The laid-back riding position gives excellent aerodynamics. The seat itself is extremely comfortable – most of the weight is supported by the rider's back, very little on the buttocks. Flevobike have developed a new covering for their seats, a very open-weave fibre mesh, which lets air circulate while remaining supportive and resilient.

Both wheels are the common 20" (406) size, and Shimano V-brakes are standard. The transmission is the Sachs 3x7 system: seven derailleur speeds, and three hub gears. Mudguards, carrier racks and lighting sets are all available.

If there's a Flevobike more streamlined than the Fifty-Fifty, it's the Alleweder. Described at greater length in Encycleopedia 4, this fully-faired tricycle is available in two forms. The first, popular option is the 33.5kg aluminium Alleweder, a monocoque design which you can assemble youself – or order as a complete machine. There's also the lighter (27kg) – but unavoidably more expensive – Carbon Alleweder, a beautiful creation of curved carbon-fibre composite. Both versions have full suspension, excellent brakes and bodywork adjustable to suit the weather.

Flevobike

Flevobike have been building recumbents since 1989, and now employ eleven people. They are proud of their innovative approach: there's a lot of development work constantly underway behind the scenes. Sometimes a project takes on a life of its own – this was the case with an aluminium tandem made for fun by a Flevobike employee: it's now developed into a special project for schools, an educational kit which is also available to the public. Flevobike is also active in racing. Together with the Dutch HPV Club they organise 'Cycle Vision' every first weekend of June: a feast of racing on the RDW car test track in Lelystad. Flevobike has a shop in Dronten, not far from Lelystad, and sells plans and parts for people who want to build their own HPV. Export is no problem, either direct to customers or through retailers. Their UK agents, Wheels within Wheels, import the Oké-Ja, Flevo's entry-level medium-wheelbase two-wheeler, and the rest of the range to order.

Flevobike, De Morinel 55, 8251 HT Dronten, NETHERLANDS.
Tel +31 321 337 200 Fax +31 321 337 201
Email flevobike@wxs.nl Website http://www.ligfiets.net/flevobike
UK Agent: Wheels within Wheels.
Tel +44 161 612 6354 Fax +44 161 612 6514

In the Netherlands, the Fifty-Fifty costs around f 2990, and the aluminium Alleweder from f 3495 (in kit form) or f 5095 (complete). The Carbon Alleweder costs from f 15500 (complete). Prices will vary worldwide.

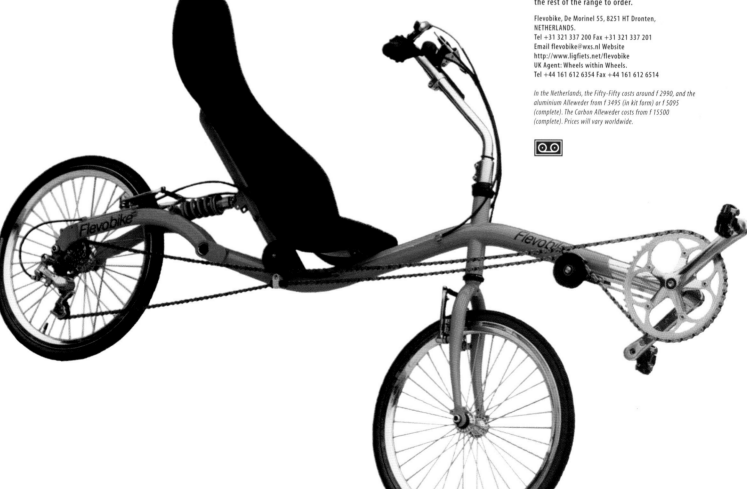

CULTY

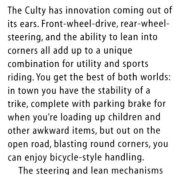

The Culty has innovation coming out of its ears. Front-wheel-drive, rear-wheel-steering, and the ability to lean into corners all add up to a unique combination for utility and sports riding. You get the best of both worlds: in town you have the stability of a trike, complete with parking brake for when you're loading up children and other awkward items, but out on the open road, blasting round corners, you can enjoy bicycle-style handling.

The steering and lean mechanisms are independent, giving a normal ride on gentle curves, and automatic tilt when you need it. The end result, after much research and refinement, is a dynamic but forgiving machine. There is a bit of a knack to riding it, but one that comes with just a few minutes' practice. Even 'non-sporty' riders soon find that even on rough ground, balance is effortless. Excellent traction comes from the front-wheel drive and forward centre of gravity. The relatively high seat (60cm, 24") makes mounting and dismounting easy even for the less agile.

The load-capacity is huge: there might be a crate of bottles between the rear wheels, a box of groceries under the main beam, and two small children behind the seat. And the handling is perfect even when the trike is fully laden. When loading up, the parking brake also locks out the tilt mechanism.

The Culty's chromoly and stainless-steel frame has front and rear suspension, is around 170cm long overall, and the rear wheel track is 63cm. Fold down the seat, and in two minutes flat it'll fit in the back of a small car. There's a choice of Sachs 7 and 12-speed hubs, and also a combination of seven-speed and Schlumpf Mountain Drive – to give a super-wide 712% gear range. Wheels are 20" (406) with Sachs drum brakes. The Culty is made in red, black and blue: custom colours also available.

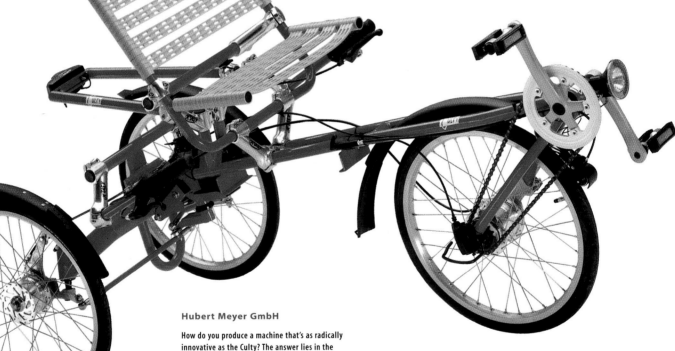

Hubert Meyer GmbH

How do you produce a machine that's as radically innovative as the Culty? The answer lies in the combination of Hubert Meyer and Thomas Poreski's widely differing areas of experience. Hubert has a successful machine-tool making business, and Thomas combines his vast experience of cycling with a job as scientific advisor to a German member of parliament. The Culty went into production in the middle of 1997, and has been refined ever since. Now that they feel that they have perfected the standard model, Thomas and Hubert are turning their attention to producing custom-built models. They have developed an electric power-assist system, and various types of fairings are also available.

Enquiries and orders: Culty, c/o Thomas Poreski, Herderstr. 29, D-72762 Reutlingen, GERMANY.
Tel +49 177 277 7592 Fax +49 7121 204 085
Email culty@liegerad.com
Manufacturer: Hubert Meyer GmbH, Birkenfelderstr.11, 75180 Pforzheim, GERMANY.
Tel +49 7231 972810 Fax +49 7231 972812

In Germany a 7-speed Culty costs from DM3989, DM4287 with 12 gears, and DM4670 for the 14-speed version with Mountain Drive. Framesets are also available. Prices will vary worldwide.

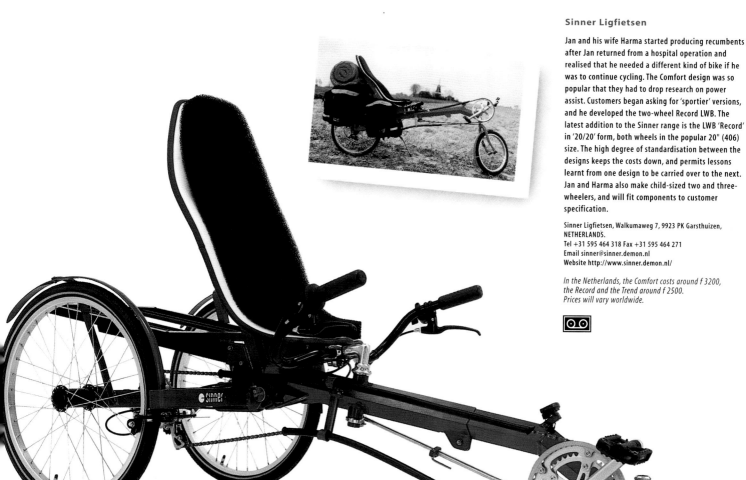

Sinner Ligfietsen

Jan and his wife Harma started producing recumbents after Jan returned from a hospital operation and realised that he needed a different kind of bike if he was to continue cycling. The Comfort design was so popular that they had to drop research on power assist. Customers began asking for 'sportier' versions, and he developed the two-wheel Record LWB. The latest addition to the Sinner range is the LWB 'Record' in '20/20' form, both wheels in the popular 20" (406) size. The high degree of standardisation between the designs keeps the costs down, and permits lessons learnt from one design to be carried over to the next. Jan and Harma also make child-sized two and three-wheelers, and will fit components to customer specification.

Sinner Ligfietsen, Walkumaweg 7, 9923 PK Garsthuizen, NETHERLANDS.
Tel +31 595 464 318 Fax +31 595 464 271
Email sinner@sinner.demon.nl
Website http://www.sinner.demon.nl/

In the Netherlands, the Comfort costs around f 3200, the Record and the Trend around f 2500. Prices will vary worldwide.

SINNER COMFORT TRIKE

Are you a Sinner? Jan Roelf de Vries is. The Dutch traffic police took exception to a power-assisted prototype he was riding, and gave the company its name. Since then, Sinner have, ironically, become established as one of the Netherlands' most respected producers of practical recumbents.

The original Sinner is the Comfort, an aluminium trike weighing around 16kg. The seat is supportive and comfortable, and an optional open-mesh foam pad can be added to provide firm support with excellent air circulation – minimising the sweaty back syndrome. Standard gearing is seven-speed derailleur, but 21-speed or a Nexus seven-speed hub gear are optional. Both rear wheels are driven, with hub freewheels, giving good traction. The Comfort has a large and solid rear carry rack, on which child seats or a large (70 litre) box can be fitted by the manufacturers. All Sinners have integral mudguards and LED rear light, and a dynamo front light is available as an option. Many other components can be specified, including hydraulic brakes and a neatly-mounted cycle computer. The low weight and

small wheels make the Comfort quick and agile – impressively so for a design based on comfort and practicality.

Sinner also make two-wheeled models, the Record LWB and the Trend SWB, both with 20" (406) front and 26" (559) rear wheels. The Record is also available with 16" (340) front and 20" (438) rear wheels, the same as the Comfort, or with two 20" wheels. All versions are made from square section aluminium, and are adjustable for leg-length using a telescopic boom. Adjustment is easy: the square frame means that there is no rotation and realignment required, simply check the chain tension and ride.

Any Sinner recumbent makes a fine mounting for a child seat. Sinner also produce a neat hitch to turn two Comforts into one articulated tandem for family outings – indeed, you can add as many units as you like, making a 'bike train'. The front wheel of the rear trike is released and the fork is attached the back of the lead bike, safely cushioned by a further suspension elastomer.

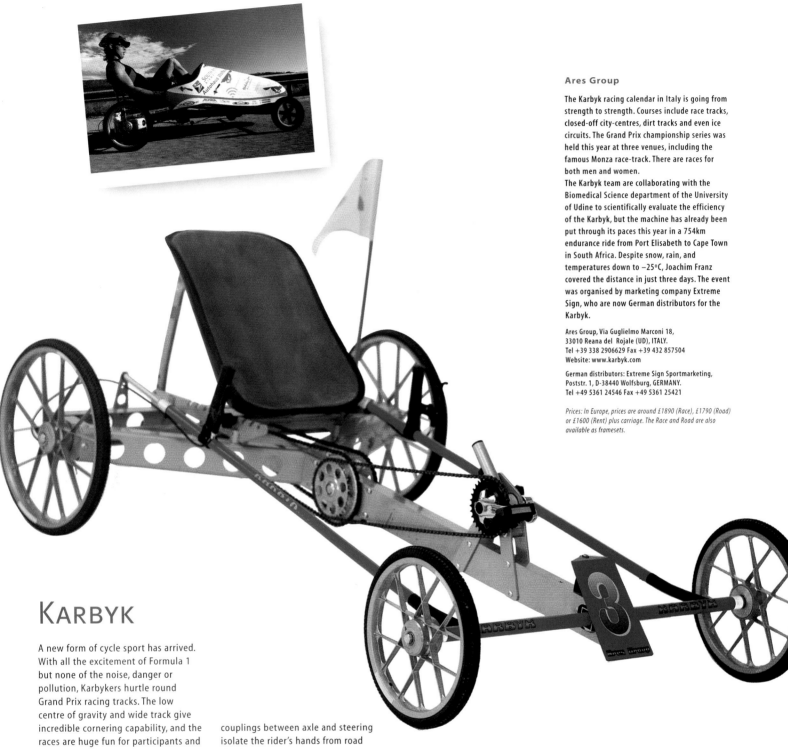

Ares Group

The Karbyk racing calendar in Italy is going from strength to strength. Courses include race tracks, closed-off city-centres, dirt tracks and even ice circuits. The Grand Prix championship series was held this year at three venues, including the famous Monza race-track. There are races for both men and women.

The Karbyk team are collaborating with the Biomedical Science department of the University of Udine to scientifically evaluate the efficiency of the Karbyk, but the machine has already been put through its paces this year in a 754km endurance ride from Port Elisabeth to Cape Town in South Africa. Despite snow, rain, and temperatures down to −25°C, Joachim Franz covered the distance in just three days. The event was organised by marketing company Extreme Sign, who are now German distributors for the Karbyk.

Ares Group, Via Guglielmo Marconi 18, 33010 Reana del Rojale (UD), ITALY. Tel +39 338 2906629 Fax +39 432 857504 Website: www.karbyk.com

German distributors: Extreme Sign Sportmarketing, Poststr. 1, D-38440 Wolfsburg, GERMANY. Tel +49 5361 24546 Fax +49 5361 25421

Prices: In Europe, prices are around £1890 (Race), £1790 (Road) or £1600 (Rent) plus carriage. The Race and Road are also available as framesets.

Karbyk

A new form of cycle sport has arrived. With all the excitement of Formula 1 but none of the noise, danger or pollution, Karbykers hurtle round Grand Prix racing tracks. The low centre of gravity and wide track give incredible cornering capability, and the races are huge fun for participants and spectators alike.

The Karbyk was developed principally for competition, but there are three versions: the Race, Road, and Rent. They share the aluminium chassis, with a differential driving the rear wheels, and it is easy to upgrade from one model to another. The Road version is aimed at utility and touring use, while the Rent is a great machine for theme parks, hire outlets and tourist resorts. The padded seat is made from carbon fibre or fibreglass, and can tilt and slide to fit. Drum brakes on each of the rear wheels are controlled individually, letting the rider use the strength of both hands for maximum deceleration. 'Hose'

couplings between axle and steering isolate the rider's hands from road shock.

The transmission on the Race and Road is a combination of 24-speed Shimano 105 and Grip-Shift; the Rent is a low-maintenance single-speed machine. Other than this, the main difference between the three models is wheel size: The Road has 20" and 24" wheels, the Rent 16" and 20" and the low-profile Race has 12" and 16". The wheelbase is 1360mm, and the overall length for the Race is 1708mm. Total weight is between 24 and 28kg.

The Karbyk is available in a choice of ten colours, and accessories include mudguards, chain guard, lights, horn, and flag. A fairing and an electric-assist system are under development.

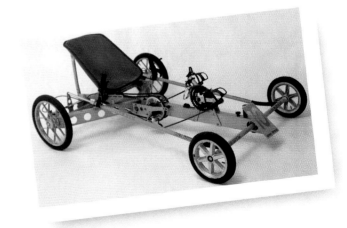

GREENSPEED SUITCASE TRIKE

Greenspeed

Ian Sims produces a wide range of trikes, from sleek racing machines to the Tandem Touring Trike (featured in Encycleopedia 4). He has made trikes for riders of all weights, sizes and capabilities – from a 450lb man to children with disablities, as well as hand-cranked machines. Greenspeeds have seats that are an integral part of the frame, and are made to measure. Six inches of precise length adjustment is provided through a telescopic boom. Ian's inventive mind is never at rest. He is now working, for example, on practical fairing designs for touring and commuting. Email and the Internet allow him to liaise quickly and cheaply with customers around the world.

Greenspeed, 69 Mountain Gate Drive, Ferntree Gully, Vic 3156, AUSTRALIA.
Tel +61 3 9758 5541 Fax +61 3 9752 4115
Email ian@greenspeed.com.au
Website http://www.greenspeed.com.au

Agents in Europe: HP Velotechnik, Goethestr. 5, 65830 Kriftel, GERMANY.
Tel +49 61 92 41010 Fax +49 6192 910218
Email pulvermu@stud.uni-frankfurt.de

S&S Machine, 9334 Viking Place, Roseville, CA 95747, USA.
Tel +1 916 771 0235 Fax +1 916 771 0397
Email: steve@sandsmachine.com
Website: http://www.sandsmachine.com

In Australia, the S&S tourer costs around A$5150 and prices will vary worldwide.

A recumbent trike is an exciting machine to tour on, but can be difficult to take on a bus or a train. The size that makes the trike stable and comfortable can make it awkward to transport. Ian Sims has now added S&S Bicycle Torque Couplings to his proven and respected touring trike, to create a machine that fits in a couple of suitcases. The seat is detached by removing a bolt at the front, and undoing the two small S&S couplings at the rear. The frame then splits just behind the handlebar pivot. The brake and steering mechanisms remain connected when the trike is packed, greatly reducing the adjustment needed when the trike is assembled.

In a matter of minutes, the trike can be packed into two standard suitcases, one suitcase for the frame and wheels, and one for the the seat, leaving enough room for your clothes and more. Or you could use one suit case and a backpack.

S&S couplings are actually stronger and stiffer than the tubes they join, so handling and stability remain excellent. Gearing starts with a Sachs 3x7 at the back, with either a triple front ring or a Schlumpf Mountain Drive. This gives either 63 or 42 gears, with a very wide range, making the trike suitable for both heavy and fast touring. Independent hub brakes on the front wheels and centre-point steering allow braking with either hand without veering off-line. A rear mudguard, flag and mirror are standard equipment, and rear rack and front mudguards can be fitted. The frame is aircraft-grade 4130 chro-moly steel and the wheels are 20" (406) all round. When packed, the trike and cases weigh around 20kg. The only non-standard tool needed for the packing and unpacking is a small spanner for the S&S couplings.

ENCYCLEOPEDIA RECUMBENTS

BikeE Corp

The BikeE was launched in 1993, and was the first quality compact wheelbase recumbent, designed to prove that comfort, handling and performance are not mutually exclusive. With a large base of satisfied customers BikeE are fulfilling their aims of bringing recumbents into mainstream cycling. A strong network of dealers in the USA and beyond make the BikeE readily available, and easily-adjustable to the demands of the individual rider.

The BikeE Corporation was founded by David G Ullman, Richard Rau and Paul Atwood. A Professor of Design and Mechanical Engineering, a graduate in Automotive Technology, and a long-term recumbent rider respectively, their knowledge and experience has helped make the BikeE one of the most popular recumbent bikes on the market.

Proving that a BikeE keeps its looks, the machine in the main image was in regular use for some months before we took the photos. The owner has made a few changes to the standard specification, adding, for example, bar-ends and a cycle computer.

BikeE Corp., 5460 SW Philomath Boulevard, Corvallis, 97333-1039 Oregon, USA.
Tel +1 541 754 9747
Fax +1 541 753 8004
Email BikeEvol@aol.com

In the USA, prices range from $650 to $1995, and will vary worldwide.

BikeE

Tempting America to fall feet-first into cycling, the BikeE must be one of the most accessible recumbents around. The high seat, feet-first riding style and relatively low bottom bracket make the BikeE an easy bike to ride. It's just the vehicle to persuade upright riders from their perches.

Long enough to offer excellent stability at high speed, yet short enough for excellent slow-speed manoeuvrability, the BikeE AT (Air Technology) has reassuring handling in all conditions. A rear swingarm suspension system, incorporating a damped compressed-air shock absorber, soaks up the bumps – then there's further cushioning from the seat. The air shock can be pumped up to take account of different conditions or rider weight, and the system avoids the 'pogo' effect that makes many suspension systems hard work.

Twist shift gear changers on the handlebars operate the 21 gears: the Sachs 3x7 system gives a gear range

wide enough for touring yet simple enough for just cruising round town.

The seat is five-way adjustable, with a very comfortable cushioned base, and slides up and down the aluminium backbone, making adjustment for different riders quick and simple. The AT and rigid-frame BikeE CT are both available in two frame sizes. The standard frame fits riders of up to 6'3" (190cm), while the XL frame will take riders up to 6'9" (205cm), and is also recommended for heavier riders of over 6'1" (185cm). The XL frame is a good choice for an average-height rider wishing for more rear carrying capacity. There is a wide range of good quality tyres available for the 16" (349) front and 20" (406) rear wheels.

Both versions of the BikeE make practical, comfortable bikes with a surprising turn of speed. Whatever speed you go, you ride on a comfortable seat and with your eyes up – so enjoy the scenery!

Pashley PDQ

The PDQ ('Pretty Damn Quick') from Pashley is a nicely-judged combination of the comfortable and practical, and has been well received by riders looking for an exciting all-round recumbent which might become their one and only bike. It's based on the famous Counterpoint 'Presto' design by Jim Weaver in the States, from whom Pashley acquired world rights. They developed and refined the concept over several years before introducing it to the UK market.

Pashley opted to avoid conventional frame suspension, to keep down weight, complexity and cost. Given the short wheelbase this decision would normally result in a body-jolting ride. The PDQ gets round this with an ingenious seat design, with an aluminium frame pivoting on the front mounting, supported at the back on an elastomer ring which smooths out rough-road vibration and takes the sting out of unexpected pot-holes and speed humps. The comfortably-wide seat can be fine-tuned to fit your body shape: simply adjust the fabric tension by tweaking the Velcro straps. This Velcro-fastened mesh holds the whole seat together. Undo all the straps, remove the seat cover and the seat frame slides effortlessly apart, detaching from the main frame in one straightforward movement. The handlebars adjust vertically and pivot forwards from the headset for easy access when climbing aboard, and the whole handlebar assembly folds down along the top of the front boom. These

two features, combined with the Sachs Centera quick-release hub in the front wheel, give an easy and rapid pack-down for transportation.

Riding the PDQ is a real pleasure, not just because of its smooth and stable riding characteristics, but also because of its versatility. It can cope with almost anything which might come your way: different riding surfaces, varying traffic conditions, very slow and very fast speeds – always with the safety-net of the reassuringly-powerful V-brakes. The 20" (406) wheels, short wheelbase of 95cm (37.5") and practical seat height at about 52cm (20.5") mean balance is easy and steering stable, even when manoeuvring tightly.

The one-size frame with sliding front boom fits riders with leg measurements between 29" and 37" (74 to 94cm). Dual-sided VP-131 pedals, clipless on one side and conventional cage on the other, allow for most styles of footwear, and the PowerGrip-operated Sachs Centera 3x7 transmission is so versatile that commuting is as enjoyable as touring. The PDQ weighs 13.5kg. Extras include rear carrier, mudguards and large luggage bag for behind the seat.

Pashley Cycles

Pashley's diversity in specialised bikes is unrivalled in Britain. They supply high-quality cycles for the public, and also all manner of cycles to industry, food and beverage companies, film studios, special needs hospitals, and more. The same company that produces workbikes for the British post office also makes the Tube Rider for California-style cruising. Pashley make tricycles to carry 200kg, and 'mountain' unicycles ('Munis') for adventurous individuals. From their factory in Stratford-upon-Avon come quality bikes and trikes for children, alongside the lightweight spaceframe of the fully-suspended Moulton APB. Innovation is constant: they've recently come up with the PDQ3, a wonderfully stable tricycle version of the PDQ. Another development is the Starburst 'Rocket' ice-cream vending tricycle, with electric-assist power and five-tune sound chip.

Pashley are looking for distributors to take their range further afield.
Pashley Cycles, Masons Road, Stratford-upon-Avon, Warwickshire, CV37 9NL, UK.
Tel +44 1789 292 263 Fax +44 1789 414 201
Email info@pashley.co.uk
Website www.pashley.co.uk

In the UK the PDQ costs from about £899, and the PDQ3 about £1299. Prices will vary worldwide.

HORIZONT-TOP

Recumbents are famous for their comfort, and for their speed. But – as with any engineering product – there is always a trade-off between the two. The Horizont-top, with its combination of low drag and well-designed suspension, is designed to give the rider a good helping of both. But a comfortable ride is no good without a comfortable fit – so the Z&Z team have developed a special steering-tube extension, which in combination with an 'Aheadset' stem and narrowed-down MTB bars offers a generous degree of adjustablity. The seat is available in three sizes, and has a leg-length adjustment range of 220mm.

Suspension systems can often add quite a weight premium. However, the Horizont-top's designers have ignored the general convention – transplanted from the car and motorbike industries – which assumes that the whole frame must be suspended. They have produced a neat 'Rinkowski'-type design, in which the seat swings on a front pivot, and road shock is absorbed by the spring assembly visible above the rear wheel. And while wind resistance is usually less of a problem with recumbents than uprights, Z&Z shave a few bushels off the Horizont-top's drag coefficient by opting for a relatively prone rider position, together with over-seat steering. The frame is made up from Mannesmann

CroMo steel. Three sizes are available: 'small' fits riders 1.5m to 1.75m, 'medium' covers 1.65m to 1.9m, and 'large' fits riders 1.9m to 2.05m tall. Components are a mix of Shimano STX and RX100, and wheels are 20" (406) and 26" (559).

The end product is a bike that is lively enough to be fun and practical around town, but still comfortable enough for longer trips, with luggage-carrying capacity to match. A rear box can be fitted, and an extra low-rider pannier rack is available to mount under the seat. With both systems your luggage also benefits from the suspension.

Also in the Horizont range are the Swing and Fast, both featured in last year's Encycleopedia. The Swing features under-seat steering and a similar suspension system to that fitted to the Horizont-top. The Horizont-fast is the racing version: the frame is simpler and lighter, and is fitted with extra-narrow over-seat handlebars.

Zweirad und Zukunft

In Germany, obtaining a good apprenticeship can be almost as much a cause for celebration as getting into university. Zweirad & Zukunft ('Two-wheelers for the Future'), a charitable organisation for youth training and education, place great emphasis on training at their workshop, with eighteen apprentices at any one time. They're also helping to redefine the traditional 'two-wheeler mechanic' qualification, which covers both pedal and petrol-powered vehicles. Conventionally, the focus is on motorbikes and mopeds, but not at Z&Z! Here, human-power rules. Partnership arrangements with like-minded local businesses mean that trainees can often enjoy useful and interesting work placements with these companies.

Zweirad & Zukunft, Fahrradkulturwerkstatt in Altona e.V., Gaußstraße 19, 22765 Hamburg, GERMANY.
Tel +49 40 395285 Fax +49 40 390 3221

In Germany, the Horizont-top costs around DM2790, the Horizont-swing DM2890, and the Horizont-fast DM3500. Prices will vary worldwide.

TRIPENDO

Turn a corner on a bicycle, and you lean instinctively, so that weight and centrifugal force combine along the line of the bicycle. It's different on a tricycle. There is normally no way to lean, and the centrifugal forces must be resisted by wheels and frame, which must be made strong and heavy. Small wheels are needed to resist the sideways forces, although larger wheels make for a more comfortable, easy-rolling ride. The riding position must be kept as low as possible to prevent overturning on corners, although a higher riding position would be more pleasant in traffic.

To overcome all of these problems, you need a leaning tricycle – but this is a vehicle whose design presents formidable technical challenges. The Tripendo's solution is an ingenious parallelogram linkage, dual-wishbone suspension system which gives an intuitive, stable and comfortable ride. Rider, frame, and all three wheels lean in parallel by up to 26°, controlled by the right-hand control lever. The left-hand lever controls the steering angle of the front wheels. The combination of these two motions compensates for any corner at any speed. Centre-point steering gives predictable handling, even on rough surfaces.

It's also tremendous fun. The steering takes just a few minutes to get used to. You only really use one control lever, the other just being used for small corrections. Once you've mastered it, it's a blast! You can power through corners which would otherwise require serious acrobatics on a non-leaning trike, and there's no

worry, as there is on a bike, that a wheel will break loose and dump you.

The 'Standard' Tripendo has a fibreglass frame, a V-brake on the rear wheel and hydraulic-operated Sachs drums at the front. The 29kg carbon-fibre 'Carbon' version uses Formula disk brakes. Both feature swing-arm rear suspension. A good fit is achieved by sliding the bottom bracket, and an internal tensioner means that you don't need to adjust the chain length. The chain is kept away from the rider's clothing. Two frame-sizes fit riders between 1.60 and 1.95m tall. The 26" (559) wheels (spoked or carbon fibre) are driven by a 24-speed transmission, controlled by an EGS Synchro-Shift. A Rohloff 14-speed hub gear is also available, as is an electric power-assist unit.

LW Composite GmbH

When Frank Schliewert decided to make himself a bike he wanted three things: comfort, safety and fun. A mechanical engineer by profession, he took up the challenge of making a three-wheeler with all the fun of a bicycle through the bends, and developed his prototype leaning tricycle, which we featured in Bike Culture Quarterly 10. He has since worked closely with thermoplastic fibre-composite specialists LW Composite GmbH and bodywork designer Michael Conrad to develop the design, launching it as the Tripendo in late 1998.

LW Composite GmbH, Industriestr., D-35683 Dillenburg, GERMANY.
Tel +49 2771 392492 Fax +49 2771 392489
Email LW-Composite@tripendo.com
Website http://www.tripendo.com

In Germany, the standard, fibreglass model costs around DM 5916, the carbon fibre version around DM 7946. Carbon wheels cost an extra DM 1900. Prices will vary world-wide.

VELVET QUIX

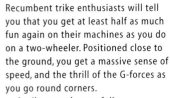

Recumbent trike enthusiasts will tell you that you get at least half as much fun again on their machines as you do on a two-wheeler. Positioned close to the ground, you get a massive sense of speed, and the thrill of the G-forces as you go round corners.

A trike must be carefully constructed to resist these forces, and to handle predictably even under extreme conditions. With eleven years of experience in recumbents, Veloladen have come up with the Velvet Quix, a fast yet sturdy tricycle, well-equipped to bring tricycle fun to everyday riding or for touring. The centre-point steering geometry has been carefully developed to give stable, light handling, yet the practicality shows through with mudguards, carrier rack and lighting. Overall weight is around 19kg.

The frame is powder-coated TIG-welded steel, with the rack and seat frame made of aluminium. The wheels are 20" (406) front and 26" (559) rear, and the Alex hollow-section aero-rims are shod with Continental Top Touring 2000 tyres. The track is 820mm, overall width is 885mm, and with a rider with 900mm leg-length, overall length will be around 2.055m. The Sachs 3x7 transmission gives 21 gears, and Teflon tubes prevent the chain oiling your trousers.

The main brakes on a trike are at the front, so the Quix is equipped with Sachs drum brakes in each front wheel. The drums are operated by hydraulic Magura Hydro-Stop pistons, to give maintenance-free, well-balanced and powerful stopping. A Tektro V-brake at the back offers further reassurance, and the lever has a catch which can lock the brake for parking.

Veloladen Liegeräder

Velvet is the brand name for bikes made by Veloladen, who have fifteen years experience in building and selling bikes from their shop in Bergisch Gladbach, set in green countryside near Cologne. In that time they have seen the recumbent scene explode, from a motley crew of designers and manufacturers producing expensive, short production-run machines, to the situation today – where the recumbent bike is finally being recognised for what it is: a practical, valid member of the cycle family. That family is well represented at Veloladen; they cover tandems, hybrids, town bikes, children's bikes, trailers and 'specials' – and retain a big interest in recumbents. Veloladen also have a substantial hire fleet. For the last five years they have hosted the 'Bergisch Gladbach Recumbent Day'. This annual event gives recumbent riders from across the world an opportunity to meet up, hang out and – if they wish – to compete in the Bergisch Championships.

Veloladen Liegeräder, Dolmanstr. 20,
D-51427 Bergisch Gladbach, GERMANY.
Tel +49 2204 61075 Fax +49 2204 61076
Email info@veloladen.com Website www.veloladen.com

*In Germany, the Quix costs from around DM5498.
Prices will vary worldwide.*

SCOOTERBIKE

'Sit down and put your feet up'. For years, recumbent enthusiasts have been telling the world that diamonds are not forever, that the recumbent format can offer comfort, speed, and safety. The world is, finally, starting to listen. A new class is emerging: medium-wheelbase, easy-to-ride mainstream recumbents.

The ScooterBike sits more than comfortably in this new category. It is designed so that anyone can jump aboard and ride off, first go. The handlebars, gear-shifter, mirror and front wheel are all positioned well within the rider's field of view. The comfortable seat is high enough to allow good visibility – for the rider and for approaching car drivers – and can be readily adjusted without tools, and the components have been selected for their low-maintenance characteristics.

The most striking aspect of the ScooterBike is its swooping lines: the elegant, laid-back design gives it a distinctive charm, and should help woo even the most sceptical 'recumbents aren't for me' cyclist. It borrows much of its styling from the new generation of laid-back motor-scooters, and even has a rigid top-box as standard. One, highly adjustable, frame size is available, to fit riders between 1.55 and 2.00m in height.

Two versions are available: the ScooterBike 'Easy' has a midnight blue, powder-coated CroMo frame with Dynamount BDV-6 rear suspension, whereas the 'Pro' is fitted with an ST8-RC shock-absorber unit. The 'Pro' also has front suspension, courtesy of a Cannondale DD-50 Headshok, along with Nexus seven-speed gearing, rather than the four-speed on the Easy. The 'Pro' also has an upgraded set of anti-lock roller brakes. Wheels are 16" (305) and 20" (406). Total weight is around 17kg, including lights, rack and mudguards.

Veloladen Liegeräder

The ScooterBike is the product of 15 years collaboration between Veloladen team members Klaus Schröder and Ortwin Kürten, and independent designer Norbert Nattefort. Veloladen (German for 'Bike Shop') have been making and selling innovative bikes for many years, and now sell their recumbents under the name Velvet. Their Quix recumbent trike is featured elsewhere in this Encycleopedia. With the Velvet Scooterbike they set out to design a modern, intuitive city bike, that was practical, stylish, and suitable for 'young and old, large and small'. The similarity with motor-scooters is quite intentional – they're all the rage in the countries of mainland Europe. Klaus, Ortwin and Norbert are currently developing a front fairing, which will, they say, continue the emphasis on cool looks combined with genuine usefulness. They also have plans to produce an electric booster-motor.

Veloladen Liegeräder, Dolmanstr. 20,
D-51427 Bergisch Gladbach, GERMANY.
Tel +49 2204 61075 Fax +49 2204 61076
Email info@veloladen.com
Website www.veloladen.com

In Germany, the Easy costs around DM2598, and the Pro around DM3998. Prices will vary worldwide.

V-200

"The Flux V-200 'comfort bike' provides a comfortable, relaxed and upright riding position, straightforward and reliable steering and gears, problem-free running and has room for the shopping." This was the judgement of the ADFC (Germany's national cycling organisation) on awarding the V-200 the title 'Bicycle of the Year, 1999'.

The medium-wheelbase recumbent is a relatively new development, and one that is winning a lot of converts to the idea that sitting back in a comfortable seat is actually a pretty smart way to ride a bike. The V-200 makes it plain that recumbents have come of age, with polished styling, elegant lines and plenty of 'street cred'.

The rider enjoys all the benefits of a recumbent seat and rear suspension, but is positioned high enough to be able to see well in traffic, and also be visible to other road users. The relaxed, medium-wheelbase geometry provides the forgiving handling. This is a bike designed for negotiating traffic jams, and with similar overall dimensions to a 'normal' bicycle, taking the V-200 on public transport should be no problem. There's plenty of room for luggage for shopping or for when you want to take it touring: you can fit two large panniers under the seat, and a third

behind the rider's back. Low maintenance was a top design priority, right down to the puncture-resistant tyres (with reflective sidewalls).

The powder-coated CroMo frame comes in two sizes: S/M for riders around 155cm to 183cm tall (5'1" to 6'), and the L size for riders 178cm to 200cm (5'10" to 6'7"). The V-200 is equipped with Tektro V-brakes front and rear, wheels are 16" (305) front and 20" (406) rear, and customers can choose between a Sachs Centera 8-speed transmission, or the 3x7 hub/derailleur gearing system from Sachs/SRAM. The overall weight for the 8-speed version, including mudguards, lights, mirror, stand, and CroMo rack, is around 16.1kg.

Flux Fahrräder GmbH

Christian Uwe-Mischner – Cum, to his friends – has a long history in the recumbent scene. He's been making them since the early 1980s, and is also a familiar face at race meets. His best known products to date include the ST-E and ST-2 – short-wheelbase recumbents set up for sports or touring – and his Z-Pro; a very striking, ultra-low, long wheelbase racing machine, demonstrating Cum's ability to understand the recumbent market in all its variety.

Flux Fahrräder GmbH, Kreuzbreitlstr. 8, D-82194 Gröbenzell, GERMANY. Tel/Fax +49 8142 53180

In Germany, the V-200 costs from around DM2198. Prices will vary worldwide.

Manfred Klauda

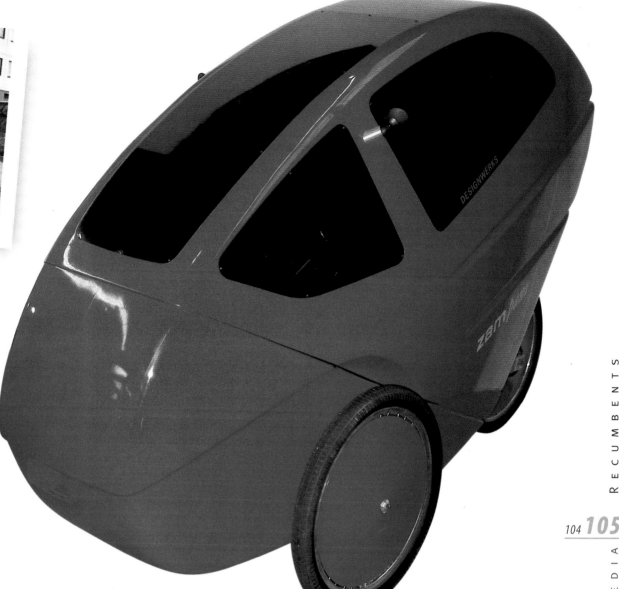

ZAMPANO

The message is getting through: pedal power is the future. But many people are still reluctant to commit themselves to a mode of transport that leaves them exposed to the elements, and fully-enclosed HPVs have a reputation for being 'for enthusiasts only'. No longer!

The Zampano is a velomobile designed with practicality and straightforwardness in mind. It doesn't look home-made, it doesn't need an assistant to help you get in, and it's not so heavy that you can't use it in hilly areas.

The manufacturers stress that while the vehicle shown here is a three-wheeled prototype, the production machine will be a four-wheeler. Unfortunately, pictures of the final version were not ready as we went to press. However, the bodywork and general appearance of the machine are otherwise very similar.

With four wheels you can expect easy-going handling characteristics: this is very much a machine aimed at the ordinary person in the street who wants a predictable, dependable and,

above all, reliable machine. Getting inside is as easy as anything: just lift the canopy. The bodywork hinges right back, and with a wheel in each corner the vehicle is extremely stable as you get in.

The Zampano is built around a fully-suspended aluminium chassis. Transmission is via hub-gears, with a choice of seven or twelve speeds plus reverse. There are drum-brakes fitted in each wheel, and there's an additional parking brake. The clam-shell glass-fibre canopy is easily removed on warm days, and for in-between weather you have the option of just taking off the top part of the fairing. The interior is well ventilated, and has 120 litres of luggage capacity. Overall weight is around 30kg (22kg if you remove the fairing). The overall length is 210cm, and the height is 132cm. A 12V lighting system, indicators, horn, mirror and a hand-operated windscreen wiper are fitted as standard.

Tretauto GmbH

Velomobile designers are sometimes rankled when their machines are compared to children's pedal-cars. But not Manfred Klauda. He actually owns a pedal-car museum in Munich, in which the hundred-year history of the motor car is mirrored in child-size miniatures.

But Manfred's exhibits don't just sit there gathering dust. He's in the Guinness Book of Records for riding a 60 year old pedal-car 612km in seven days. And it is his experience of pedal-cars which led him to get involved in velomobiles, aiming to develop a practical product that covers the middle ground between cars and bicycles. Right from the start, Manfred's goal has been to target ordinary folk, people who are interested in 'high tech' only if it means 'easy tech'.

Early development work on the Zampano was carried out by the Berkut team in Moscow, whose B-317 velomobile was featured in Encycleopedia 4. They built several prototypes for Manfred. In 1997 he started working with the German design consultancy Kuntz, who have brought the Zampano to production.

Tretauto GmbH, Westenriederstr. 41,
D-80331 München, GERMANY.
Tel +49 89 2904121 Fax +49 89 22802773

*In Germany, the Zampano costs around DM 7000.
Prices will vary worldwide.*

WIZARD

Not many sports-recumbents have been round the world, but the Hurricane has. One proud owner is a Dutch airline pilot. After parking his 747 in Australia he likes to unwind by going for a spin on his dream machine. He picked the Hurricane for its lively, speedy handling, and also because it is compact enough to take on board the aircraft. Another owner, from Holland, was touring in southern Spain, and when the time came to return, simply disassembled the bike (it takes about 10 minutes) and took a coach home.

The Hurricane was developed four years ago, to meet demand among Dutch and German recumbent enthusiasts for a fast, compact and aerodynamic recumbent. The original steel-framed version is still available, and Challenge have recently introduced the Hurricane Luxe, with an all-aluminium frame and hydraulic suspension.

Low down and lightweight, the Hurricane is ideal for covering distance. If you want to take it touring, racks and special Radical panniers can be fitted, and as the coach-traveller found, getting to or from your destination should be no problem. The front boom pulls out, the seat comes off, and the 20" (406) wheels don't take up much space either. Disassembled, no part is over one metre in length. Equipped as standard with Magura HS-12 hydraulic brakes, the Hurricane Luxe weighs around 14kg (but can be reduced to 11.5kg with special lightweight parts).

Customers asked Challenge if they could fit front suspension and a chain-cover to the Hurricane. This turned out to be impossible without a complete redesign – there just wasn't the room above the front wheel.

So redesign they did – and the result is the Wizard, an all-round touring/commuting bike. It's still compact, lively and nimble, but with its 26" (559) rear wheel and 52cm seat height (17cm higher than the Hurricane) the Wizard is just a little more suited for everyday use. The chain cover keeps trousers clean, and there's room for standard panniers (up to 25kg) on the stainless-steel rear carrier. Full dynamo lighting (with an LED rear light) and mudguards come as standard.

Like the Alu Hurricane, the Wizard has an aluminium frame, and both bikes are fitted with SRAM 3x7 gears. The standard finish is a two-layer powder-coating, but both bikes have the option of an anodised main frame.

Challenge b.v.

Challenge b.v. dates back to 1990, when Paul Voerman began building bikes at home. In 1992 production moved to a factory, with frame construction at two nearby frame-builders. With the surge of orders over the last few years, this out-sourcing has proved to be a great asset. Paul's not constrained by existing production facilities. As he puts it: "Where once I used to pick up the phone and ask for five frames, I now just ask for fifty. That's really all there is to it."
There are now five people working at Challenge, including Paul's father, who is responsible for building prototype frames. Their range includes the Wing recumbent off-road tourer with 26" (559) wheels, and the latest project is an economy version of the Wizard, the Focus, priced at under 2000 guilders and with full suspension.

Challenge b.v., Anklaarseweg 35-37, 7316 MB Apeldoorn, NETHERLANDS.
Tel +31 55 5212405 Fax +31 55 5213173
Website www.ligfiets.net/challenge
Agents in Germany, Denmark, UK and Belgium: see page 144.

In Holland, the Alu Hurricane costs around f 3490. The steel version costs around f 2990. Prices will vary worldwide.

TOXY

If there's one thing that can set two recumbent owners off on a long and heated discussion it's the relative merits of mesh and solid seats. Mesh seats are comfortable and offer good ventilation, while the solid type – popular in mainland Europe – can offer excellent back support if a good fit, and can feel more solid to press against when pedalling hard.

The Toxy from Quantum Spezialräder neatly sidesteps the debate, offering a choice of mesh or solid seats (in three different sizes), on mountings which let you adjust either model for both seat height and angle. You can also of course adjust for leg-length: the Toxy will fit riders between around 1.5m and 2.00m tall.

Another important choice is between above-seat steering, or handlebars below the seat. Again, it's largely a personal preference, and again, the Toxy offers you the choice. Flexibility is the hallmark of this multi-purpose machine. To further adapt the machine to your needs, you can choose front and rear fairings, wheel discs, rear box, racks for four panniers, and more. The versatility extends to the bike

itself: the lightweight aluminium frame and lively steering combine to provide a sparkling ride that is ideal for zipping around town, yet with front and rear suspension, the experience is relaxing enough to suit long-distance touring. Front and rear wheels are both the popular 20" (406) size, and low-maintenance, industry-standard components are used to ensure that obtaining spares is never a problem, even away from home. The transmission uses either the Sachs 3x7 system or Neos 24-speed derailleur gears. Mounting points for luggage, water bottles, fairings or other accessories are provided as standard on the Toxy frame.

Overall weight is around 15kg for a typical machine. Standard finish is a powder-coated red, but yellow and black are available on request, as are Magura hydraulic brakes and dynamo lighting. Also in Quantum's catalogue is a long list of spares, and even a selection of specialist tools.

If that still isn't flexible enough for you, buy a frameset and build up a bike yourself!

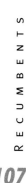

Quantum-Spezialräder

Arved Klütz has been making innovative bikes from his factory north of Hamburg since 1994, after completing his studies in mechanical engineering and business studies. He started producing bikes under the name Quantum-Liegeräder (Quantum Recumbents), but his latest project is an upright machine codenamed the 'Modular Bike', so it's now Quantum Spezialräder (special bikes) instead.

The 'Modular bike' is an upright machine, with 20" wheels and full suspension. Arved describes it as a continuation of the 'Toxy concept', with its universal frame-size and ability to be fitted with a huge range of extra components. The geometry can be altered according to the rider's size and preference, and it can be set up for general everyday use, for long-distance touring, or even as a load-carrier, with heavy-duty racks front and back. And as a bonus, the 'Modular Bike' is also capable of folding up for easy transport.

Quantum-Spezialräder, Arved Klütz, Steinstr. 5, 25364 Hörnerkirchen/Elmshorn, GERMANY.
Tel +49 4127 92283 Fax +49 4127 92284

In Germany, the Toxy costs from around DM 2570. Prices will vary worldwide.

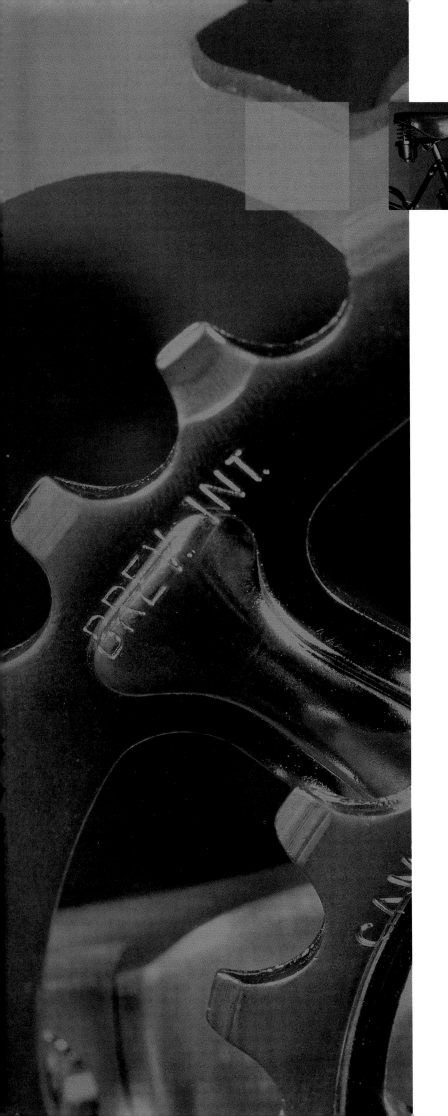

Accessories

You might be on the most expensive bike in the world, but if you can't get the indexing to stay tuned, or your panniers keep bouncing off, or the saddle doesn't suit your anatomy, then you might just as well be on the cheapest. Producing a good bike is not just about building a frame and bolting on the bits. Selecting the right components is just as much part of the design process as angles and stress-points.

And what might justifiably be called the right bike for you in the shop still needs to become your bike. It's more than just a question of handing over the money. Although few of us can afford a custom-built machine, one of the joys of cycling is that we can all fine-tune our machine to what we want and keep doing so, as our needs change and useful new products come onto the market. A different saddle can banish the pain in the seat, a handlebar extension, the crick in the neck. Age can be accepted gracefully with a wider range of gears. Someday you'll find the ideal all-purpose pannier or a pair of well-cut shorts with roomy pockets to carry your valuables. And someone will produce the ultimate multi-purpose tool to allow you to deal with any contingency: from a puncture to an appendectomy!

Since you yourself are the engine which will carry anything extra you put on your bike, you need to spend well and spend wisely on new components and accessories: if they don't work you'll pay the price double.

Cloud 9

How can you make a stem turn heads? Sculpt it of course, into a dynamic form which is stiff, strong and above all functional, a heady organic combination of art and engineering.

The Cloud 9 stem from Super Innovative Concepts is the first of a range of products being developed by a team led by Trevor Combs, an inventive young designer with a mission to come up with cycle components like nothing else on earth. He is clear that his products must be more than styling exercises: 'form must enable function' to bring clear rider benefits. In the case of the stems, this means being able to remove the stem from the handlebars without having to disassemble brakes, gears, grips and all – instead, simply unscrew and remove.

It also means that the stems are stiff, robust and lightweight.

The Cloud 9 is available in two versions, heat-treated 356 T6 aluminium alloy or carbon-reinforced thermoplastic. Both are designed to fit 'Aheadset'-type steerers. The aluminium Cloud 9 AL is a four-bolt, two-piece design, offered as 'no rise', or with +/−10° rise, and in 90, 100, 110, 120 and 130mm extension. Total weight is just 223g for the 130mm version. A range of powder-coated colours is available.

The hinged-cap Cloud 9 Thermo stem is a real head-turner, with its, two-bolt construction. But certainly no scales-turner, at 218g for the longest extension option. It's made from carbon-reinforced thermoplastic, with titanium hardware, and is available in the same extension lengths and angles as the aluminium version. The Thermo stems are made in a range of colours, and because the pigment is incorporated into the thermoplastic, the colouring is 100% scratchproof.

ENCYCLEOPEDIA ACCESSORIES

Super Innovative Concepts

Trevor Combs has been a mountain-biker for years, and it was a natural decision to base his Master's thesis at the Pratt Institute design college on the design of cycle components. He didn't expect that he'd ever end up manufacturing the parts himself, but things just kept happening… The first stems were launched by Super Innovative Concepts in late 1998. SIC have benefitted from a close partnership with manufacturing experts seconded from the US military: an unexpected 'peace dividend' from the end of the cold war is that defence technology teams have been suddenly told to find civilian applications for their work. The US Technology Transfer Program offers upcoming small and medium size companies access to cutting-edge research and production facilities which, says Trevor, were instrumental for the manufacture of a product that is an elegant match of beauty and effectiveness.

SIC, 811 Russell Avenue, Suite J, Gaithersburg, MD 20879, USA.
Tel +1 301 527 2337 Fax +1 301 527 6370
Email sicdesign@aol.com

In the USA, both thermoplastic and aluminium versions of the Cloud 9 cost around $169.95. Prices will vary worldwide.

VK STRONGBOX

Cyclists and baggage handlers don't always hit it off. Baggage handlers see bikes as sharp, greasy and awkward, and bike-owners see baggage handlers as clumsy and unappreciative of their fragile machines. The only failsafe solution is to make your bike look like 'normal' luggage – this also gets around any special 'fees' for bicycles, or even outright bans on some forms of public transport.

The VK Strongbox, from Dutch company VK International, conceals your bike in a very solid 9kg impact-resistant ABS plastic case. Just remove both wheels, and use the lengths of foam plastic provided to separate and protect the components. The 120 x 90 x 28cm case has four wheels on the bottom for easy movement and can be secured with two locks.

Cycle tour operators, large families or cycling clubs will appreciate VK's mass-transport system: a carrier to secure six large-wheeled bikes. A gas spring holds them perfectly still. A bicycle without mudguards can be fitted in 3 seconds and a bicycle with mudguards in 15 seconds. The steel carrier can be fitted on a trailer or

in a van, or VK can supply complete trailers to accommodate 6, 12, 18 or even 24 bikes.

VK International specialise in interesting accessories. Their VK Prism-Glasses are designed for racing cyclists in search of the perfect aerodynamic posture. A racer with his head down can see the road in front via the prisms, while back, neck and head remain in a natural curve. The horizontal position which results can lead, say the manufacturers, to an aerodynamic advantage of up to 5% at a speed of 40km/h.

The two prisms are 40mm wide and provide a clear view of the entire breadth of the road. The glasses are fixed tightly and securely to the head and nose with an elastic cord. They have been primarily designed for lone cyclists such as time triallists, triathletes and long-distance cyclists. They can, additionally, reduce muscle tension in the neck and back for anyone riding with drop handlebars.

VK International

VK International's further products include the 'Aero pannier' – a frame-fit, watertight, polyester case which can house everything which might be needed on a one day tour. The VK Wheelbox is a hard-shell case to protect valuable wheels from damage. The VK Saddle Adjuster is an aluminium adapter which allows you to adjust saddle position up to 40mm forwards or back. The VK Mapholder fixes, without tools, on every type of handle bar within seconds. To protect your bike from the elements try the VK Bicycle and Duo-Bicycle Pyjamas: covers made from a very strong woven waterproof material, and with stainless steel eyelets at the bottom for a cable lock. The Duo-Bicycle Pyjamas are designed for two bikes on the back of a car, and have extra eyelets for a rope or cord to secure the cover.

VK have two solutions to wet feet problems: their Rainshoes are transparent and very tough plastic covers which you pull over your shoes if rain threatens. As they weigh just 20g, they're easy to fold up and take with you on your bike. VK Latex Rainshoes use an elastic material for a snug fit. You can walk in them – so they might also be useful for gardening!

VK International, Vliegertstraat 2, 6005 PR Weert, Netherlands. Tel +31 495 545 050 Fax +31 495 546 017 Agents in other countries: see page 144.

In Holland, the Strongbox costs around f 595. Trailers start at f 2200, and Prism Glasses cost around f 290. Prices will vary worldwide.

SRAM components

A change in gear

SRAM was founded with five employees in 1987 to build a revolutionary gear changer, the Gripshift. Aspiring to sell 10,000 units in the first year, they actually sold 1,000! There were a few hurdles to overcome, but they bounced back and by 1992 a million units had been produced, soaring to ten million in 1994. In 1995 every winning bike in the Men's World Cup and NORBA National Championships was equipped with Gripshift. Racing success continues to this day. Ten years on, SRAM is a global organisation, with manufacturing facilities in the USA, Ireland, Mexico, Taiwan, China, Germany, France and Portugal. They stress the American way of customer service wherever they work.

Almost a century earlier, on August 1st 1895, Ernst Sachs and Karl Fichtel founded 'Schweinfurter Präzisions-Kugellagerwerke Fichtel und Sachs' to produce bearings and bicycle hubs. The Sachs company grew into one of Germany's larger manufacturers, with interests well beyond cycling. When SRAM acquired Sachs Bicycle Components in 1997 it became the world's second-largest bicycle component manufacturer. SRAM products are available through cycle dealers worldwide.

Global headquarters Tel +1 312 664 8800 Fax +1 312 664 8826.
European headquarters: Tel +31 33 450 6060 Fax +31 33 457 0200
Website www.sram.com

SRAM

When the world thought thumbshifters, SRAM dreamed up the Gripshift: a robust and simple way to change gear. As cycling appeals to an ever-wider audience, innovative thinking, simplicity and reliability are more important than ever. 'Comfort cycling' has arrived.

A 'comfort' bike is rider-friendly: that means components which function perfectly with as little hassle and maintenance as possible. SRAM's own expertise in designing components with these qualities has been extended by their acquisition in 1997 of Sachs, for many decades Europe's largest manufacturer of cycle components.

SRAM now supply a complete range of components for both 'comfort' bikes and MTBs, including gear components, cranksets, brakes and chains. The 'Spectro' range builds particularly on the engineering expertise and reputation of Sachs, while SRAM puts its own name on derailleur drivetrain components.

The Spectro range covers an impressive range of hub gears and brakes, perfect for city and 'comfort' cyclists, offering wide gear ranges without the complexity of a derailleur system. Ranging from three to twelve speeds, Spectro hub gears are easy to use and low maintenance. The idea is to make life as easy as possible for the customer. SRAM have paid particular attention to the ergonomics: the shifting

'feel' is improved, dual-density grips offer more comfort, and it's easy to remove and reassemble the rear wheel: no adjustment is needed. Just snap the 'click-box' back on, and off you go. The range is completed by the Spectrolux universal dynamo, the '3x7' combination hub/derailleur system, and a front drum brake.

SRAM have rethought the way derailleurs work, not taking for granted that decades of road-bike derailleur developments are appropriate for MTBs. The ESP mountain-bike derailleurs have a '1:1' ratio of lever movement to derailleur movement, giving lower than usual cable tension, and more reliable indexing. The changer is bolted in a fixed position on the dropout, allowing a stronger idler cage spring to control chain-slap and chain-suck.

'Plasma' derailleurs do away with the strange 180° bend performed by most rear derailleur cables, and the more direct cable routing leads to correspondingly lower shifting effort. The ESP and 'Plasma' ranges complement each other nicely: while the ESP shifters and derailleurs work together perfectly as a finely-tuned system, the Plasma range is compatible with most current shifters. Both shift smoothly and fast, but there's a diffferent 'feel'. If you can, try them both!

LightSPIN

Dynamos may revolve, but a revolution in dynamos has been a long time in coming. The LightSPIN dynamo, from Dynosys AG in Switzerland, could be the first of a new generation.

The LightSPIN is a bottle dynamo that uses a new, patented layout for the magnets and offers previously unheard-of performance. The generator efficiency is around 95%, and with microchip-controlled management electronics the dynamo regulates its output to exactly 6.2V, whatever your speed, eliminating the problem of bulbs blowing on fast descents. Overall efficiency is around 80%. The system provides full voltage at only 7.5km/h (4.5mph). The pedal power required to run the dynamo is only 4.5 watts, a manyfold improvement on conventional bottle dynamos, and better even than any hub dynamo. Excess power is simply not generated, resulting in a dynamo that draws the same, minimum power virtually independent of speed.

The LightSPIN is available with a built-in nickel metal hydride (NiMH) backup battery. The charging and discharging of this reserve power is handled by the electronics, and the result is a light that stays on, at full power, for up to 45 minutes after you've stopped the bike. The light will automatically cut out after 4 minutes stationary – though you can just roll the bike a little to switch it back on. This full-power backup light is a revelation to those weaned on traditional dynamos: the ability to read maps, put up tents or mend a puncture with the dynamo providing the power could free many cycle tourists from the need to carry a separate, battery-powered torch. If you have a LightSPIN without the backup facility, it can be easily added with a separate upgrade kit. The LightSPIN is designed to be compatible with existing front and rear lamp units.

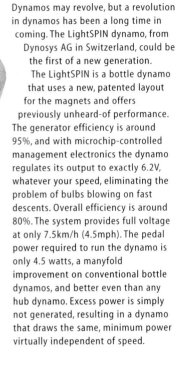

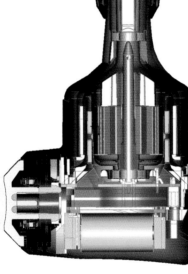

Dynosys AG

Inventor Edwin Schwaller and business partners Werner Stettler and Jean-Claude Diener set up Dynosys AG in 1995, to bring Schwaller's patented new design into production. After three years of development, the Lightspin was launched in early 1999. Edwin Schwaller has worked as a development engineer for many years, at various high-technology companies. His experience has been put to good use: much of the LightSPIN research has involved redesigning the various components for volume production in order to create a truly mass-market product. The high efficiency of the generator system has, says Edwin, resulted in interest from other users of small generator systems, including developers of commercial wind power facilities.

Dynosys AG, Hauptstr. 104,
CH-9422 Staad, SWITZERLAND.
Tel +41 62 827 4828 Fax +41 62 827 4829
Email info@dynosys-ag.ch
Website www.dynosys-ag.ch

In Germany, the LightSPIN costs around DM 130, or DM 75 without the backup battery and electronics.

Speedhub 500/14

Suddenly it was there: a 14-speed hub gear developed in secrecy by a small German company. With the Speedhub 500/14, Rohloff have done what was once considered impossible: they have launched a full-scale attack on the off-road market with a hub gear. The Speedhub 500/14 matches the range of gears on a 27-speed ATB, with an efficiency of between 96 and 98% depending on which gear you're in. Complete, the transmission weight is between that of Shimano's XT and XTR groupsets. The Speedhub gives a 526% ratio range: in derailleur terms equivalent to an ATB with an 11-28 block and a 44/32/22 tooth chainset. And it brings all the benefits of hub gears: constant chainline, low maintenance and no vulnerable derailleurs to get damaged.

The hub will shift gear with only a 13° rotation of the pedals, even under load, which gives lightning-fast gear changes from the single twistgrip control. Indexing is handled at the hub rather than at the gear lever, so there is no fear of cable stretch taking the gears out of alignment during a hard race or a long day's tour.

The Rohloff is the first hub gear to use a quick-release, although solid axles are available for frames without vertical dropouts. The Speedhub has a standard 135mm rear axle spacing. Specially-made spokes from DT Swiss are available to suit popular 26" MTB rims. As the wheel is dishless, it's much stronger than traditional freehub-type wheels, and so uses just 32 spokes. Rims smaller than around 18" are not recommended, as the spokes would run at too extreme an angle.

The Speedhub is finished in silver or as a powdercoated 'Red Baron', and mountings for disc brakes are optional: it is currently compatible with certain disks from Hope and Magura. All Rohloff hubs can be retrofitted for disc brakes.

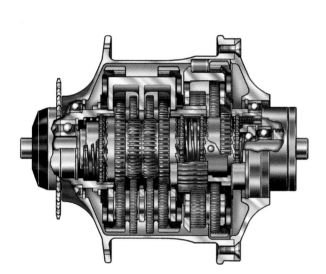

Rohloff

In 1986 Bernhard and Barbara Rohloff set out to build the finest chain the world of cycling had ever seen. Their energy and effort was rewarded a few years later, in 1990, when Rohloff chains propelled riders to victory in both of cycling's blue riband events; the Tour de France and the World Championships. They make a wide range of chain-related accessories, including 'Caliber' chain-measurers, the 'Revolver' chain tool and the excellent Oil of Rohloff. The Rohloff company logo is a raven, so, when they were given an abandoned raven chick, they felt duty-bound to raise it to adulthood. Raven-raising has now become official company policy, with several chicks given a second chance at life each year.

Rohloff GmbH, Möncheborgstr 30, D-34125 Kassel, GERMANY. Tel +49 561 875 615 Fax +49 561 875 338 Email service@rohloff.de Website www.rohloff.de

In Germany, the Speedhub 500/14 costs from roughly DM 1500. Prices will vary worldwide.

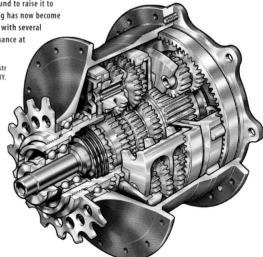

ENCYCLOPEDIA **ACCESSORIES**

SYNCHRO-SHIFT

Derailleur gears may have been around a long time, but that doesn't mean they can't be improved. French company EGS have tackled the problem head-on: developing radical designs which rethink the derailleur from first principles.

The heart of the system is the Synchro-Shift gear selector, a single spring-assisted twist-grip which operates both front and rear derailleurs in sequence to give twelve gears, in even steps and without duplication. By avoiding the extreme combinations across the block, the chain is kept straighter, it shifts more reliably and lasts longer. Avoiding the 'small-small' and 'big-big' combinations also means that less slack has to be taken up – you can use a shorter chain and a shorter derailleur cage. This reduces weight and further improves shifting performance and reliability.

The rear derailleur mechanism, thought EGS, was ripe for improvement: vulnerable, fragile, and with awkward cable entry. The alternative is the 'Up-Cage' derailleur, which runs along the chainstay and uses three jockey wheels: two tension the chain, and one controls shifting. The Up-Cage improves ground clearance by up to 9cm (3.5"), and reduces the length of chain required

by as much as 15%. This gives considerable advantages in mountain bike racing, keeping the chain away from the dirt, and the mechanism out of harm's way, and has been used to good effect by the EGS racing team. What works on the racetrack will be equally at home in the grime of everyday cycling.

Synchro-Shift gear changers are available in five different versions, and work with conventional indexed derailleurs. Up-Cage derailleurs are designed to take full advantage of the straighter chain provided by the Synchro-Shift selector and are not recommended for use with other shifters.

EGS

Frank Savard and Christian Gauthier set up EGS in April 1996 to design, manufacture and market a new generation of cycle components. The Synchro-Shift was the first, followed by the Up-Cage derailleur. Completing the system is a new 'Freeside' chainring design, designed to match the Synchro-Shift and Up-Cage combination. The 'Flash Hub' for the rear lets the wheel body be removed (to mend a puncture, for example), leaving the gears still attached to the frame, so you don't disturb the alignment. Finally, Savard has come up with the exquisite EGS 'Twin Motion' brake levers.

In July 1998 EGS improved their production facilities, setting up a joint operation with one of their suppliers to produce the Synchro-Shift range, which is now fitted to over 30 brands of mountain bikes. Specialists HMA produce the top-of-the-range X-Pro components, machined from titanium and aluminium.

EGS, 1 Rue Nungesser et Coli, BP 476, 86104 Chatellerault Cedex, FRANCE. Tel +33 549 20 22 10 Fax +33 549 85 35 42 Email info@e-g-s.com Website www.e-g-s.com

In France, Synchro-Shift prices range from 250 FF for the basic Easy, to 2600 FF for the X-Pro. Prices will be similar worldwide.

ORTLIEB

Non-cyclists often assume that cycling in the rain must be hell. Cyclists are (usually) aware that a combination of proper clothing and healthy circulation mean that it isn't really such a big deal. But what about your belongings? You can hardly expect them to put on a Gore-Tex jacket and adopt a hearty attitude.

Ortlieb have the answer. For the last fifteen years they've been producing cycling gear which is guaranteed waterproof and dirtproof. They even offer two levels of water resistance: 'Spray-Waterproof' covers items that you can leave out in quite heavy rain, whereas the 'Floating' products will do just that, should you accidentally drop them in a river.

Central to the Ortlieb range are the Front-Roller and Back-Roller panniers. The smaller front panniers can be used on a rear rack if preferred, and are great for children's bikes and recumbents. The roll-top fastening is absolutely waterproof. As with all Ortlieb panniers, the Roller bags are symmetrical, so fit either side of the bike, and they won't be lopsided when converted to a rucksack. If you prefer a more traditional style, try the Bike-Packer and Mini-Biker bags, which feature a fold-over lid. With both styles you can choose the 'Light' option, with a lighter, PVC-free fabric and the new 'Quick-Lock 2' mounting system, which

holds the bags securely to the bike over the roughest potholes. It's adjustable to fit any rear carrier rack, with tubing of 8, 10 or 16mm diameter.

Ultimate 3 handlebar bags from Ortlieb come in three sizes, and in a variety of fabrics. All share a quick-release mounting system, and a strong sub-frame. Waterproof and rigid, an Ortlieb barbag makes an excellent home for a camera, and special padding can be fitted for this purpose. Most bar-bags are fitted with generously-sized transparent map-cases, with the exception of the roll-top models.

Ortlieb make a vast range of products for cyclists, including courier bags, the 'Travel-Biker' racktop suitcase, and a handy briefcase/laptop carrier (where being 100% waterproof is of supreme importance). Many cyclists will also know of Ortlieb's other outdoor equipment: from waterbags which double as showers to drybags beloved of canoeists, to an interesting range of rucksacks with a unique waterproof zip, combining full rain protection with excellent ease of access.

Ortlieb's reputation among the outdoor fraternity is second to none: just take a look at the next long-distance cycle tourist who passes through your town. Chances are, the panniers will be Ortlieb.

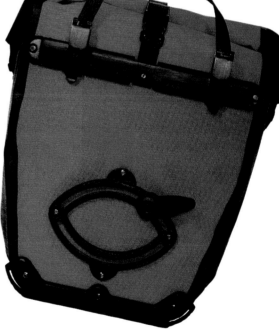

Ortlieb Sportartikel GmbH

Cycling writer Stephen McKay is a passionate fan of Ortlieb. He once worked as a sales rep for a bike manufacturer, but instead of going round in a van, was sent out on a bike. Towing three more bikes behind him, he covered some 600 miles, going from shop to shop. It was quite an ordeal, but he feels that having reliable, waterproof bags made all the difference. "The whole project was, with hindsight, quite ridiculous. The trailer was badly designed, and back-up from base was negligible. As days turned to weeks, the exhaustion and loneliness mounted, until I reached a state at which I really wasn't in a fit state to be cycling on busy roads. I honestly feel that the quality of the Ortlieb gear may have helped save my life – they were the one part of the expedition that worked properly. No matter how bad things got, I always knew that my gear was going to be 100% dry."

Ortlieb Sportartikel GmbH, Rainstr. 6, 91560 Heilsbronn, GERMANY.
Tel +49 9872 8000 Fax +49 9872 800266 Email info@ortlieb.de Website www.ortlieb.de
Agents in other countries: see page 144.

*In Germany, a pair of Back-Rollers costs around DM 169 (basic) or DM 229 (light).
Ultimate 3 bar bags range from DM 89 to DM 179. Prices will vary worldwide.*

TOONY SADDLES

Sitting on a work of art can be surprisingly comfortable – when it's been crafted by hand from your favourite saddle. 'Toony' saddles bring colour and life to almost any racing or MTB saddle, giving it a vegetable-tanned cowhide cover, individually hand-decorated. The pattern is carved into the leather in various designs, to give a 'relief' appearance – and it's coloured with special leather dyes. Several stunning 'Beasts of Burden' are available, one of which is the crocodilian 'Selle Crocal' shown here. A Toony saddle is functional, long-lasting and hard-wearing, just requiring a little grease now and again. The shape and fit of the original saddle is maintained precisely.

Kunst & Leder also make distinguished replicas of historic saddles, a special Pedersen saddle, and a wide range of leather bags for the connoisseur (featured in Encycleopedia 4 and previous issues). Often used on high-wheelers, Pedersens or Moultons, these bags will grace any fine bicycle, and with a little care, will last a lifetime.

Kunst & Leder, Stephanie Rothemund
Kunst & Leder, Galerie "Allerhand", Turnitzstr. 29,
D-91522 Ansbach, GERMANY. Tel +49 981 957 67 (12 – 18h)

Stephanie Rothemund, Esbacher Str. 2, D-91746
Weidenbach, GERMANY. Tel/Fax +49 9826 9446

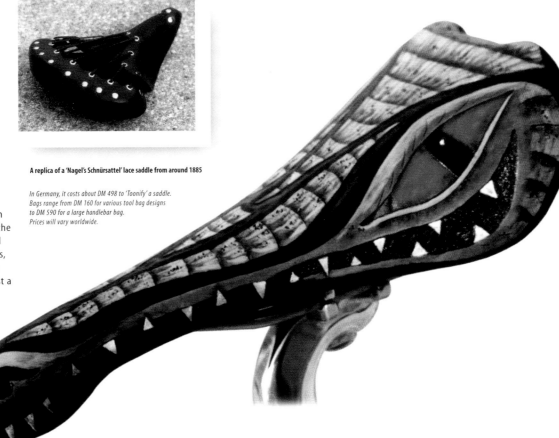

A replica of a 'Nagel's Schnürsattel' lace saddle from around 1885

*In Germany, it costs about DM 498 to 'Toonify' a saddle.
Bags range from DM 160 for various tool bag designs
to DM 590 for a large handlebar bag.
Prices will vary worldwide.*

RADICAL BAGS

Put normal panniers on a recumbent and they're often too high up, or don't use all of the available space effectively. Help is at hand in the form of recumbent-specific luggage from Dutch company Radical Design.

The 'side-pod' bags (the 'Allfa Zijtassen') are designed to be hung from the seat and the rear carrier. Various sizes are available, holding 40 to 70 litres. A slightly smaller version fits on recumbents with no rear rack.

There's often also luggage space behind the rider's back – and putting one of Radical 'Allfa Toptas' bags here also helps the aerodynamics. Three sizes are available up to 30 litres, and different models fit either narrow or wider seats.

As well as these recumbent bags, Radical make high-quality 'normal' panniers, heavy duty for prolonged use, including the massive 60L 'Discovery Tandem' model (it fits on most bikes, not just tandems). Radical can manufacture specially-adapted bags to order, including Brompton rackpacks.

Radical Design
Radical Design, Hoofdstraat 8, 9514 BE Gasselternijveen,
HOLLAND. Tel/Fax +31 599 513 482
UK agents: Comfort Cycles UK. Tel +44 1454 320 319.
Full details page 145
*In Holland, prices range from f 129 to f 399, and will vary
worldwide.*

PICNIC

Lockable storage on a bike frees you from the tedious task of carrying every item with you each time you leave your bike around in public. The Picnic from Polish company Nicator is a secure and aerodynamic solution. It's also dust and waterproof: Nicator's favourite demonstration at trade shows is to have a dozen or so goldfish swimming around in a translucent water-filled Picnic.

Easily fitted with just three mounting points to almost any bike with 24-28" wheels, the 1.3kg Picnic has a built-in steel lock for the lid. It's available in a wide range of colours moulded into the impact-resistant thermoplastic shell, and can carry around 25 litres of baggage.

The Picnic is available through distributors worldwide: see page 145, or contact Nicator direct for details. They would be interested to hear from prospective overseas agents.

Nicator s.c.
Nicator s.c., Biuro Handlowe, Lokal Nr 308, ul. Ostrobramska 101, 04041 Warszawa, Poland.
Tel 0048 22 673 6043 Fax 0048 22 673 6069
Email nicator@supermedia.pl
Website www.nicator.supermedia.pl
Agents in UK and Germany: see page 145

In Western Europe the Picnic costs about DM65. Prices will vary worldwide.

MOUNTAIN DRIVE

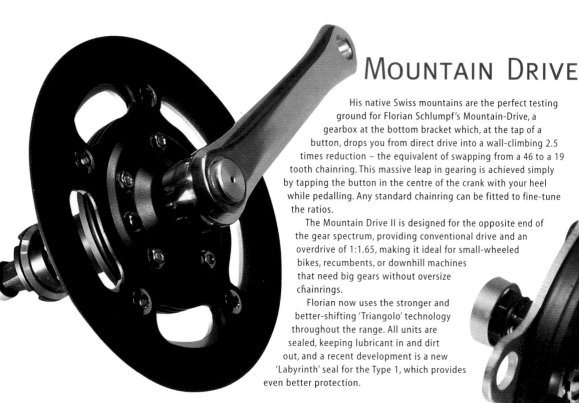

His native Swiss mountains are the perfect testing ground for Florian Schlumpf's Mountain-Drive, a gearbox at the bottom bracket which, at the tap of a button, drops you from direct drive into a wall-climbing 2.5 times reduction – the equivalent of swapping from a 46 to a 19 tooth chainring. This massive leap in gearing is achieved simply by tapping the button in the centre of the crank with your heel while pedalling. Any standard chainring can be fitted to fine-tune the ratios.

The Mountain Drive II is designed for the opposite end of the gear spectrum, providing conventional drive and an overdrive of 1:1.65, making it ideal for small-wheeled bikes, recumbents, or downhill machines that need big gears without oversize chainrings.

Florian now uses the stronger and better-shifting 'Triangolo' technology throughout the range. All units are sealed, keeping lubricant in and dirt out, and a recent development is a new 'Labyrinth' seal for the Type 1, which provides even better protection.

Florian Schlumpf Spezialmaschinenbau
Florian Schlumpf Spezialmaschinenbau,
Dorfstr. 10, CH-7324 Vilters, Switzerland.
Tel +41 817238009 Fax +41 817238364
Email schlumpf_ing@bluewin.ch
Website www.schlumpf.ch

In Switzerland, prices range from sfr.486. Prices will vary worldwide.

SPINSKINS

Did you watch the Sojourner robot reporting from Mars in 1998, and wonder at the airbag system that landed it safely? Spinskins were developed by one of the airbag's designers, Charlie Howland, and uses the same technology from manufacturers Warwick Mills. Liquid crystal Vectran fibres are woven with Kevlar to produce a tyre liner of exceptional performance. The Kevlar/Vectran weave is covered by a fabric layer, with feathered edges, to protect the tube from any abrasion. Spinskins also protect against pinch flats, by spreading the force of any impact. There are five sizes, including BMX, MTB and three different widths of 700c liner. Spinskins weigh from 34g (MTB) to a mere 14g (700c narrow). Tested on cactus-covered deserts, Spinskins brings NASA technology to the most vulnerable part of your bike.

Spinskins
Spinskins, Warwick Mills, 301 Turnpike Road, New Ipswich, NH 03071, USA. Tel +1 603 878 1565 Fax +1 603 878 4306 Email spinskins@aol.com Website http://www.SpinSkins.com/

In the USA, Spinskins cost around $39.95. Prices will vary worldwide.

BIKE BUREAU

Laptops and bicycles are two of the most useful tools in modern life, and the Bike Bureau helps the busy office commuter to keep both in good order. It's an attractive, professional-looking briefcase, which comfortably takes A4 files or a portable PC, and which fits securely onto your bike's rear carrier.

Take the Bureau off the bike, and the top flap of the double lid folds back over the rear of the bag, covering the Klickfix hooks and sealing away the wheel side of the bag, which might have attracted road dirt or spray. Folding the flap back also reveals a zip compartment for wet cycling clothing, and a smart top handle for carrying it into the office.

The briefcase has an internal document divider, organiser section, pen pockets, a key-ring holder and a removable shoulder strap. There's a choice between classic black Cotton Duck with quick-release chrome leather straps, or purple and black Cordura. Carridice say that, as with their saddlebags and panniers, Cotton Duck is by far the most popular choice, with its weather-beating performance and classic appearance.

Carradice of Nelson Ltd
Carradice of Nelson Ltd, Westmoreland Works, St Mary's Street, Nelson, BB9 7BA, UK.
Tel +44 1282 615886 Fax +44 1282 602329

In the UK, the Bike Bureau costs around £54.95 (Cotton Duck) or £49.95 (Cordura). Prices will vary worldwide.

The Pedersen bicycle as it appeared in Encycleopedia 4, fitted with hand-made 'Woodguard' equipment, from Johannes Rességuier, in Germany. For Pedersen bicycles, and Woodguards, contact: Kalle Kalkhoff, KGB, Donnerschweerstrasse 45, Oldenburg 26123, Germany. Tel +49 441 885 0389. Fax +49 441 885 0388

Listed below are some of the products featured in previous Encycleopedias, and which are not included in this edition. The list is not definitive, and we have taken out products which we know are no longer available. The contact details are the latest that we have available: some manufacturers may have moved without letting us know. The Encycleopedias published to date are named: Encycleopedia 93/94, Encycleopedia 94/95, Encycleopedia 96, and Encycleopedia 4 (covering 97/98).

A. Winther A/S
E4: Dolphin and Donkey trailers
Rygesmindevej 2, DK 8653 Them, Denmark
Tel +45 8684 7288
Fax +45 8684 8528

A.S. Engineering
E4: S-327
A.S. Engineering, c/o TNT Mailfast, MOW/MOW/10012/14, PO Box 66, Hounslow TW5 9RT, UK Tel/Fax +7 095 430 3897 Email ykpro@aha.ru

AIRO-Shield
E4: AIRO-Shield
1973 North Nellis Blvd., Suite 121, Las Vegas, Nevada 89115-3654, USA
Tel +1 702 382 7288 Fax +1 702 382 7288
Email Tom@ttinet.com Website http://www.ttinet.com/tom

AnthroTech Leichtfahrzeugtechnik GmbH i.G.
E4: AnthroTech
Rothenbergstr. 7, 90542 Eckental-Frohnhof, Germany Tel +49 9126 288 644
Fax +49 9126 288 321

ATP Green Gear Cycling
E94/5: Bike Friday, E96: Bike TwosDay. 4065 West 11th Ave., #14, Eugene, OR 97402. USA. Tel +1503 6870 487 Fax 6870 403.

Batavus
E4: Relaxx
Industrieweg 4, 8444 AR Heerenveen, Netherlands Tel +31 513 63 8999 Fax +31 513 63 8262 Email info@batavus.com http://www.batavus.com

Bebop Incorporated
E96: Bebop Pedals
8570 Hamilton Ave, Huntington Beach, CA 92646, USA. Tel +1 714 374 0200 Fax +1 7143740268 Email mrbebop@aol.com

Berkut
E4: Berkut B-317
department of 'Outlook Ltd', Adm. Marakov Street 45-91, Moscow 125 212, Russia
Tel +7 095 452 33 98 Fax +7 095 452 33 98

Bicycles by Haluzak
E4: Traverse
Bicycles by Haluzak, 2166 Burbank Avenue, Santa Rosa, California 95407 USA. Tel +1 707 544 6243 Email recumbent2@aol.com

Bilenky Cycle Works
E96: Air Tandem
5319 North Second St, Philadelphia, PA 19120, USA. Tel +1 215 329 4744
Fax +1 215 329 5380

Bjällby Recumbents
E4: Easy & Tough
Stationwej 10A, DK-3520 Farum, Denmark
Tel +45 4295 6005 (home) Fax +45 43 62 87 83 (work)

Boulder Bikes
E4: Paris-Roubaix
PO Box 1400, Lyons, CO 80540, USA
Tel +1 303 823 5021 Fax +1 303 823 5025
Email rkd_llc@indra.com
http://cyclery.com/boulder_bikes/

Bromakin Wheelchairs
E4: Bromakin Trice Conversion
12 Prince William Road, Belton Park, Loughborough, Leicestershire, LE11 5GU, UK Tel +44 1509 217 569 Fax +44 1509 233 954 Email peter@bromakin.co.uk

Carradice of Nelson Ltd
E4: Carradice Bags
Westmoreland Works, St Mary's Street, Nelson, BB9 7BA, UK Tel +44 1282 615 886
Fax +44 1282 602 329

Chronos
E94/95, E96: Chronos Hammer

2936 Avenida Theresa, Carlsbad, CA 92009, USA. Tel +1 619 942 9049 Fax +1 619 942 9049

Citytramp TransportRoller GmbH
E4: Citytramp
Teckstr. 37, D-71116 Gärtringen, Germany
Tel +49 7034 266 61 Fax +49 7034 266 61
Email 0203664323-0001@t-online.de

Condor Cycles
E4: Condor Cycles
144-148 Gray's Inn Road, London WC1X 8AX, UK. Tel +44 171 837 7641 Fax +44 171 837 5560

Crystal Engineering
E94/5, E4: Trice
Unit 1A Jubilee Wharf, Commercial Road, Penryn, Cornwall TR10 8AQ, UK Tel +44 1326 378 848 Fax +44 1326 378 848
Email tricehpv@globalnet.co.uk

Design Management AS
E4: Bicycle Lift
Teknostallen (Trondheim Innovation Centre), Prof Brochs gt. 6, N-7030 Trondheim, Norway Tel +47 7354 0266
Fax +47 7394 3861

Design Mobility
E4: Swift Folder
PO Box 1005, Eugene, Oregon 97440, USA
Tel +1 503 343 5568 Fax +1 503 683 3397
Email cat@efn.org

Easy Racers Inc.
E96: EZ-1 recumbent
2891 Freedom Blvd, Watsonville, CA 95019, USA. Tel +1 408 722 977
Email tooeasy@aol.com
http://www.easyracers.com

Extreme Engineering Ltd.
E96, E4: Rubicon
14 Fairways, Toft, Bourne, Lincolnshire

PE10 0BS, UK Tel +44 177 859 0339
Fax +44 177 859 0339
Email raywatextremeeng@msn.com

Fahrrad-Manufaktur
E4: C-140 Tourer
Zum Panrepel 24, 28307 Bremen, Germany
Tel +49 421 43857 0 Fax +49 421 43857 99

Fateba Fahrradtechnik
E96: Fateba Long Bike recumbent
Bachmann & Co, Rosenstr. 11, CH-8400 Winterthur, Switzerland. Tel +41 522 126 911 Fax +41 522 137 841

Firma Egon Rahe
E4: Eleganz
Adenauerstr. 8, 33428 Marienfeld, Germany
Tel +49 5247 800 44 Fax +49 5247 80044

Firma Veit Lehmann
E96: Tetrad hand-and-foot powered bike
Laubenhöhe 10, 69509 Mörlenbach, Germany.

Flux - Fahrräder
E93/4: ST-2 recumbent
Kreuzbreitlstr. 8, D-82194 Gröbenzell, Germany. Tel/Fax +49 8142 53180

Freedom Bikepacking
E93/4: Commuter and Limpet pannier bags
The Barn, Church Lane, Clyst St Mary, Devon EX5 1AB, UK. Tel +44 1392 877531
Fax +44 1392 877872

FutureCycles
E94/5, E96: Streetglider recumbents.
Friends Yard, London Road, Forest Row, East Sussex RH18 5EE, UK. Tel +44 1342 822847 Fax +44 1342 826726

G. Wehmeyer Zweiradteile
E96: Weco 3BS-Synchro hubs
Engerstr. 47, D-33824 Werther, Germany.
Tel +49 520 3225/6/8 Fax +49 5203227

Geoff Wiles Cycles
E4: 'W' Performance Products Hubs
45-47 Cuxton Road (A228), Strood, Rochester upon Medway, Kent ME2 2BU, UK Tel +44 634 722586 Fax +44 1634 727 416

George Longstaff Cycles
E93/4: Tandem Trike.
Albert Street, Chesterton, Newcastle under Lyme, Staffs ST5 7JF. Tel +44 782 561 966
Fax +44 782 566 044

Giant
E4: Giant MCR/TCR.
Contact your nearest dealer.

Harig Liegeräder
E93/4: Aeroproject recumbents.
Richard-Zanders-Str 48, Bergisch Gladbach, Germany D-51469. Tel/Fax +49 22 02 38455

Highpath Engineering
E93/4, E4: Eggrings
Cornant, Cribyn, Llanbedr PS, Ceredigion, SA48 7QW, UK Tel +44 1570 470035
Fax +44 1570 470035

HP Velotechnik
E4: Wavey and Streamer
Goethestr. 5, 65830 Kriftel, Germany Tel +49 61 92 41010 Fax +49 6192 910218

Human Powered Machines
E4: Lightweight Long Haul
PO Box 1005, Eugene, Oregon 97440, USA
Tel +1 503 343 5568 Fax +1 503 683 3397
Email cat@efn.org Website
http://www.efn.org/~cat

Ibis
E4: Bow-Ti
PO Box 275, Sebastopol, CA 95473, USA
Tel +1 707 829 5615 Fax +1 707 829 5687
Email ChuckIbis@aol.com Website
www.ibisycles.com

Jack Wolfskin
E96: Diogenes & Royal Flash bags
and jackets.
Postfach 1454, 64529 Mörfelden-Walldorf,
Germany. Tel +49 610 593 3787 Fax +49
62322 6415

Joe Breeze Cycles
E4: Breezer Twister
Contact national distributors below for
details of your nearest stockist

Koga BV
E4: Emotion, GlobeTraveller
Postbus 167, 8440 AD Heerenveen,
Holland Tel +31 5136 30111 Fax +31 513
633289 Email info@koga.com
Website www.koga.com

Leitra APS
E94/5, E96, E4: Leitra
Box 64, DK-2750 Ballerup, Denmark
Tel +45 48 18 33 77 Fax +45 48 18 33 77

Lightning Cycle Dynamics
E94/5: Lightning P-38 E96: Stealth, R-84
312-Ninth Street, Lompoc, CA 93436, USA.
Tel +1 805 736 0700 Fax +1 805 737 3265

Linear Manufacturing Inc
E94/5, E96, E4: Linear Tandem
RR1, Box 173, Guttenberg, Iowa 52052, USA
Tel +1 319 252 1637 Fax +1 319 252 3305

Lyonsport
E4: Adjustable stem
1175 Plumtree Lane, Grants Pass, OR97526,
USA Tel +1 541 476 7092
Email lyonsport@aol.com

M5
E96: M5 recumbents
Brak Straat,11, 4331 - TM, Middelburg,
Netherlands. Tel +31 118 628 759
Fax +31 118 642 719

Main Street Pedicabs
E4: Pedi-Cab
3003 Arapahoe Street, Suite 222, Denver,
Colorado 80205, USA Tel +1 303 604 2330
Fax +1 303 604 2404 Email
pedicab@usa.net http://www.pedicab.com

Merlin Metalworks
E4: Merlin Road bike with S and S Coupling
40 Smith Place, Cambridge, MA 02138, USA
Tel +1 617 661 6688 Fax +1 617 661 6673
Email dfox@merlinbike.com
http://merlinbike.com

Mesicek
E96, E4: Mesicek High Bicycle
Nerudova 257, 69701 Kyjov, Czech
Republic Tel +42 629 5653 Fax +42 629
5653. Or Kalle Kalkhoff, KGB,
Donnerschweerstrasse 45, Oldenburg
26123, Germany. Tel +49 441 885 0389.
Fax +49 441 885 0388

Mirrycle Corporation
E96: Mirrycle Mirrors & Bells
6101 Ben Place, Boulder, USA, Co 80301,
USA. Tel +1 303 4423495 Fax +1 303
4479273

Montague Corporation
E96: Triframe folding tandem
432 Columbia St., Ste 29, Cambridge,
MA 02140, USA. Tel +1 617 491 7200 Fax
+1 617 491 7207

Montara Mountain Bike
E4: MP200 STEALTH Pedals
61 Clarendon Road, Pacifica, CA 94044,
USA. Tel +1 415 359 1326
Email mtb@montaramtb.com
www.montaramtb.com

Nightsun Performance Lighting
E4: Nightsun XC
995 South Fair Oaks Drive, Pasadena, CA
91105, USA. Tel +1 818 799 5074 Fax +1
818 799 0923

Ostrad GmbH
E96, E4: Ostrad SWB, E94/5 Ostrad LWB,
Winsstr. 48, 10405 Berlin, Germany Tel +49
30 443 413 93 Fax +49 30 443 413 94
Email OstradGmbH@aol.com
http://www.as-c.de/ostrad/

Pamir Engineering
E4: Pamir Tools
PO Box 323 Fairview, PA, USA Tel +1 814
474 2228 Fax +1 814 474 2228
Email pamireng@aol.com
http://members.aol.com/pamireng

Peter Busse Sicherheitstechnik
E4: Pitlock Security System
Liegnitzer Str. 15, 10999 Berlin, Germany
Tel +49 30 611 2092
Fax +49 30 611 2093

PIVOT-Liegeräder
E4: Harpoon
Ahornstr. 15, 88069 Tettnang, Germany
Tel +49 7542 54656 Fax +49 7542 5981

PJ Taylor Cycles
E93/4, E94/5: Victorian E96: Discoverer
mobility tricycles
375 Birchfield Road, Redditch, Worcs, B79
4NE, UK. Tel/Fax +44 1527 545262

Plastron Products
E4: Bike Lid
10434 NE 17th St, Bellevue, WA 98004,
USA. Tel +1 206 455 9014 Fax +1 206 455
1750 Email wrw1958@worldnet.att.net
Website www.bikelid.com

Radnabel
E94/5, E96, E4: Radnabel ATL
Jakobsgasse 19, 72070 Tübingen,
Germany. Tel/Fax +49 7071 238 96

RANS Recumbents
E4: Zero-G
4600 Hwy 183 Alternate, Hays, KS 67601,
USA Tel +1 913 625 6346 Fax +1 913 625
2795

Reflectalite
E4: Bicycle bulb service
24 Orchard Road, Brentford, Middlesex,
TW8 0QX, UK Tel +44 181 560 2432
Fax +44 181 847 2035

Ride-Rite Bicycles Inc.
E4: Advanta SR-1
6322 114th Avenue S.E., Bellevue,
Washington 98006, USA Tel +1 206 228
8006 Fax +1 206 271 4017 Email
Bob_Riley@msn.com
http://www.BikeRoute.com/RideRite.htm

Roberts Cycles
E93/4: Small-sized & custom frames
89 Gloucester Road, Croydon, Surrey, CR0
2DN, UK. Tel +44 181 684 3370 Fax +44
181 683 1105

S and S Machine
E4: Bicycle Torque Couplings
9334 Viking Place, Roseville, CA 95747,
USA. Tel +1 916 771 0235 Fax 0397 Email
steve@sandsmachine.com
http://www.sandsmachine.com

Santana Cycles Inc
E4: Santana Tandems
Box 206, La Verne, CA 91750, USA
Tel +1 909 596 7570 Fax +1 909 596 5853
Email santanainc@aol.com
http://www.santanainc.com

Schauff GmbH
E4: La Luna, Wall Street Duo
Postfach 1669, D-53406 Remagen/Rhein,
Germany Tel +49 2642 93640 Fax +49
2642 3358 Email schauff@aol.com

Schmidt Maschinenbau
E96: Schmidt's Original Nabendynamo
Aixer Strasse 44, 72072 Tubingen,
Germany. Tel +49 707 138870.
Fax +49 707 138876.
Email schmidt.maschinenbau@gmx.de

Schramm Spezial-Fahrräder
E96: Triset modular load-carrying trike
Richthofenstrasse 29, 31137 Hildesheim,
Germany. Tel +49 5121 76 0373 Fax +49
5121 760326

Schubert & Schefyk KG
E4: Guylaine WL
Magdeburger Str. 12, 64372 Ober-
Ramstadt, Germany. Tel +49 6154 52466
Fax +49 6154 52467

schulz + weber
E4: TransSport
Postfach 10 29 31, 66029 Saarbrücken,
Germany Tel +49 681 985 0902
Fax +49 681 985 0903
Email schulz_weber@t-online.de

**Showme Products Christian
Schumacher GmbH**
E4: Emotion Three
Bahnhofstr. 2, D-84088 Neufahrn i. NB,
Germany Tel +49 8773 7399 Fax +49 8773
91 02 81

SideKids
E4: SideKids
6717 Palatine N, Seattle 98103, USA Tel +1
206 784 1190 Fax +1 206 789 3202

**Sparta Rijwielen- en Motorenfabriek
B.V.**
E4: Silver Bullet
Postbus 5, 7300 AA Apeldoorn,
Netherlands Tel +31 55 355 0922 Fax +31
55 355 9244

St John Street Cycles
E96: D.O.G. full-size folding racer, Thorn
Kiddy Cranks for tandems, Thorn Discovery
expedition tandem
91/93 St John Street, Bridgwater,
Somerset, TA6 5HX, UK. Tel +44 1278
441502 Fax +44 1278 431107

Steco Metaalwaren-fabriek bv
E96: Attache-Mee pushchair carrier
Wolweg 34, NL-3776 LP, Stroe, Holland.
Tel +31 34 2441441 Fax +31 34 2441584

Swallow Tandems
E4: Swallow Tandems / Tandemania
The Old Bakery, LLanrhaeadr Ym
Mothnant, Oswestry, Shropshire SY10 OJP.
Tel +44 1691 780050
Fax +44 1691 780110
Email info@swallow-tandems.co.uk
http://www.chaucer.ac.uk/swallow/
sw1.htm

Tauber
E4: Bicone
Beatrixlaan 2, 1815 JN Alkmaar,
Netherlands Tel +31 7251 12495
Fax +31 7251 50246

The Cutting Crew Ingenieurbüro GmbH
E4: Trac-Pearls
Am Mühlberg 16, 61348 Bad Homburg
v.d. H. Tel +49 6172 928 681 or 2
Fax +49 6172 23 729

Thijs Industrial Designs
E93/4: Thys Funfiets
Koorkerkstraat 10, 4331 AW Middelburg,
Netherlands. Tel/Fax +31 118 634 166

Thorpe Consulting
E4: Mako
PO Box 250, Ruislip, Middlesex, HA4 8UU,
UK. Tel +44 0976 800 682 Tel +44 976 800
682 Email flashgd@msn.com

Timbuk2 Designs, Inc
E4: Timbuk2 bags
5327 Jacuzzi Street 3E-2, Richmond, CA
94804, USA Tel +1 510 526 0597 Fax+1
510 526 0599 Email
brennan@timbuk2.com
http://www.timbuk2.com

Tom Board
E4: Tom Board Frames
The Bicycle Workshop, 27 All Saints Road,
London W11 1HE, UK. Tel +44 171 229
4850 Fax +44 171 221 0411

Tubus Transport Systems
E93/4: tubular steel carrier racks
Overbergstrasse 22, D-48145 Münster,
Germany. Tel +49 251 131781 Fax +49 251
131783

URBICO B.V.
E4: UBiCS
PO Box 160, 6190 AD Beek (L), Netherlands
Fax +31 46 437 9342
Email urbico@ilimburg.nl

Valdenaire
E4: Traffic and Mercurius
BP 103-88204 Remiremont, Cedex,
France Tel +33 329 23 23 46
Fax +33 329 62 12 33

Vision Recumbents
E4: Vision R44/5
ATP Vision, 952 Republican St., Seattle, WA
98109, USA Tel +1 206 467 0231 Fax +1
206 467 0175 Email atpvision@aol.com

Vredestein Fietsbanden b.v.
E4: Monte Carlo tyres
Vredestein, Postbus 24, 7000 AA
Doetinchem, Holland Tel +31 314 370 555
Fax +31 314 370 500

Weldite Products Ltd
E4: Trailfix Tools
Harrier Road, Barton-upon-Humber, North
Lincs, DN18 5RP, UK. Tel +44 1652 660000
Fax +44 1652 660066

Worksong Cycles
E93/4: Worksong full-size portable
8 Dagmar Road, Wood Green, London, N22
4RT, UK. Tel +44 181 888 5650

Zzip Designs
E93/4, E94/5, E96, E4: Zzipper fairings
PO Box 14, Davenport, CA 95017, USA
Tel +1 408 425 8650 Fax +1 408 425 1167
Website http://www.diskspace.com/zzip/

*For information about ordering any
of the four previous Encycleopedias,
see pages 138/139.*

Across the world human power is a moving experience, with the energy of our bodies offering an eloquent and caring alternative to the sadness and sameness of inappropriate motorisation. Cyclists are everywhere. They may be on world tours, or riding to the next village to see relatives. They may be carrying a hundred watermelons through the streets of Bombay, or courier-riding in Manhattan, touring English country lanes or powering over the French Alps in a peloton. And the bike is a great leveller – whether on a full-suspension titanium recumbent tandem or a Hero roadster with a design little changed since the 1880s, whether you're a director of a multinational company, a top professional mountain bike rider, or a window-cleaner, it's still just you and your bike out there, doing your own thing beneath the vast and vacant skies.

In *Encycleopedia* (and in our *Bike Culture Quarterly*) we try to bring the worldwide community of cyclists together. In the following section eight readers from five continents report on the various cycling scenes in their home countries.

Why do the British never explore Britain?

LYNNE CURRY from Bristol is mystified.

The British passion for leaving the country at every opportunity is so baffling. We prefer to shoot off to France, and are currently engaged in a love affair with Italy. When I look back on our last long trip, though, I think fondly of Stewartby (Bedfordshire, England). It would be exaggeration to say it appeared like an oasis as it hove into view without announcement. It was less exotic than fascinating, a model village built by the local brickmaker for his workers, named after him (which used to be done with little vanity), with its own public clock tower and meeting hall, and houses arranged around neat lawned greens. Daventry is another warm memory. Daventry has no glamorous image, but is an underrated typical small English market town, with friendly people and a choice of two pavement cafes.

Out there in England – in the undiscussed and (one might think) unremarkable hinterland of the notable tourist honeypots is a strange, mesmerising and foreign land which has its own existence away from tourism. Ninety-nine per cent of the British have never indulged themselves in an exploration of their own country at a human pace and may never know its unspoiled, untouristy, unselfconscious pleasures.

This is no reason for visitors from elsewhere to make the same mistake. So don't go to Oxford and Cambridge, which are full of foreigners. Go to Oxshott and Carstairs, or Ossington and Carlisle. There are one or two key things a visiting cyclist should know about the British and our relationship with bicycles. The first, undeniable truth is that most still regard the bike as poor men's transport. We have memories of factories turning out, flooding the streets of industrial towns with manual labourers pedalling home for their tea. So we look down on people on bikes, believing them to be too poor, or too mad, to do the trip in a car. However, if ever you are in trouble on your bike – if you fall off, or it goes wrong – the British will rush out to help you, pluck you off the ground if necessary. If you run out of water and ask someone in their garden to fill your water bottle, they will scuttle into their kitchen in delight, flattered to be asked. If you cannot find anywhere to camp, go into a village pub. Within an hour someone will have offered you their back garden, or the pub garden, or the community centre garden. And breakfast the next morning. There are great reserves of warmth in the British, a hidden stock of hospitality waiting to be tapped.

Above: Britain has miles of quiet county roads linking delightful villages.

Right: Cyclists in Oxford.

But along with this buried generosity comes an odd gullibility. We British do not merely watch car advertising; we apparently believe it. Our bodies may sit for four hours in a hot metal box on the M5 motorway, but our soul is on that empty mountain road in the Scottish Highlands, cornering at silly speeds. So road manners are pretty bad, and getting worse. Motorists will pass you too fast and too close, so the best solution is to seek out the smaller roads – 'B-roads', or unclassified roads. An Ordnance Survey map (1:50,000) is vital for every area you intend to explore.

The British climate is mixed – bring waterproofs in all seasons – and so is the terrain. There are Scottish hills, long and rhythmic, and Welsh hills, short and vicious. Devon and Cornwall have golden beaches and romantic, rocky coves. Wales has blue hills and mists, white beaches and crags. The sights will take your breath away but so, unfortunately, will the climbs. Inland, cycling the Cotswolds, the Mendips or the Pennines can be hard, if rewarding, work. There

are really no parts of Britain that could not be recommended to a cyclist, provided you have a good map to keep off the most congested roads. Even the cities: London on a bike is wonderful, especially on a bank holiday, when the locals aren't at work. Use a good London cycling map and the growing cycle path network.

Birmingham, an old and modern working city, is a horror in a car and a pleasure on a bike. Wherever you are, within a few miles, the terrain and the character of the landscape will change dramatically: from the tall gates of the landed gentry on their estates, to pit villages, with their terrace houses and back yards. We are supposed to be a congested country, but a cyclist will find plenty of great empty spaces. If you can

come to Britain only once, come in June, and go to Scotland – anywhere in Scotland, really. Edinburgh is wonderful, but so is Glasgow (both have their own maps specifically for cyclists). The sights will burn your eyes; the people are great; the seafood is marvellous; the gorse smells like heaven.

Don't camp – camping is the same everywhere – but stay in bed and breakfast accommodation, which (especially inland) is usually in people's homes. It is good value, and such a privilege. The Americans charge a fortune for this, but it's regarded here as a cheap option. I don't know why, as it's much more interesting than anonymous hotels. The exception is at Cape Wrath, in the far north west. Stay at the Cape Wrath Hotel, a large

fishing lodge with white cotton sheets and large white baths. Here you can watch the locals in the bar, some dressed maybe in kilted finery, alongside a party of rich louts from the commercial sector of London, who will have driven there in a selection of embarrassing cars. Here you can see the British class system in all its horror. But why not save up and stay a while? Arrive in May and leave in late September, before it gets too cold. Pedal slowly, and breathe in the scent of the hedgerows and the flowers, the docks and the works. Ask for favours, ask for help, ask for advice, ask for the local speciality. Have no fear of the natives except behind the wheel. Put your trust in Ordnance Survey and discover the many countries in this small island.

Contacts
Cyclists' Touring Club: Cotterell House, 69 Meadrow, Godalming, Surrey, GU7 3HS. Tel +44 1483 417217 email cycling@ctc.org.net, website
British Tourist Authority (representing English, Scottish, Welsh tourist boards): Thames Tower, Black's Road, W6 9EL Tel +44 181 846 9000, website http://www.visitbritain.com (they also have offices in 43 countries)
Sustrans (co-ordinating and building a long-distance National Cycle Network, made up of a combination of traffic-free tracks and quiet roads): 35 King Street, Bristol, BS1 4DZ. Tel 0117 929 0888, website http://www.sustrans.org.uk
The Bycycle Club (run by the publishers of *Encyclepeodia*) is principally for UK members, and does not offer touring information. Tel +44 1904 654654

The land of the free

Bicycle activist CHARLES KOMANOFF focuses on how the role of the bicycle is being defended and celebrated in the land of the free.

U S bicycle activists are looking for new forms of expression. Traditional cycling advocacy is scoring victories, but they're piecemeal – a bike lane here, some new racks there. Solid wins, but not the sea-change cyclists want: their city or region transformed into a truly bike-friendly area.

In-your-face activism is still around: New York cyclists are painting life-size police-chalk outlines of pedestrians and cyclists 'killed by automobile', with name and crash date emblazoned underneath. The riders, hauling their stencils and spray-paint on a kiddy trailer, have made over a hundred of these 'street memorials', to widespread approval. The group are also adding police fatal accident reports to a database, chronicling the thousand victims of cars in pro-car Mayor Giuliani's first four-year term of office.

Elsewhere, bike activism seems to have retreated from the streets. Critical Mass rides have fizzled out in the face of motorist violence, bashings in the media, police clampdowns... and too few riders. Access – to elected officials, agency staff, funders – is now the order of the day. In cities like New York, Philadelphia, Chicago, Seattle and Portland (Oregon), professionally staffed advocacy groups are defending previous cycling gains and forcing incremental progress.

But the beacon of full-on campaigning is San Francisco. SF has the country's outstanding grassroots cycle advocates, the San Francisco Bicycle Coalition (SFBC), and the one ongoing mass ride, the original Critical Mass – still going strong after 70-odd monthly rides, with participation in the thousands. Together, the Coalition and the Mass are the utopian cyclist's dream, offering both the opportunity to agitate for better cycling and the rush of euphoria from riding on streets liberated from cars.

Critical Mass stands on its own, a self-perpetuating 'organized coincidence', and SFBC are free to defend it as the alter-image of the daily 'Car Mass' that ordinarily goes unremarked – while focusing on their own campaigns. SFBC membership has grown ten-fold in just five years, to 2000, and volunteers with staying power lead campaigns for transit access, car-free parks, driver accountability, and humanised streets.

This summer, however, the city administration junked a major bike project which it had been planning with the SFBC – an on-street lane network painstakingly mapped from dozens of de facto routes carved out by cyclists over the years. The surprise rejection has inflamed the cycling community and ignited a new season of intense activism.

One response comes in the form of Bike Summer '99: a two-week San Francisco cycle-fest to finally create a cycle-friendly American city. In this vision cycle activists, environmentalists, sustainability enthusiasts and other planetary citizens converge on San Francisco next August and fill the city with cycling energy. Activities will include daily 'Reclaim the Streets' events, nightly mass rides, 'car lifts' to clear bike lanes, bike rack raisings, petition-gathering, teach-ins, manifestos, film screenings, street theatre, art exhibits, bike safety and skills training, cultural history bike tours and family rides – and more.

Staging Bike Summer will take immense effort, and the SFBC will be in constant overdrive. But the place and the moment seem right. If not San Francisco, where? If not now, when? To make the velorution, we must live the velorution. To live the velorution, we must make the velorution!

STEPHEN McKAY

In Zürich, the 'Züri rollt'
project provides free
loan-bikes for tourists and
locals alike.

**MIRIAM STEINMANN tells us how
Switzerland is just a little bit different.**

A little bit different

We Swiss are a curious mixture of the old and the new; a nation of mountain peasants who have seen Switzerland's standard of living go through the roof in the last couple of generations. Cycling is important here. You might see men cycling along with machine guns across their backs, off to their quarterly target practice. Pretty much all of the men here aged between eighteen and forty-five have to join the army, and keep a gun and ammunition at home in case someone invades. Or you might pass a group of ladies heading off to the opera, dressed up to the nines, astride bikes that range from disintegrating roadsters to space-age (but spotless) mountain bikes.

Switzerland is a great country for cycle-tourists. You usually know where you are with the weather, and we've managed to resist the temptations of mindless industrialisation. We've got mountains, if you like mountains. And if you want flat bits, we do that too. People often assume that it's Alps, Alps, Alps here, but the terrain really is very varied. The high mountains are to be found in the south and east, in Wallis, Tessin and the Graubünden. To the west lies the Jura region, where you will find hills, mountains and plateaux. The central 'Mittelland' features fairly spiky hills, too, but the land levels out as you move north towards Lake Constance. So there's something for everyone in Switzerland. Plenty of white-knuckle off-road routes, as well as many kilometres of quiet roads that lead you gently down through quiet and peaceful valleys. There's even one route in Ticino where you can get off the train at Faido, and then ride the 30 kilometres down to Biasca without ever touching the pedals. And

with Switzerland, you get four cultures in one: the German-, French-, Italian- and Romantsch-speaking areas are all culturally quite distinct. Add to that the fact that the Swiss 'nation' is nothing more than a confederation of 23 highly independent Cantons, and you start to get the picture.

Culturally, too, we're pretty well set up for cyclists. Despite the high level of car ownership here, and the excellent public transport, cycling is widely respected, both for leisure and for practical purposes. Every year, schoolchildren go on an annual *Schulreise* ('school trip'), and this frequently takes the form of a cycle tour. So in the summer months you will often see long lines of children cycling along, accompanied by a couple of pedal-powered teachers. And while there is something of a car cult here, with a particular focus on US gas-guzzlers, cycling isn't looked down on in quite the same way as in English-speaking countries. Thus it's not uncommon to find that even higher class hotels have bike sheds around the back. And there are all sorts of cyclist-specific services, ranging from supervised parking to bike washing facilities. Our railway service (the SBB) runs special cycle holidays, and also a network of bike hire-points. You can even do a one-way hire, for an extra fee. And in Zürich we have the 'Züri rollt' project, where you can borrow a 21-speed town bike for the day, free of charge.

Like many things in this country, cycling is quite closely regulated. For example, all bikes are supposed to carry a registration sticker, which costs sfr4.00 a year, from any post office or supermarket. This simply provides third party insurance. And if someone is convicted of riding dangerously, s/he can actually be

banned from cycling for a month or two. But don't be put off: in many ways we're surprisingly easy-going: and the upside of all this regulation is that cycling is seen, more or less, as part of the transport mainstream. Every spring and autumn, local community centres set up drop-in bike workshops, with tools and assistance laid on. Helmets are not mandatory, and cycle paths are completely optional. Taking bikes on trains is seen as fairly normal, albeit with a few restrictions. You can also usually put your bike on trams and boats, and sometimes buses too, for a fee. But don't be fooled by our low overall crime rate (money laundering aside): bike theft is as common here as anywhere else, at least in the cities. Drivers are pretty civilised in the German- and French-speaking areas, but in the Italian-speaking part they're, erm, rather Italian.

A new national network of cycling routes called *Veloland Schweiz* has just been opened up, sponsored by the national railway, the tourism bureau, and several transport agencies. This network comprises nine long-distance routes, covers most of the country and offers different cycling conditions for different abilities. In conjunction with using the routes network, cycle tourists can book themselves and their bikes into designated hotels and guest-houses along the way. The routes are well signposted, and there is a host of back-up literature. In addition, any bookshop will stock guides to routes of extraordinary variety taking you all over Switzerland, the tree-house of Europe.

The Swiss Tourist Office is at Tödistr. 7, Postfach, CH-8027 Zürich, Tel +41 1 288 1111, postoffice@switzerlandtourism.ch

A Powerhouse for new ideas

STEPHEN McKAY

SILKE FELDHUSEN, from Braunschweig, introduces us to the German scene.

Germany: the home of BMW, Mercedes Benz, Volkswagen, and motorways with no speed limit. But it's also a great place to ride a bike. It's a beautiful country, and cycling is taken very seriously here, both as a leisure pursuit and as practical transport. However, there is a downside to this… if there is a bike-path running alongside a road, you *must* use it. No matter if it means dodging pedestrians, dogs and three-year-olds on their first trike. And although you technically have right of way at side roads, you always have to assume you don't. It's deemed to be more efficient for cyclists to be removed from cars wherever possible. This makes cycling less attractive for everyone except beginners, and segregation means that drivers and cyclists forget how to deal with each other safely.
A more helpful phenomenon is the practice of opening up one-way streets as contraflows for cyclists. These roads are marked 'Radfahrer frei' ('except cyclists').

Cycle tourism is booming. More and more families are choosing cycling holidays, and scenic cycle routes are being signposted every where. As local communities discover that cyclists make good customers, hotels and B&Bs are springing up along the main cycling routes. The youth hostel network is also very good – it is possible to cycle across the whole country, hopping from one hostel to the next. I've never had any problems getting a bed, as a single traveller. 'Wild' camping in the countryside is illegal, though I've always got away with it. You can also sometimes pitch your tent on youth hostel grounds.

Bikes can be taken on almost any train, except on the ICE (Inter City Express). Book well in advance, especially during the summer, as the number of bikes on each train is sometimes limited to eight. Look out for a small bicycle symbol on timetables.

You'll find a bike shop in every small town. In certain cities, such as Braunschweig and Berlin, there are public workshops; wonderful places where you can fix your bike yourself or with help from volunteers.

Too much of a good thing?

The pro-segregation transport policy in Germany has led to an increase in conflict on shared-use paths. Although it is not yet a major problem, growing numbers of in-line skaters, cyclists and pedestrians and even horse-riders are all fighting over limited amounts of space. The resulting accidents and punch-ups are starting to attract interest in the mainstream press. One paper reported recently that at one kindergarten in Wäschenbeurener, leaders are having to take special safety measures when they take groups on the shared-use path that runs past their premises: an adult walks at the front and back of the line of children, each carrying a red warning flag. Local residents are also copying tactics used when a fast road takes motor-traffic through residential areas: making wooden 'dummy children', designed to look as if they're about to run out in front of speeding cyclists.

Fortunately, and partly as a result of campaigning action by the national German cycle club (the ADFC), there has recently been a change in traffic legislation. All cycle paths must now meet certain specific standards, including minimum width, surface quality and safety aspects. Cycle paths which do not meet these standards should in theory be declassified, and their blue signs removed – leaving cyclists free to ignore them and use the road. Unfortunately, many local authorities are ignoring this change in the law. On cycle paths which run alongside main roads, bikes are supposed to have right of way over cars turning into or out of side roads, but no sensible cyclist relies on drivers to remember this.

All in all, the German experience shows how the apartheid approach to road planning – which has its adherents across the world – avoids the root of the problem: the basic culture on our roads. Only when the streets are filled with bikes, and motorists ride regularly themselves, will they be truly safe for people to use

Stephen McKay

ERNST PLATZ

Versuchung.

Radfahrer-Postkarten
Verlag v. M.Seeger Stuttgart.

You'll find a bike shop in every small town. In certain cities, such as Braunschweig and Berlin, there are public workshops; wonderful places where you can fix your bike yourself or with help from volunteers.

Above: A cycling postcard by the German artist Ernst Platz, 1897.

The cycle routes set out for tourists are magnificent. They usually follow river valleys, offering few serious challenges for the less athletic cyclist. The tour along the Weser river, for example, runs from the North Sea to Hannoversch Münden: a total of 450 km. You can stop there, or continue along either the Werra or Fulda rivers, which join here to become the Weser. Another popular river route follows the Danube. The German part runs from Donaueschingen to Passau; my favourite area is in the Swabian Alb, at the beginning of the tour. From Passau you can ride on to Vienna (the most popular section), Budapest or even as far as the Black Sea.

The tour along the Altmühl Valley from Beilngries to Kelheim is also very special. The Altmühl is a small river winding through beautiful landscape, old towns and villages before joining the Danube. If you enjoy hills and mountains, try the Taunus, the Rhön, the Harz mountains, the Erzgebirge, and – of course – the Alps. I'd also recommend the Rhine, Neckar, and Mosel rivers, the Baltic and North Sea coasts, the lakes of Mecklenburg, Rügen Island, Holsteinische Schweiz and the Lüneberg Heath.

The Germans themselves vary as much as the regions. The same goes for the local languages, which range from the Frisian 'Platt' of the North Sea shore to the rugged dialect of deepest Bavaria. But of course, everyone understands High German, and most people know at least some English. Culturally, too, Germany is a varied land. Until the last century, 'Germany' was no more than a very loose grouping of relatively independent bishoprics, principalities and kingdoms. This has led to the development of all sorts of cultural peculiarities around the region. Get on your bike and see for yourself.

Pedal East

Japan is known abroad more for its car industry than for its cycling. But, as MASAYA KOMAI reports, there's plenty of interesting pedal-power going on.

Japan is very much a cycling country, but not like any other. Cycling here is all about getting to the shops or the railway station, often on a folder or electric bike, and long distance touring is regarded as rather weird. The Japanese may be amazed when they encounter cycle-tourists, but can be very supportive: people in rural areas will sometimes help you out with gifts of food. Although we do have a few nutters, car drivers are generally pretty considerate, even on narrow roads. The general crime rate is also low, so – relatively speaking – Japan may be one of the safest countries for cycling.

Japanese roads are narrow, and very crowded in the cities. The rules for cyclists are pretty vague: you can choose whether to ride on the pavement or the road. The latter is generally better. Roads can be particularly steep near the ocean coasts, so a map with topographic information is a must. But watch out if you're thinking of hiring a bike: most machines available are absolute junk. You will often see abandoned bikes lying in the streets: bike shops frequently refuse to service bikes that they didn't originally sell, and the humidity here takes its toll on componentry. Perhaps this is why Japanese manufacturers often experiment with shaft-drive machines, with their much-reduced maintenance requirements. But you won't see tandems: you can ride them in two, enlightened districts but otherwise they are banned in Japan.

Look out for roads where cycling is prohibited, especially fly-overs. Also, be aware that in cities cyclists are not allowed to turn right at large intersections. You must perform a 'two step turn', which means that you pull over on the left, cross the road, wait until the traffic light changes and then cross the road again. You then set off again, on the new road. This sounds rather convoluted, and it is, but bear in mind that the medical system in Japan is not as comprehensive as in some other countries. The ambulance service is run by the fire department, and its crews receive less training than is common elsewhere. Finding a hospital for emergency admissions outside of office hours can sometimes be complicated, especially out in the suburbs.

Taking bikes on public transport is easy, as long as you do it the Japanese way. This entails buying or making a 'Rinko' bag, which takes a standard bike with its wheels removed from the frame. You can take your Rinko on most buses and trains, with the exception of some long distance bus routes. Japanese Railways charges 270 yen per trip, and you may have to pay a small fee on local bus services. On ferries, you have a choice of paying a baggage fee for your bike in a Rinko, or a (higher) cycle fee for taking your bike on whole. All domestic airlines take Rinkos free as long as you don't exceed your overall weight allowance.

Where to ride? One of my favourite rides is to Kawayu Onsen, a hot springs area accessed via a superb cycle route. There's nothing like leaping into a hot spring with a can of beer after a bike ride. The route runs through Wakayama region: you can get there from Kansai International Airport in Osaka by taking a train via Hineno and Wakayama city to Kiitanabe. Jump off here and assemble your bike. Take National Route 42, heading South, and as you crest Kobiro peak you'll see Kawayu Onsen laid out before you. ('Kawa' means river in Japanese and 'yu' means hot water.) The springs are next to a river, near Kajika-so Youth Hostel (tel 0735-42-0518), and you can use them 24 hours a day. Swimsuits optional.

There are also other springs nearby, including Yunomine Onsen and Watarase Onsen, and an interesting Shinto shrine called Kumano-hongu-taisha. After enjoying all this, you could take the Route 168, which runs along the beautiful Kumano river down to Shingu station. (Further information from the Hongu Tourist Association. Tel 0735-42-0735.)

I also recommend riding through the Shimanto river valley, where it runs through green forests at Shikoku, and the old fishing village on Sado Island is worth a visit.

There are many cycling events held across Japan, including the annual Tour de Kumano in November, which takes place near Kawano-yu. Further information on this and other events can be obtained from the Japanese Cycling Association. Another, rather unique, cycling phenomena is our world-famous Keirin track racing. This is perhaps more like greyhound racing than any type of cycle-sport you may be familiar with. Based around gambling (a very popular pursuit here), Keirin racing involves nine riders blasting out of their numbered stalls: about 90 metres in front a 'human hare' is there for the catching. The idea is to tuck in behind him (he gets a bike, too!), and stay there for the first three laps or so. He cranks up the pace, and just before the final lap, he peels off. At this point all hell breaks loose. The riders vie, or even wrestle, for a good position as they enter the final sprint.

And if your feel like something a little more relaxed, you could do worse than spend a few hours at The Bicycle Culture Centre in Tokyo. Here you'll find an intriguing collection of antique bikes, bicycle art and associated bits and pieces.

OUR GEOGRAPHY AND CLIMATE

Japan is made up of four major islands (Honshu, Shikoku, Kyushu and Hokkaido) and more than 4,000 smaller ones. They form a crescent 3,000 km (1,860 miles) from North to South. Nearly 70% of Japan's land area is mountainous and 66% of the country is covered with forest. All areas except Hokkaido have a hot and very humid rainy season which lasts from early June to mid-July, and the southwestern part of Japan is often hit by typhoons between August and October. Hokkaido is covered with snow for half the year: the best time for cycling there is from June through to September. In Summer, the humidity is high, with the temperature on the more Southern-lying islands often above 35˚C. So the best season for cycling in the rest of Japan might be Spring and Autumn, though this does mean a harsh temperature difference between day and night.

Left: Unicycling is part of the school curriculum.

Below: An image from the Bicycle Culture Centre.

ACCOMMODATION

In Japan we have Cycling Terminal Facilities – 57 of them across the country. They provide, amongst other things, accommodation, and hire bikes. They are run by local councils, and cost 5000 yen per night, including breakfast and dinner. Reservations are required, and bike hire costs 200-500 yen per four hours. For further information, again contact the Japan Cycling Association. Business Hotels in the suburbs charge about 6000 yen per night. Youth Hostels are 3000-5000 yen, depending on the location.

If you prefer to camp, you'll find campsites marked on maps, but youth hostels are popular with Japanese cyclists. They're also great places to meet other cyclists, exchange information, and make new friends. It's best to join your local youth hostel association before you go away. Membership is valid for any Japanese youth hostel, and gets you a discount. But watch out: some parts of Japan don't have any hostels. But perhaps the best option are *minshuku*: family-run guest houses, with prices from 5000 yen a night. Here you'll get full-board, and a friendly, informal atmosphere.

The best general-purpose map for cyclists is probably 'Road Atlas Japan', a 1:250,000 topographic road map published by Shobunsha (tel 03-3262-2141), ISBN 4-398-20101-7. There's also an excellent English-language guide book, *Cycling in Japan*, edited by Bryan Harrell and published by Hilary Sagar, ISBN 4-7700-1742-1.

Since Japan is mountainous, there are quite a few tunnels. So, you'll need lights and reflective gear. But don't expect to pick up cheap Japanese bike components: prices here are high, and that includes bike-bits. Helmets are not compulsory in Japan, but I'd recommend one – along with good rain gear. And don't forget: we ride on the left here!

Contacts:
Tokyo Tourist Information Centre: +81 3 3502-1461 (toll-free in Japan 0120 2228000)
Kyoto Tourist Information Centre: +81 75 371-5649 (toll-free in Japan 0120 444800)
West Japan Railway Company: http://www.westjr.co.jp/kou/english/index_e.html
Japan Cycling Association: jca@ma4.justnet.ne.jp
The Bicycle Culture Centre: c/o The Bicycling Association of Japan, Jitenshakaiken No. 3 Building, 1-9-3 Akasaka Minato-ku, Tokyo 107, Japan, Fax +81 3 3586 1194 +81 3 3586 1194, email

One minute CARLOS CORDERO was writing up his PhD thesis in law, the next he was a full-time cycle-activist. What happened?

Orders from Above

'd just popped in to the local telephone company, to pay my bill. I'd always been in the habit of bringing my bike in with me, to stop it getting stolen. But this time the porter blocked my way. I explained that I couldn't park it outside as there were no racks and I was concerned for the security of my machine. "I'm sorry, young man," he replied, "these orders are from above".

I managed to find a secure parking place, some half a kilometre away, but as I was walking back I decided to abandon my thesis and start to concentrate on the rights of cyclists in Peru. At that time the World Bank had just launched a plan to build a brand new network of cycleways in the northern part of the capital; I worked on this project for three years, before going on to launch Ciclored, which campaigns on cycling and general transport issues here in Peru.

So, that's my story. But what does my country have to offer visiting cyclists? Well, it depends a lot on where you go. Some of the cities on the Pacific coast can be pretty grim; Lima seems to be copying Los Angeles in the way it's developing. But if you are in the capital there is a nice ride along the seafront in the Miraflores and Chorillos districts. And on Sundays, the Avenida Arequipa is closed to motor traffic. This takes you for five kilometres through the historic city centre to the sea, and if you're lucky you'll encounter

a few 'cultural spectacles' on the way. Speaking of which, we've got plans for an annual bicycle fiesta there, with displays, dances and games for adults and children alike. We are very aware that the bicycle is more than a means of transport: it also gives a 'new' way of relating to our neighbours, on the streets and squares. To the south of Lima lies the Reserva Natural de Paracas, which is absolutely ideal for cycling. A mixture of desert and ocean, all on-road, and with masses of birds of prey and old sea-dogs for company.

Last year a group of us went up to Huarez, seeking out cycle-touring routes for a sustainable tourism project. A great place to visit, it's five hours bus ride from Lima, heading northwest, and is 2600 metres above sea level. The best time to go is between May and October – the rest of the year is rain, rain, rain. If you do make it to Huarez, I recommend that you hire a local cycle guide for a day and take the opportunity to explore the area where the two Andean mountain ranges meet. It's one of the most amazing spectacles I've ever seen.

Ciclored is currently researching in Puno, which is right on the Bolivian border, by Lake Titicaca, the highest navigable lake in the world. Only thirty kilometres down the road is Juliaca, a trading town with streets so full of bikes and trikes that it could be compared with Holland. On the route between Titiaca

and Juliaca lie the ruins of Sillustrani; this is also a good camping spot, next to a beautifully peaceful lake.

In Cusco you will find Machu Pichu, the lost city of the Incas and absolutely unmissable. If you like adventure on a bike, there's a great trip that runs from the Inca capital deep into the forest, before reaching the Manu National Park. The route involves bus and boat rides, stretches where you have to get off and push your bike, and of course, plenty of arduous cycling. It's not easy, but it's something you'll never forget.

It's possible to hire mountain bikes, but if you're planning to spend more than a week in any one place, I recommend you try to bring your own. Hiring gets very expensive, and it's only possible in certain areas. If you go in a group, or fancy joining up with one, a guide is well worth having. You'll normally get information about hiring guides from tourist agencies and hotels.

Peru is a welcoming and hospitable country. If you feel like visiting, drop me a line and I'll try to help.

CICLORED: San Juan 242, Lima 33, Peru.
Tel: +51 1 2717024, fax: +51 1 4472675
email: ccordero@amauta.rcp.net.pe

Come rain or shine

There are around 3.2 million bikes in Norway, which is about twice the number of cars in the country. And a third of the bikes you'll see on our roads are manufactured in Norway. However, it's the same old story when it comes to road planning: cycling still comes second to driving for the 'powers that be'. Nevertheless, the country as a whole is pretty switched on to pedal power. 57% of all Norwegians use their bikes at least once a week during the six summer months; that's a 40% rise in six years.

What do we use our bikes for? Well, mainly to get to work and for recreational trips; rather less for shopping. Many Norwegians – especially families – take their bikes on holiday to Denmark, France and the UK. And some of us also ride during the winter, despite the drifting snow and sheet ice. Spiked tyres are becoming very popular amongst winter riders.

Cyclists tend to stay on-road, but the state of some of our roads actually requires off-road bikes. One of the most popular trips is along the old construction road that runs beside the Oslo-Bergen railway line, where it crosses the Hardangervidda. This is one of Europe's largest mountain plains, and offers a rich variety of flora and fauna during its short snow-free season (July-September). There are plenty of cyclists about, but no cars (you'd need a Land Rover).

There are many other possibilities for cycling in the mountains. You will find signposted routes between Røros and Lillehammer, and you can buy special maps from Troll Cycling. Another favourite of mine is the Lofoton Islands, which is right up in the north of the country. There's a stunning route on Lofoton that sandwiches you between sheer cliffs and the Arctic sea. Another region to consider is along the southern coast; you can enjoy a nice ride along minor roads between Oslo and Kristiansand. There are other signposted routes, too, and you can get free information on them from the organisation 'Cycle Tourism in Norway'. There is also a book in English by Chris Heymans (published by Syklistenes Landsforening) which describes the area around Stavanger. Off-road cycling is prohibited in some areas, but generally it's okay. As a local, I recommend the roads and tracks. They're usually wild enough. You should also consider bringing your hiking boots...

There's usually plenty of sun, but we do sometimes have lengthy spells of rain. This is especially the case in the mountains and in the western and northern parts of Norway, where there can also be a fair bit of wind. However, these are also the areas with the most fantastic scenery. Don't be afraid of Norwegian weather, the climate is good for cycling. Just remember your waterproofs.

Transport planning in Norway has tended to separate us from drivers, and put us in with the pedestrians. This has, of course, been a disaster, with conflict on shared-use paths and cyclists having to give way to motorists at every junction. There is no obligation to use the cycle paths (except on certain expressways). Syklistenes Landsforening has been

It is often said that Norwegians are born with skis on their feet. But perhaps it would be more accurate to say that they are born attached to pedals: three quarters of them own bicycles. TROND BERGET, Secretary General of Syklistenes Landsforening (the Norwegian Cyclists' Association), reports.

campaigning for years against the policy of 'getting cyclists out of the way of motorists', and changes are gradually being made.

Crossing fjords is an increasing problem for cyclists. Our coastline used to be punctuated with hundreds of ferry crossings, but sadly these are dying out as more and more tunnels are built for motorists' convenience. Cycling is banned in these tunnels, but you can usually take a bike through on a bus. The Norwegian Public Roads Administration will send you a free tunnel guide for cyclists on request.

You can also take your bike on local trains outside the rush hour, for 40 Kroner. On medium- and long-distance trains you pay 80 kroner and you must send your bike 24 hours in advance (on the Oslo-Bergen train you need to give 48 hours notice).

There are some excellent books on cycling in Norway, but all are in Norwegian apart from Chris Heymans'. The Norwegian Public Roads Administration publishes a free cycle touring map containing descriptions and route guides for twelve different tours. I personally recommend our 1:250000 road maps. 21 sheets cover the whole country, each costing 50 Kroner plus postage. Larger scale city maps are also available. Oslo in particular is not very easy to

cycle in or out of: the routes are poorly signposted, with several stretches of roads that with heavy car traffic and no alternatives for cyclists. Having a good map helps a lot, and I recommend the one that Cappelen publish, covering the Oslo Fjord area at a scale of 1:150000. They also produce a map of Oslo city showing all cycling facilities. Most Norwegian cycle maps can be ordered from Syklistenes Landsforening.

Norway offers real challenges and breathtaking beauty. It's a land everyone should cycle in at some time in their lives.

Syklistenes Landsforening (Norwegian Cyclists' Association), P.O. Box 8883 Youngstorget, N-0028 Oslo, Norway. Tel +47 22 47 30 30
Norwegian Public Roads Administration, P.O. Box 8142 Dep., N-0033 Oslo, Norway. Tel +47 22 07 35 00
Troll Cycling, P.O. Box 373, N-2601 Lillehammer, Norway. Tel +47 61 28 99 70
Cycle Tourism in Norway, P.O. Box 448 Sentrum, N-0104 Oslo, Norway. Tel +47 22 00 25 00

The future is bright

Natural wonders and wilderness are on offer to cycle tourists visiting Australia, but Australian cyclists themselves are beset by right wing reactionism and a deadening car culture. NEIL IRVINE, former editor of *Australian Cyclist*, describes the state of cycling in his native country.

Above: Cycling in the Blue Mountains, New South Wales.

Below: An Australian Bush cyclist from the 1890s.

Australia, the wide brown land, is home to Pauline 'Rights for Whites' Hanson and compulsory bicycle helmets. It's also home to Tour de France stars Stuart O'Grady and Neil Stephens, and to two-time Race Across America winner Gerry Tatrai. Household names, but nevertheless cycling is still very low in the public consciousness.

Fortunately, the outlook for cycling is not totally bleak. Each Australian State has an active group of cyclists campaigning for better facilities, with some success. For instance, in my home state of New South Wales, the government is engaged in a study to produce a metropolitan cycle network for Sydney. Western Australia, which hosted the 1996 VeloCity conference at Fremantle, is building veloways alongside the Perth rail network. South Australia is blessed with a keen cyclist as Transport Minister, and Victoria is building a Principal Bicycle Network in and around Melbourne. Most local government areas have a bicycle plan, often in its second or third revision. A few have even been implemented. Critical Mass also keeps cycling in politicians' thoughts with regular themed rides in most major cities. Urban cyclists can often take their bikes on public transport – trains and, in Sydney at least, harbour ferries – for no charge, off-peak. Studies have been done in parts of the country of fitting bike racks to city buses. For cross-country travel, touring coaches carry bicycles in their luggage bays for a fee, while long distance trains accept boxed bicycles. Domestic airlines will also fly your bike, usually for a fee.

Where is best to cycle in Oz? If you're looking for tranquillity away from traffic, there are many options. Islands have great potential as cycling getaways and Australia is blessed with many of them. Our island state,

Tasmania, is a very popular summer cycle-touring destination. It has its own island escapes, including Maria Island off the east coast and Bruny Island, south of Hobart. Both come highly recommended as mountain bike touring venues. The Larger Kangaroo Island, part of South Australia, is great for adventurous cycle explorers. Rottnest Island, off Fremantle, Western Australia, is accessible by fast ferry and has a near car-free network of sealed roads perfectly suited to the basic bikes which visitors hire in droves. Lord Howe Island, a 90-minute flight into the Pacific from Sydney, features a 25 km/h speed limit, a maximum 400 tourists at any one time (plus 300 locals), and hire-bicycles as the favoured mode of tourist transport. (The locals, like typical Australians, all drive everywhere on the island's abbreviated road system. That's so you know they are locals). But you don't visit Lord Howe Island just to cycle. The walking in this World Heritage listed paradise is also a major attraction.

If you stay on the mainland, recognised cycle touring areas include the New South Wales Southern Highlands and Snowy Mountains, New England (northern NSW), the Gold Coast hinterland (south-east Queensland), Cairns and the Atherton Tableland (north Queensland), Victoria's Alps and Great Ocean Road, and the south-west of Western Australia. There is a book (available from Bicycle New South Wales) describing a cycle touring route between Sydney and Brisbane. All these areas are suitable for road bikes. Determined MTB tourers will enjoy South Australia's Flinders Ranges, Victoria's Grampians, WA's northern Kimberley region, NSW's Kosciusko National Park and the forests of that state's south coast. Ultimate challenges abound: there are the trans-Australia routes from Perth to Sydney via the Nullarbor Plain; Adelaide to Darwin via

Useful contacts:
Bicycle New South Wales, Level 2, 209 Castlereagh St Sydney (GPO Box 272, Sydney NSW 2001). Tel +61 2 9283 5200 Fax +61 2 9283 5246, email bikensw@ozemail.com.au – books, touring guides and advice
Australian Cyclist magazine: PO Box 344, Berry NSW 2535. Tel/Fax +61 2 4464 3255, email suewebber@shoal.net.au
Bicycle Federation of Australia.
Website: www.bfa.asn.au – details of cycle campaigning groups in each state.

Alice Springs (all sealed roads) or the rugged MTB trip along the Great Dividing Range from Wilson's Promontory, Victoria, (which is the southernmost mainland point) to Cape York, Queensland (the northernmost).

When do you want to go? Bearing in mind that Australia stretches from about latitude 10 degrees south to over 43 degrees south, there is a huge climatic variation. The tropical north is best avoided during 'The Wet', roughly spring and summer, while the south gets bitterly cold in winter. In between there is virtually always somewhere you could be cycling right now. But remember, June is midwinter here.

Major participatory cycling events generally take place in spring or summer. Bicycle NSW and Bicycle Victoria, the country's largest cycling organisations, run both one-day and multi-day events. Cycle Sydney (September) and The Great Melbourne Bike Ride (March) attract thousands of ordinary people to celebrate cycling on closed road routes. The Big New South Wales Bike Ride (March/April) and Great Victorian Bike Ride (November/ December) take a different route across their respective states each year. For nine days, around 2,000 cyclists cycle and camp at towns along the way. The Sydney to the 'Gong Ride (November), Australia's equivalent of the London to Brighton, attracts 10,000 cyclists annually. They ride the beautiful coast south of Sydney to the steel city of Wollongong on a 90 km route.

Australian Cyclist, a bi-monthly magazine, available from many newsagents and by subscription, lists all the dates of the aforementioned and many other rides in a calendar each issue.

Where pedals come first

Pedal-power is still an intrinsic part of daily life in many parts of the world. It's appropriate technology for everyone, East and West. If the hundreds of millions of cyclists in the world all used motor cars there would soon be social mayhem and climate catastrophe.

ALL PHOTOGRAPHS ON THIS PAGE BY SUE DARLOW

Bike Culture Weeks '99

Open Road, who publish Encycleopedia, Bike Culture Quarterly and Bycycle Magazine also organise Bike Culture weeks for their readers. For 1999 there will be two Bike Culture Weeks at the historic city of York, one at Ford Castle in Northumberland, and one in France. These are very international events, with a unique atmosphere. For the year 2000 and beyond, contact Open Road's office on +44 1904 654654.

York Weeks

We are returning to our successful 1998 venue at the magnificent Queen Margaret's School in Escrick Park. We have exclusive use of this former country house, in extensive grounds, which offers access to the rolling Yorkshire Wolds, the North York Moors, and easy-riding flatlands to the south. There is also a Sustrans bike path straight to the centre of York and a regular bus service.

York is probably Britain's best preserved historic city, and is also regarded as the most cycle-friendly. We live and work in York, so we know all the best rides, and the top places to visit.

The rooms are single and double, and offer a high standard of comfort. Some can be converted into family rooms, if needed, and all are close to communal kitchens for coffee making etc.

The week includes free use of indoor and outdoor swimming pools, nine-hole golf course, croquet, tennis, squash, badminton, five-a-side football etc. Also included is a guided tour of York (on foot). There will be a maximum of around 100 participants on each week to maintain sociability. If you wish your booking to span more than a single week, you simply pay pro rata for the extra days.

Ford Castle Week

We have exclusive use of the historic Ford Castle, set within the delightful village of Ford, in a beautiful valley in rural Northumberland on the edge of the Cheviot hills, six miles from the Scottish border, and ten miles from the famous Northumbrian coast and Holy Island. This is a border country of ancient castles and churches, stately homes, friendly pubs and tea-rooms; an area characterised by its network of quiet, virtually traffic-free roads. The landscape is magnificent, but this means that there are very few routes which avoid the hills, and the rides will be more demanding than York. The historic town of Berwick on Tweed is twelve miles away, with a 45 minute train connection to Edinburgh. Berwick is also less than an hour from Newcastle on the train, allowing our foreign visitors to arrive by North Sea ferry. Both Edinburgh and Newcastle have airports.

Ford Castle (parts of which go back to the 14th century) is owned by Lord Joicey. Rooms include singles, twins and some family rooms. Most have superb views over the battlements and the surrounding countryside. There is also a small campsite in the adjoining castle orchard and a separate annex, the Clock Tower. The public rooms are magnificent, and the secluded courtyard will be a fine arena for trying out lots of different bikes, where knights in armour may once have jousted.

Also included in the price are a guided tour of the castle, croquet, snooker, a grass tennis court and indoor games. All the meals are table service. There will be a maximum of around 80 participants to maintain sociability.

"The atmosphere was superb, the rides were great, and everyone felt included. We made so many new friends."
Horst Alt, Germany

"The ride leaders were great! They were all willing to adjust their speeds for a variety of cycling abilities. I enjoyed the juggling, the slide show and video show very much. I got more than expected. The people were great, mostly open to new experiences - a wonderful group."
Jean Seay, USA

Bike Culture Weeks for 1999 include seven nights (six nights for France) and contain all the following:
- *Breakfast and three course evening meal (with a vegetarian option)*
- *A choice of at least three different guided rides each day, which should appeal to everyone on the holiday*
- *A full programme of evening talks, films, and live entertainment, including (for the English holidays) a ceilidh*
- *A social room with (for the English holidays) a bar*
- *Fix-your-bike and maintenance classes*
- *(For the English holidays) a pick-up service to and from the station on the first and last day*

- *A wide selection of interesting recumbents and other unusual bikes, supplied by Open Road, for you to try out*
- *A try-out day to which cycle manufacturers are invited with their cycles*
- *A wet weather programme (this does not cover entrance fees to museums, stately homes etc)*
- *Undercover bike storage*
- *A pick-you-up service if you or your bicycle break down*
- *Plenty of activities for families with children*
- *The chance to meet and ride with other cyclists from around the world*

Normandy

For the third year running we return to La Grange d'Espins. Our holiday is based at this ancient but comfortable gîte d'étape, in an area of delightfully quiet country roads and easy-going off-road cycle routes. Few of the roads are completely flat, but most serious hills can be avoided. La Grange d'Espins is about 20 kilometres south of Caen, and five kilometres from the delightful wooded hills of the Suisse Normande. We have exclusive use of the gîte, which was once a farm, and forms a secluded courtyard bordered by the remains of an 14th Century priory, all within 12 hectares of meadow, and very close to several ancient forests, with many well signed cycle routes through them. Good quality mountain bikes are available for hire at the Gîte. There are 50 beds in thirteen rooms, and camping alongside, with the usual camping facilities.

Some of the rides are led by Alain Rouillier, the owner of the Gîte. Alain and Isabel Rouillier live on site with their children, and are keen cyclists. There are facilities for volleyball, table-tennis, seven-a-side football and horse-riding on site (book the latter in advance), with swimming, archery, canoeing, and paragliding nearby. For reasons of conviviality this holiday is restricted to 80 participants.

We will suggest a touring programme for those from the group who wish to stay in Normandy for an extra week.

All Bike Culture Weeks were fully booked last year, so we recommend that you book early. The deposit is 20% of the total. The full amount is payable six weeks before the holiday starts. No refunds for cancellations within six weeks of the start date. Discretionary discounts are available for larger families and group bookings. Please enquire by telephone. All prices include value-added tax.

Dates for 1999
York: *July 31st to August 7th and August 7th to 14th.*
Ford Castle: *August 29th to September 5th.*
Normandy: *7th to 13th June.*

Costs
Adults pay £295 for seven nights in York, with campers paying £215. Adults pay £275 in France, with campers paying £199. For Ford Castle adults pay £339 and campers £239. Children 7-15 years pay half price on all holidays, children 3-7 pay quarter price, and under threes are free of charge. UK participants who are members of Open Road's Bycycle Club receive a 5% reduction for everyone in their party.

Full details are available from the York office of Open Road Ltd,
The Danesmead Wing,
33 Fulford Cross,
York YO10 4PD
UK
Tel: 01904 654654 If there's a time zone problem please use the answerphone.
Fax: 01904 654684
E-Mail: holiday@bcqedit.demon.co.uk

Other publications from Oper

Bike Culture Quarterly

A radically different no-ads subscriptions magazine for the thinking cyclist. It's a lively international forum for the practical and the off-beat, the traditional and the radical. It covers cycle design and technology, people-profiles, cycle touring, cycling art and literature, big issues, ideas, insights, inventions and visions. BCQ lives by the quality of its editorial alone: the absence of advertising makes it great value per page. Shortlisted twice in the US for Best Small Publication of the Year, it's larger than A4, and

usually contains at least 60 full pages of editorial, mostly in colour. BCQ is totally international in its outlook, and is also published by Open Road in a German language edition.

Previous Encycleopedias; a full set

Encycleopedia has been going for five issues now. You can still obtain a full set of back issues, each crammed with innovative cycling ideas, products and other editorial. Few products are repeated issue on issue (apart from some classic designs). There are colour-feature descriptions of around 500 different cycling products from 450 small and imaginative cycle manufacturers. You will find a complete set to be an astonishing reference work to the best ideas in cycling, from many countries, over the last five years. And one of these Encycleopedias (1994/95) has a complete full colour edition of Bike Culture Quarterly bound into it. Pictured left is Encycleopedia 4, covering 1997/98. This was published as simply 'Encycleopedia' in the USA, with a different cover.

The Encycleopedia Video

Seeing bikes on the page is one thing, seeing them in action is quite another. You can order, to accompany the very book you are reading, an hour-long video showing more than half of the featured products in action and in close-up, and covering other topical cycling themes. You can see how folders fold, how trailers hitch and fold, how the riding position on recumbents looks, and so on. Each featured product is described in a minute-long section, with a useful English commentary. This video benefits from a considerable new investment programme from the publishers, Open Road. It is provided in either NTSC (N. America) or PAL (W. Europe) formats and is available in the UK for £8.00 including postage, with equivalent prices from our agents in other countries. See page 138 for details.

All prices and ordering information are set out overleaf

Road

Open Road, publishers of this book, also offer stimulating cycling magazines for anyone with an open mind and a love of good words and fine images. We are unique in the world, and are sure that if you have enjoyed Encycleopedia, you will also enjoy our other publications.

Bycycle Magazine

This magazine for the thinking cyclist is intended primarily for the UK reader, although much of the editorial is also of international interest. Bycycle gives you lots of sharp journalism on issues, events, products and people. It's a 64-page magazine, almost full colour, and keeps up a ratio of three pages of editorial to one of advertising. It is not available in a German edition.

Binders

Both **Bike Culture** and **Bycycle** have specially made binders, which contain 12 issues; the former in maroon, the latter in blue, and both with gold lettering.

BCQ Bound sets

Your chance to enjoy what will soon be one of the most sought-after collector's items: the first 12 issues of Bike Culture Quarterly (Summer 94 to Spring 97) in a purpose-made maroon and gold binder. It's virtually a book in twelve parts, with over 800 adverts-free pages (almost 600 of them in colour) of the best cycle writing, making it, we believe, the biggest, most comprehensive cycling reference works ever compiled. It's timeless stuff – as fresh now as when it was written. You can read it as a book, or you can remove and replace each issue individually, in seconds. It's an ideal gift for any cyclist, with life-long value.

As a non-subscriber ordering everything separately you would have to pay at least £84.50 (or equivalent in your currency), depending on postage. We offer you the package, representing three years of our best work, including binder and postage for £45.00 in the UK – prices from agents in other countries are on page 138.

Why? Because we believe you will like it so much that you will want to become a subscriber! We recommend that you do not delay: certain of the early issues had a low print run: it will soon be impossible to obtain a complete set.

David Eccles Prints

We commissioned David Eccles, one of Britain's foremost cycling illustrators, to produce original images of 19th century cycles in the form of a limited edition set of four linocuts. Conceiving an image and printing it from a block of cork linoleum is a rare and delicate craft. A linocut has a limited capacity for printing due to the fragility of the material. David produced 75 individually numbered and signed sets of the four prints before cancelling each block. Because both the printing and the inking are done by hand no two prints will be exactly the same.

The paper, made entirely from 100% cotton and acid-free, has been specially made by hand for this edition by Chris Bingham of Ruscombe Valley Paper. It replicates exactly paper made in the mid-to-late 1700s. For our purposes we had the making hot-pressed by the Wookey Hole Mill.

These prints are offered individually and, subject to availability, also in sets of all four prints. Each print is numbered, signed and dated by the artist.

The prints have all been window-mounted on 46cm x 41cm acid-free conservation board. For practical reasons, we cannot supply the prints ready-framed.

1. Dursley Pedersen Tandem

2. Mergamobile

3. Alpha Bantam circa 1898

4. Bicycle racing, mid 1880s

All prices and ordering information are set out overleaf

Other publications from Open Road

	USA / Mexico / Canada	postage	Australia / New Zealand	postage	Germany / Austria	postage	Switzerland	postage	UK / Rest of World	UK Postage (...New Zealand)	Other European Postage	Rest of World Postage	Choices	Quantity	Total Price
Publications															
Encycleopedia 99: the Video	$ 12.00	—	A$ 21.00	—	DM24,-	—	SFr20,-	—	£ 8.00	—	£ 3.50	£ 5.00			
*Encycleopedia 97/98 (no video)	$ 12.00	$ 4.00	A$ 25.00	A$ 5.00	DM30,-	DM8,-	SFr24,-	SFr7,-	£ 8.00	£ 2.50	£ 3.50	£ 5.00			
Encycleopedia 96 (no video)	$ 9.00	$ 4.00	A$ 25.00	A$ 5.00	DM20,-	DM8,-	SFr15,-	SFr7,-	£ 6.00	—	£ 2.00	£ 3.50			
Encycleopedia 94/5 (inc BCQ3, no video)	$ 9.00	$ 3.00	A$ 18.00	A$ 2.50	DM20,-	DM8,-	SFr16,-	SFr7,-	£ 6.00	—	£ 1.25	£ 2.00			
Encycleopedia 93/94 (no video)	$ 7.50	$ 2.50	A$ 15.00	A$ 2.50	DM14,-	DM8,-	SFr12,-	SFr7,-	£ 3.50	—	£ 1.25	£ 2.00			
BCQ 1 – 12 set in binder	$118.00	—	A$120.00	—	DM135,-	—	SFr115,-	—	£ 45.00	—	£ 15.00	£ 20.00			
BCQ single issues (not BCQ3)	$ 9.50	$ 2.00	A$ 12.00	A 1.50	DM18,-	DM4,-	SFr16,-	SFr7,-	£ 6.00	£ 1.00	£ 1.50	£ 2.00	Issue(s):		
Subscriptions															
Bike Culture Quarterly, (4 issues)	$ 38.00	—	A$ 50.00	—	DM75,-	—	SFr65,-	—	£ 24.00	—	—	—	Start at BCQ Issue…		
Bycycle (6 issues)	$ 39.00	—	A$ 55.00	—	DM54,-	—	SFr44,-	—	£ 14.95	£ 5.00	£ 5.00	£ 9.00	Start at Bycycle Issue…		
BCQ (4 issues) + Bycycle (6 issues)	$ 72.00	—	A$ 99.00	—	DM121,-	—	SFr103,-	—	£ 28.00	£ 15.95	£ 15.95	£ 19.95	Start at BCQ Issue… Bycycle Issue…		
Open Road Art															
David Eccles limited edition print	$100.00	$ 15.00	—	—	DM195,-	DM15,-	SFr160,-	SFr12,-	£ 65.00	£ 5.00	£ 10.00	£ 20.00	Print 1/2/3/4		
David Eccles limited edition (set of 4)	$350.00	$ 15.00	—	—	DM660,-	DM15,-	SFr530,-	SFr12,-	£220.00	£ 5.00	£ 10.00	£ 20.00			
													Total		

(for how to pay see opposite page)

The video is VHS, and sent in the format usual in the country of order, unless you tell us otherwise.

Prices as at 1/1/99, and subject to alteration.

* The Encycleopedia published in 97/98 is known as just Encycleopedia in the USA (published there by the Overlook Press) and as Encycleopedia 4 elsewhere.

Note: We also have agents in Norway, the Netherlands and New Zealand.
See the page opposite for prices and how to contact them.

Visit our Website on http://bikeculture.com/ On-line ordering services are available

Date ☐☐/☐☐/☐☐   If cheque enclosed please tick ☐   Your unique reference number (if you have one) ☐☐☐☐☐☐

DELIVERY ADDRESS

Name Mr / Mrs / Ms _____

Address _____

Post Code _____

Telephone (daytime) _____

CREDIT CARD DETAILS (Not available in Germany)

Name Mr / Mrs / Ms _____

Address (if different) _____

Post Code _____

Signature _____

Visa/Delta ☐   Access/Mastercard ☐   Eurocard ☐

Card Number ☐☐☐☐ ☐☐☐☐ ☐☐☐☐ ☐☐☐☐

Issue Number ☐☐   Expiry Date ☐☐/☐☐

Switch ☐

Switch Number ☐☐☐☐ ☐☐☐☐ ☐☐☐☐ ☐☐☐☐

Issue Number ☐   Valid From ☐☐/☐☐   Expiry Date ☐☐/☐☐

How to order

1. Make your choice from the ordering table opposite.

2. Add up the prices. Choose the price column for your country.

3. Check on this page for details of where to send your order and how to pay. Note that you can usually order by telephone if you wish.

4. Finally, fill out the form with your details, and send off your order and payment. We'll get the goods to you within 28 days, but usually a lot sooner.

USA, Mexico and Canada

Orders are handled by:

George Otto Junior, Open Road USA, 104 S. Michegan Ave., Suite 1500, Chicago, IL 60603.
Tel 312 201 0101 ext 304. Fax 312 201 0214. Email 74733.1624@compuserve.com. Visa/Mastercard payments accepted.

Deutschland, Österreich und die Schweiz

Alle Bestellungen aus Deutschland, Österreich und der Schweiz für Einzelausgaben (BCQ oder Encycleopedia), Jahresabonnements, T-Shirts, Videos usw. werden von Kalle Kalkhoff, KGB, Donnerschweerstr. 45, 26123 Oldenburg bearbeitet. **Tel:** 0441 8850389 **Fax:** 0441 8850388

Für weitere Informationen und Preise von Einzelexemplaren, rufen Sie KGB an und sprechen Sie mit Kalle.

Zahlungsmodus

Soweit Sie über ein Konto in der Bundesrepublik verfügen, senden Sie bitte mit Ihrer Bestellung einen Verrechnungsscheck an KGB in deutscher Währung.

Die Schweiz

Unsere neue Postscheckkontonummer für Schweizer Abonnenten ist 87-601949-5 KGB Kalle Kalkhoff

Senden Sie bitte Ihre Bestellung an KGB und den Betrag in Schweizer Währung an dieses Konto. Verwenden Sie andernfalls einen Euroscheck. Bitte denken Sie daran, 'Oldenburg' als 'Ort' anzugeben und Ihre EC-Kartennummer auf der Rückseite des Schecks zu vermerken. Euroschecks müssen ebenfalls in DM notiert werden. English versions of Bike Culture and Encycleopedia can be sent by KGB on request.

Dieses Plakat (DIN A2) von David Eccles im Fin-de-Siècle-Stil ist auf hochwertigem Papier gedruckt und für DM25,- plus DM10,- Versandkosten ausschließlich von KGB erhältlich.

Netherlands

Subscriptions and all other orders, and supplies to shops, are handled by:
Luud Steenbergen, Trapperkracht, Soerabayastr. 4, 3531 EB, Utrecht. **Tel/Fax:** 030 296 1015

Prices as at 1.1.99. They include single item postage, but please add an extra ƒ10 when ordering more than one item: **Enc99 Video:** ƒ24.00. **Enc4:** ƒ37.50.

Enc93/94: ƒ15. **Enc94/95:** ƒ25. **Enc96 no video:** ƒ25. **BCQ 1-12 inc binder:** ƒ150. **Single BCQ:** ƒ15.
Binders: ƒ20. **BCQ 4 issue subscription:** ƒ59. **BYCYCLE 6-issue sub:** ƒ64.
BYCYCLE 6-issue sub + BCQ 4-issue sub: ƒ114.

New Zealand

Orders are handled by:
Cycle Works, PO Box 33051, Christchurch.
Tel: (03) 3386803 **Fax:** (03) 3386231 **Email:** bikes@tpnet.co.nz

Australia

All Australian orders are handled by:

Ian Sims, Greenspeed, 69 Mountain Gate Drive, Ferntree Gully, VIC 3156.
Tel: (03) 9758 5541 **Fax:** (03) 9752 4115 **Email:** ian@greenspeed.com.au
Ian accepts credit cards, cheques or money orders made out to Greenspeed.

UK and Rest of the World

Please direct all subscriptions, orders and subscription enquiries to:
Open Road Mail Order, Unit 1, East Riding Business Centre, Annie Reed Road, Beverley, East Yorkshire, HU17 OLF, UK **Tel:** +44 1482 880399 **Email:** openroad@nite-direct.demon.co.uk
UK customers can use the FREEPOST address:
Open Road Mail Order, FREEPOST NEA 3279, Beverley, East Yorkshire. HU17 OBR

If the automatic answering service is running, please speak slowly and clearly and make sure you include relevant card details. We accept almost all credit and debit cards. If you want us to phone you back, tell us how. We always aim to phone back within 24 hours.

All cheques and Eurocheques must be payable to Open Road Ltd. If using a Eurocheque, please send your order in Pounds Sterling, putting 'Beverley, England' as the 'Place'. Credit card payments must be made in Pounds Sterling only. When using your card by post please indicate the type of card, expiry date, registered card address, the name as it appears on the card, the card number, and the name and address for delivery. For debit cards please add issue number and 'valid from' date.

We do not accept cheques from non-UK bank accounts made out in Pounds Sterling. If you are paying in a currency other than Sterling, please ensure that you are sending enough money at the current rate of exchange.

Editorial enquiries, and enquiries about Bike Culture holidays should go to:
Open Road Ltd, The Danesmead Wing, 33 Fulford Cross, York YO10 4PD, UK
Tel: +44 1904 654654 **Fax:** +44 1904 654684 **Email:** peter@bcqedit.demon.co.uk

Norway

Penny and Chris Heymans, PedalNor, Kløverveien 10, 4300 Sandnes, Norway. Tel 51 66 40 60
Fax 51 66 48 70 Email pedal@robin.no Website http://www.robin.no/pedal
Enc99 Video: 100NOK. **BCQ 4 issue subscription:** 280NOK. **BCQ 12 issues:** 800NOK.

Keeping bike culture
in your neighbourhood

When you buy a bicycle you take home a machine which will become either a personal friend or an expensive liability, or, more likely, something between the two.

For anyone who rides regularly, a cheap bike is never exactly that, because it will soon bring you big repair bills and personal disruption as components begin to give up the ghost. For long periods this 'cheap' bike sits at home, until the time can be found to buy and fit a replacement part, or to take it (by car?) to the bike shop. Then the day comes when the owner decides that cycling wasn't much fun anyway: the bike was a heavy beast, and might as well stay out of sight and unrepaired. Besides, it had begun to rust...

Yet cycle technology has never been more welcoming. You can buy bikes, accessories and clothing which will do their job, give you great pleasure, and last for ages. But you are unlikely to get this in a big cut-price department store, or from a mail order catalogue. When you go to a specialist bike shop you may pay more, but you will also receive more. You are more likely to be advised by experts who are daily cyclists themselves. You will probably see a wider real choice than in a department store, especially with higher-priced bikes. You may be able to try on a range of clothing. Above all, you are less likely to be sold something which will give you long-term problems.

A specialised shop will assemble and adjust your bike with care, before you take it on the road. They can offer you maintenance advice, and are more likely to give you good after-sales service. So going to your local bike shop can bring real personal benefits. But your decision as to how and where you spend your money also plays a part in the struggle of specialised cycle shops against the powers of Mammon in the big sheds on the edge of town.

Good specialist bike shops are essential to the fabric of a society which values cycling. This is why Encycleopedia supports such shops strongly. A good bike shop is part of the local community. We list on the following pages some of the bike shops which stock Encycleopedia. They are in many different countries, and reflect their local cycling cultures, but the simple fact that they sell such a book as this is a reasonable indication that they are caring shops.

It is the specialised shops who are taking an interest in the kind of bikes you see in Encycleopedia. These machines are often expensive to keep in stock and take considerable knowledge to explain. It also usually takes many times longer to demonstrate and sell an unconventional cycle than it does to sell a cheap mountain bike from the Far East. Some of the shops listed will stock quite a few of the products which you see in Encycleopedia, others will stock hardly any, but they all have details, from us, the publishers, of how to source the products in Encycleopedia. However, a shop may decline, for very understandable reasons, to source a product for you. After all, they have no prior knowledge of which products we will put into Encycleopedia. They may suggest you try sourcing from a different shop. If all else fails, contact us.

A few manufacturers prefer to deal with customers directly. This is usually because their products are too specialised, or may require a degree of custom building, or perhaps, being big and bulky, they take up too much space in the average shop. However, you or the manufacturer may prefer to have the machine delivered to your local bike shop for assembly, final fitting and after-sales service.

We hope you will support the cycle shops listed over the following pages, or any local bike shop which makes an effort.

Encycleopedia Shops

AUSTRALIA

Canberra

Canberra Cycles Pty Ltd
70 Newcastle Str., Fyshwick, Canberra 2609. Tel 026 280 4984 Fax 026 239 1257 Email ccycless@enternet.com.au
Mo-Fr 8.00-18.00, Sa 8.00-16.00, Su 10.00-15.00
All kinds of bikes from $100 to $6,000, including dual-suspension MTBs and recumbents.

Mitcham

Cycle Science Mitcham
478 Whitehorse Road, Mitcham, VIC 3132. Tel 03 9874 8033 Fax 03 9874 8442 Email freedhpv@connexus.apana.org.au
Mo-Th 9.00-18.00, Fr 9.00-21.00, Sa 9.00-17.00
A wide range of accessories and bicycles including recumbents for sale or hire. We custom build in steel or aluminium.

Perth

Quantum
64 Farmer Street, North Perth, WA 6006. Tel 089 443 3407 Fax 089 443 8687
Hrs Mo-Fr 9.00-18.00, Sa 9.00-12.00

Victoria

Greenspeed
69 Mountain Gate Drive, Ferntree Gully, VIC 3156. Tel 03 9758 5541 Fax 03 9752 4115
Email ian@greenspeed.com.au Website www.greenspeed.com.au

AUSTRIA

Baden

B.I.E.R Fahrrad-Studio
Jägerhausgasse 20, A-2500 Baden. Tel 02252 47690 Fax 02252 47690 Email ambrosch@ping.at
Website http://ourworld.compuserve.com/homepages/fahrradstudio/
Hrs Tu-Th 10.00-12.00 & 15.00-18.00 Sa 10.00-12.00
We specialise in recumbents and trailers. A sensible range of city bikes, MTBs and good accessories.

Salzburg

Velo active
W-Hauthaler Strasse 10, A-5020 Salzburg. Tel 0662 435595 Fax 0662 435595/22

Vienna

Cooperative Fahrrad GmbH (VSF)
Mollardgasse 20, A-1060 Vienna. Tel 01596 52 56 Fax 01596 52 574
All kinds of pedal-power for the big city and beyond.

BELGIUM

Ghent

De Ligfiets
Lange Violettestraat 217, B 9000 Ghent. Tel/Fax 09 223 4496
Hrs Thursday 6-9 pm, by appointment.
The Belgium recumbent specialists, hire and sale, M5, Challenge, Flevobike, Speedliner, Optima, Windcheetah. With more than 8 years of daily recumbent use we know what we're talking about.

CANADA

Victoria

Fairfield Bicycle Shop, Ltd.
1275 Oscar St., Victoria, BC V8V 2X6. Tel 250 381 2453 Fax 250 384 2453 Email fairbic@islandnet.com
Practical bikes for the real world. Commuters' oasis in an MTB desert. Frame building, cycle repair courses, cycling coalition involvement.

Vancouver

Reckless: the bike store
1810 Fir St (at 2nd ave), Vancouver, BC V6J 3B1. Tel 604 731 2420 Fax 604 266 9090 Email dragan@rektek.com
Quality rentals, guided or independent tours, full service repairs, and unrelentingly friendly service! We speak French, Italian, Spanish, Japanese, German & Cantonese. Free air and free oil any time!

Toronto

Bikes on Wheels Cooperative Inc
309 Augusta Avenue, Toronto, Ontario M5T 2M2. Tel 001 4169 662453
Bikes and accessories. We are a worker co-op. We advocate the use of human-powered vehicles. Burley, Ibis.

DENMARK

Copenhagen

Christiania Cykler
Oster Port Open Mo-Fr 10.00-17.30, Refshalevej 2, DK-1432 Copenhagen K.
Tel 032 954 520 Fax 031 544 593
A highly professional, enthusiastic shop within the famous Christiania commune, yet attracting customers from all over Copenhagen. Specialisms: Pedersens and MTBs.

Copenhagen

Dansk Cyklist Forbund
Rømersgade 7, DK-1362 Copenhagen K.
Tel +45 33 32 31 21 Fax +45 33 32 76 83
Email dcf@inet.uni-c.dk Website www.dcf.dk

FRANCE

Paris

Bicloune (Le Comptoir du Cycle)
7 Rue Froment, 75011 Paris. Tel 0148 054775 Fax 0148 054770
Specialists in international bikes, particularly Dutch bikes and parts, eg Gazelle, Batavus, also for Schwinn and Scott. Antiques department: complete bicycles, spare parts, catalogues and postcards.

GERMANY

D-06108 Halle/Saale

Fahrradies (VSF)
Bermburgerstr. 25. Tel 0345 290 9727 Fax 0345 290 9728
Mo-Fr 10.00-12.00, 13.00-19.00 Sa 10.00-15.00
A lovely shop in a historic town, and well worth a visit! Featured in BCQ

D-10119 Berlin

Velo B (VSF)
Gips Strasse 7. Tel 030 283 90809 Fax 030 283 90815

D-10405 Berlin

Ostrad (VSF)
Winsstr. 48. Tel 030 44341393 Fax 030 44341394.
Email ostradGmbH@aol.com
Mo-Fr 10.00-18.30 Th 12.00-20.00 Sa 10.00-13.30
The cycle shop with a difference. Highly qualified mechanics. Accessories, recumbents for sale and hire, competent advice, also planning recumbent weekend tours.

D-10997 Berlin

Christiania Bikes (VSF)
Köpenicker Strasse 8b.
Tel 030 618 8015 Fax 030 611 3697

D-18055 Rostock

Radhaus (VSF)
Goetheplatz 1. Tel 0381 455203 Fax 0381 455204

D-20144 Hamburg

The New Cyclist
Grindelberg 45, Hamburg, Tel 040 422 0658, Fax 040 422 0659
Mo-Fr 10.00-19.00 Sa 10.00-13.00
Proprietor: Michael Schäfer. Frame builder. Exclusively custom-built tourers and MTBs. Full selection of folders and recumbents. English frames a speciality.

D-21029 Hamburg

Pro Velo (VSF)
Serrahnstr 1-2 D. Tel 040 721 3109 Fax 040 721 2988
Hrs Oct-Feb Tu-Fr 10.00-18.00 Mar-Sep Tu-Fr 10.00-20.00 Sa 10-16
Advice, service, hiring, city bikes, touring bikes, racing bikes, load carrying bikes, tandems, recumbents, folders, children's bikes, trikes, trailers, MTBs, BMX, clothing, parts etc.

D-22765 Hamburg

Zweirad und Zukunft (VSF)
Gaußstr. 19. Tel 040 393992 Fax 040 3902302
Hrs Tu-Fr 10.00-13.00 & 15.00-18.00 Sa 10.00-18.00
Closed on Mondays.
Self-help workshop. Recycling and ecological repairs. Buying and selling: city bikes, touring bikes, children's bikes, recumbents, tandems and trailers.

D-22765 Hamburg

Rad & Tat GmbH (VSF)
Am Felde 2. Tel 040 395667 Fax 040 392154

D-23552 Lübeck

Sattelfest GmbH (VSF)
Kanalstr. 70. Tel 0451 704687 Fax 0451 7063742,
Hrs Mo-Fr 9.00-18.00, Sa 9.00-14.00
Town bikes, tourers, racers, folders, recumbents, trailers, clothing. Specialising in vehicles and parts for durability and all-weather performance. Tandem and recumbent hire

D-24106 Kiel

Fahrradies (VSF)
Adalbert Strasse 11, Ecke Knorr Strasse. Tel 0431 332016 Fax 0431 336381

D-24118 Kiel

Velocenter (VSF)
Knooperweg 165. Tel 0431 803991 Fax 0431 85053

D-24939 Flensburg

Velopedes (VSF)
Neustadt 7. Tel 0461 46699 Fax 0461 45590

D-26123 Oldenburg

Die Speiche GmbH (VSF)
Donnerschweerstr. 45. Tel 0441 84123 Fax 0441 83471
Hrs Mo-Fr 9.30-13.00 14.00-18.00, Sa 9.30-13.30
All kinds of cycles, trailers, cycle bags, helmets and accessories, as well as good advice and renowned quality service. Bike loans, self-help workshop, and courier-service next door.

D-26123 Oldenburg

KGB (VSF)
Donnerschweerstr. 45. Tel 0441 885 03 89 Fax 0441 885 03 88
Mo-Fr 10.00-13.00 & 14.00-17.00
Largest Pedersen, Galaxe and high bicycle exhibition in Germany. Distribution centre for Bike Culture Quarterly and Encycleopedia. Not really a cycle shop, but worth a visit!

D-27211 Bassum

Per Pedal (VSF)
Hindenburg Strasse 12. Tel 04241 7388 Fax 04241 7307

D-29525 Uelzen

Die Speichenstimmer (VSF)
Sternplatz 5. Tel 0581 2023 Fax 0581 2024
A full selection of bikes: touring bikes, recumbents, MTBs, and accessories.

D-29549 Bad Bevensen

Fahrradhaus (VSF)
Medingerstr. 20. Tel 05821 1305 Fax 05821 41353, Mo-Fr 8.30-18.00 Sa 9.00-13.00
We are amusing, honest, committed, friendly, prepared, competent, critical, brave, naive, curious, self-exploiting, conscientious, tolerant, but above all cyclists!

D-30171 Hannover

Räderwerk GmbH (VSF)
Marienstr. 28. Tel 0511 717174 Fax 0511 2832140
Hrs Mo Tu Th Fr 10.00-18.00, Mi 14.00-18.00, Sa 10.00-13.00
'Museum of the Modern Bike'. Encycleopedic selection available: 30 recumbents, 10 trikes, 10 folding bikes, load carriers, child trailers, cycles for disabled cyclists bought and sold.

D-30175 Hannover

Drahtesel (VSF)
Volgersweg 58. Tel 0511 348 1512 Fax 0511 311638

D-33102 Paderborn

Fahrradladen Pigal (VSF)
Bahnhof Strasse 64. Tel 05251 37284 Fax 05251 31288

D-34134 Kassel

Fahrradhof Kassel (VSF)
Frankfurter Strasse 285. Tel 0561 471132 Fax 0561 473338

D-37073 Göttingen

Ultra Rad
Nikolaikirchhof 12. Tel 0551 484113 Fax 0551 484113

D-37073 Göttingen

Velo Voss GmbH (VSF)
Nicolai Strasse 21. Tel 0551 484236 Fax 0551 56237

D-37077 Göttingen-Weende

Radweise Fahrräder GmbH
Breite Str. 18, Göttingen Weende. Tel 0551 34533 Fax 0551 34533
Mo-Fr 9.30-13.00 15.00-18.00
Useful, individualistic bikes for everybody. All three proprietors manage the shop, but also work as a team. If you have any questions, we'll answer them!

D-38106 Braunschweig

Radhaus (VSF)
Heinrich Strasse 25. Tel 0531 339650 Fax 0531 337146

D-40223 Düsseldorf

Cycle Service
Oberbilker Allee 57b. Tel 0211 340399 Fax 0211 3180250, Mobile 0172 219 6291
Hrs Mo-Fr 10.00-20.00 Sa 10.00-16.00
Recumbents, touring bikes, MTBs, hire bikes, and specialised bikes of all kinds.

D-42285 Wuppertal

Radfinesse (VSF)
Haspeler Strasse 10. Tel 0202 81512 Fax 0202 81512

D-44135 Dortmund

Das Rad GmbH
Brüderweg 14. Tel 0231 529324 Fax 0231 551320

D-44795 Bochum

Hase
Marec Hase, Karl-Friedrich Strasse 88.
Tel 0234 946 9050 Fax 0234946 9099

D-47051 Duisburg

Radwerk Fahrradladen (VSF)
Oberstr. 42. Tel 0203 24032 Fax 0203 288116
Hrs daily until 20.00
Service, recumbents, tandems, trailers and everything needed for cycling.

D-48151 Münster

1 2 3 Rad
Sentmaringer Weg 113. Tel 0251 9745890 Fax 0251 9745891

D-48413 Münster

Drahtesel
Servatiiplatz 7. Tel 0251 511228 Fax 0251 56252
Mo-Fr 10.00-13.30 & 14.30-19.00, closed Wed mornings, Sa 10.00-15.00
Large selection of accessories and clothing available, specialises in tandems, Koga-Miyata, Villiger, Trek, Cannondale, Giant. Shimano Service Centre, cycle manufacturer.

D-50226 Frechen Königsdorf

Lowrider
Starenweg 3. Tel 02234 967131 Fax 02234 967132
Hrs Mo-Fr 10.00-13.00 & 14.00-18.00 Sa 10.00-14.00 and by appointment.
Specialises in racing, city, touring recumbents, tandems, trailers, transport bikes. Service: hire, accessories, literature, regular recumbent meetings and tours, used recumbents.

D-50672 Cologne

Zwei plus zwei (VSF)
Bismarkstr. 56-62. Tel 0221 951 4700 Fax 0221 951 7020
Mo-Fr 10.00-18.00 Sa 10.00-15.00 Apr-Sep Mo-Wed 10.00-18.00, Th-Fr 10.00-20.00, Sat 10.00-16.00.
200 sq/m of special cycles. Specialises in trailers, folding bikes and scooters.

D-50678 Cologne

Stadtrad (VSF)
Teutoburger Strasse 19. Tel 0221 328075 Fax 0221 9322258

D-51427 Bergisch Gladbach

Veloladen-Liegeräder (VSF)
Dolmanstr. 20. Tel 02204 61075 Fax 02204 61076
Mo-Fr 12.00-18.30 Th 12.00-20.00 Sa 10.00-14.00
THE recumbent store with a huge selection, know-how, and objective advice. Proprietors: Ortwin Kürten & Klaus Schröder. Members of the VSF & German HPV Association.

D-53111 Bonn

Stahlroß (VSF)
Dorotheen Strasse 1-3. Tel 0228 694209 Fax 0228 658794

D-53840 Troisdorf

VamBike (VSF)
Alte Poststr. 21. Tel 02241 78645 Fax 02241 83357
Email liegerad@aol.com
Hrs Mo-Fr 10.00-13.00, 13.30-18.30 except Wed and Sat 10.00-14.00
Advice on high quality cycle technology for that special pedalling experience. Recumbent specialists.

D-55116 Mainz

Der Fahrrad-Laden Berens & Reus GmbH (VSF)
Albinistr. 15. Tel 06131 225013 Fax 06131 230017
Hrs Tu-Fr 10.00-13.00 & 14.30-18.30 Sa 10.00-14.00
Closed on Mondays.
Full selection! Also Brompton, Birdy and Bernds folding bikes.

D-59379 Selm

Trekking-u. Fahrradfachhandel
Ludgeri Strasse 62. Tel 02592 981575

D-60389 Frankfurt-am-Main

Radschlag (VSF)
Hallgartenstr. 56. Tel 069 452064 Fax 069 453284
Tu-Fr 11.00-18.30, Th 11.00-20.00, Sa 9.30-13.30
The internationally-minded cycle shop in cosmopolitan Frankfurt – English, French, and Turkish spoken. Trailers, folding bikes, tandems and recumbents.

D-60437 Frankfurt-am-Main

Die Fahrradscheune-Spezialräder
Alt Harheim. 27. Tel 06101 48958 Fax 06101 48958.
Frankfurt's special cycling shop! Independent cyclists (and those who want to become independent cyclists) will find everything they need!

D-60487 Frankfurt-am-Main

Per Pedale GmbH (VSF)
Leipzigerstr. 4. Tel 069 707 23 63 Fax 069 772084
Mo 10.00-18.30 Sa 9.00-13.30

D-61231 Bad Nauheim

Radladen Erstrad
Dietmar Schneidler, Am Gradierbau 1. Tel 06032 4791

D-63067 Offenbach

Fahrradgesellschaft H.+D. Meyer OHG
Bahnhofstr. 18. Tel 069 815832 Fax 069 889977
Email so.w@sn-icht
Hrs Tu-Fr 10.00-13.00, 15.00-18.30 Sa 10.00-14.00
Specialise in Moulton and Pedersen since 1982, folding bikes, tandems, no rubbish.

D-65468 Trebur

Fahrrad-Claus (VSF)
Astheimerstr. 58. Tel 06147 7915 Fax 06147 1329
Hrs Mo Tu Th Fr 9.00-12.30 & 14.30-18.00
Family business since 1920. From children's bikes to touring bikes: recumbents, folding bikes, bike hire, trailers. Test rides available. Special needs? Ask!

D-70176 Stuttgart

Radladen Doppelaxel GmbH (VSF)
Lerchenstr 40. Tel 0711 226 1515 Fax 0711 226 1984,
Hrs Tu-Fr 10.00-18.00, Sa 9.00-14.00
Many recumbents, city bikes, Brompton, Pedersen, recumbents, touring bikes and many accessories, 100m2 floor space.

D-71254 Ditzingen Stuttgart

Pedalkraft F. Eberhardt Spezialräder
Hirschlander Str. 2. Tel 07156 8369 Fax 07156 34034
Hrs Mo-Fr 9.00-13.00 & 15.00-18.30
Folding-bikes and recumbents: Brompton, Birdy, Bernds, Moulton, Galaxe, Montague folding tandems, Radius, Bevo.

D-72764 Reutlingen

Transvelo (VSF)
Planie 22. Tel 07121 470726 Fax 07121 470727

D-73119 Zell u. A.

Fahrradladen Zell (VSF)
Bach Strasse 4. Tel 07164 6263 Fax 07164 6601

D-76133 Karlsruhe

Rad & Tat (VSF)
Wald Strasse 58. Tel 0721 22238 Fax 0721 26458

D-76726 Germersheim
Haasies Radschlag (VSF)
Marktstr. 22. Tel 07274 4863 Fax 07274 779360
Hrs Mo-Fr 10.00-12.30, 14.30-19.00, Sa 9.00-13.00, Closed Wednesday mornings.
Pedersen book publisher – organises the 'alternative cycling fair' in Southern Germany – large selection of special bikes and trailers. Test-rides available.

D-77933 Lahr
Rad & Tat
Werder Strasse 65. Tel 07821 29458 Fax 07821 29458

D-77948 Friesenheim-Schuttern
Radhiesli
Im Oberdorf 25. Tel 07821 67446 Fax 07821 62965

D-78050 VS-Villingen
Tour-Räder im Zentrum GmbH (VSF)
Obere Strasse 12/1. Tel 07721 54416 Fax 07721 57664

D-78462 Konstanz
Radial (VSF)
Konradigasse 13. Tel 07531 22532 Fax 07531 29274

D-79106 Freiburg/Br.
Radhaus Fahrradhandel GmbH (VSF)
Münchhofstr. 4. Tel 0761 280832 Fax 0761 280838
Hrs Mo-Fr 9.00-13.00 & 15.00-18.30 Sa 10.00-14.00
City and touring bikes but also specialised bikes: Birdy, Friday, Brompton, Galaxe, Pedersen, Radius recumbents and many trailers.

D-80799 München
Radl - R (VSF)
Kurfürsten Strasse 8. Tel 089 349110 Fax 089 345520

D-83093 Bad Endorf
Muskelbetriebene Fahrzeuge (MBF)
Poststr. 1. Tel 08053 2374 Fax 08053 2397, Mobile 0172 6014786
Human powered vehicles for the open-minded. Test-rides and hire. TWIKE, recumbents, Pedersen, high bikes, folding bikes, transporter bikes, trailers, cycles for the disabled.

D-84307 Eggenfelden
Bike, Trike and Fun
Pfarrkirchener Strasse 25. Tel 08721 912895
Fax 08721 912894
Sale and hire of recumbents, folding bikes, transport bikes, other specialised bikes, child trailers and transport trailers.

D-90419 Nürnberg
Ride on a Rainbow (VSF)
Adam-Kraft Strasse 55, Tel 0911 397337 Fax 0911 396078

D-90478 Nürnberg
Velo Radsport GmbH (VSF)
Köhnstr. 38. Tel 0911 473611 Fax 0911 467707
Hrs Mo-Fr 10.00-18.00 Sa 10.00-18.00
Closed Wednesday
Cycling culture and service! Robust quality city and touring, child and transport trailers, folding bikes, MTB specialist/full-suspension test bikes.

D-90762 Fürth
Zentralrad Fürth (VSF)
Most Strasse 25. Tel 0911 746090 Fax 0911 770579

D-91054 Erlangen
Freilauf GmbH (VSF)
Lazarettstr. 4. Tel 09131 202220 Fax 09131 201710
Hrs Mo-Fr 10.00-19.00 Sa 10.00-16.00
A full quality range. We have a fascinating selection of child trailers, tandems, folding bikes, recumbents and Pedersens.

D-91522 Ansbach
Fahr' Rad! (VSF)
Reuter Strasse 3. Tel 0981 13501 Fax 0981 13501

D-91564 Neuendettelsau
Radladen (VSF)
Linden Strasse 9. Tel 09874 1835 Fax 09874 1835

D-93053 Regensburg
Fahr Rad Laden A.C.H.T. GmbH (VSF)
Furtmayrstr. 12. Tel 0941 7000365 Fax 0941 7000546
Hrs Mo-Fr 10.00-18.00, Sa 10.00-14.00
Pedersen, recumbents, transport cycles, Rollfiets – all waiting for your test ride!

D-96049 Bamberg
Mück's Radladen
Schrottenberggasse 2. Tel 0951 578 53 Fax 0951 57809
Mo-Fr 10.00-18.30, Sa 10.00-14.00
In the heart of the old town. Top-class city bikes, MTBs, recumbents, Pedersens. Our aim has always been to build our business around our customers' wishes and needs.

D-97070 Würzburg
Fahrradstation (VSF)
Bahnhofplatz 4. Tel 0931 57445 Fax 0931 57465

D-97912 Lauda an der Tauber
Bio Bike/Forum (VSF)
Rathausstr. 33, Zehntplatz. Tel 09343 65400
Fax 09343 65407
Michael Malich offers child-trailers, recumbents, velomobiles and more!

REPUBLIC OF IRELAND

Dublin
Square Wheel Cycleworks
Temple Lane South, (Off Dame Street) Dublin 2.
Tel 01 6790838
Hrs Mo-Fr 8:30-6:30 Sat 10:30-6:30
A centre of Cycle Culture, with a full repair and bike parking service. Occasional holidays.

NETHERLANDS

Amsterdam
Het Mannetje, Transportrijwielen
Frans Halsstraat 26A, 1072 BR Amsterdam.
Tel 020 679 2139 Fax 020 471 5217
Production and sales of transporter bikes, transporter tandems and tricycles. Specialist in the transport of two or more children on one bike. Motto: 'Freight under your own steam' (vracht op eigen kracht). A machine for every load up to 250kg.

Amsterdam
Tromm Tweewielers
Europaplein 45 t/o RAI, 1078 GV Amsterdam.
Tel 020 6642099
Specialist in folding bikes (35 models) and mountain bikes. Importer of quality English folding bikes. Trailers and scooters.

Eindhoven
De Liggende Hollander
Tourslaan 33 en 41, 5627 KW Eindhoven.
Tel 040 242 4368 Fax 040 242 4368
Sale and hire of recumbents, trailers and folding bikes. Open days for potential customers. Organises recumbent cycling holidays.

Den Haag
Kemper
Piet Heinstraat 42, 2518 CJ Den Haag. Tel 070 345 9696
Folding bike and recumbent specialist, trailers and tandems. Also hire of recumbent and folding bikes. Accompanied try-out touring runs for those interested in recumbents.

Haarlem
Optima Cycles
Gierstraat 55, 2011 GB Haarlem. Tel/Fax 023 53 41502
Email Optima28@worldaccess.nl
Design, building, sale and hire of recumbents and parts. Folding bikes, transporter bikes and necessary spare parts. Sale and hire of trailers. Pedersen and Bike Friday (official dealer).

Rotterdam
Bikers' Best
Noordsingel 3, 3035 EG Rotterdam. Tel 010 4662916
Widely competent cycle shop with everything for racing, ATB and hybrid cycles, BMX/freestyle, cruisers, recumbents, tandems, trailers, clothing. Sale and repairs, try-out and trade-ins possible.

Utrecht
Trapperkracht
Soerabayastraat 4, 3531 EB Utrecht. Tel 030 296 1015
Fax 030 296 1015
Sale and hire of products for cycling with children: Baby Bike, trailers, trailerbikes and tandems. Sale and hire of luggage trailers. Specialist in heavy transport using pedal power. Tricycles, and consultant for disabled cyclists. Subscription service and back copies of BCQ and Encycleopedia.

Utrecht
Wim Kok Fietsplezier
Nachtegaalstraat 51, 3581 AD Utrecht. Tel 030 2315780
Fax 030 2316675
All-round excellent cycle shop for touring, recumbents, ATB, hybrids, tandems, scooters. Folding bike and trailer specialist. Many unusual lines, clothing, helmets, etc.

NORWAY

Sandnes
Pedalnor
Kløvereien 10, 4300 Sandnes, Norway. Tel 066 40 60
Fax 066 48 70 Email pedal@robin.no Website http//www.robin.no/ped
Agents for Bike Culture. Arrange Cycle tours in Lofoten Islands and West Norway.

SWITZERLAND

CH-6011 Kriens
Velociped (VSF)
Luzern Strasse 16. Tel 041 3205351 Fax 041 3112077

CH-4500 Solothurn
Velo-Werkstatt
Baselstr. 47A. Tel 032 623 4676 Fax 032 623 4676
Tu-Fr 9.00-12.15 u. 13.30-18.30 Sa 9.00-12.15 & 13.30-16.00
To describe our shop in 20 words is impossible. Imagine it for yourself instead.

CH-4900 Langenthal
Velorama
Spitalgasse 3. Tel 063 922 9650
Hrs Mo We Th Fr 9.00-18.30 Sa 8.00-16.00
Special bicycles and custom work. Tourers, recumbents and town bikes. Accessories and clothing.

UNITED KINGDOM

Channel Isles

Guernsey
Ian Brown Cycle Shop
Route Militaire, St Sampsons, Guernsey, Channel Isles GY2 4DZ. Tel 01481 41308 Fax 01481 41309
Email ianbrowns@aol.com
Hrs Mon-Sat 8:30 - 5.30
Specialised cycle dealer, run by cyclists, not just bicycles, but trailers, trikes, and trailerbikes. No VAT and no disappointed customers.

ENGLAND

Bath
Avon Valley Cyclery
Rear of Bath Spa Train Station, Bath, Avon BA1 1SX.
Tel 01225 442442/461880 Fax 01225 446267
Email sales@bikeshop.uk.com
Hrs 9 - 5,30 seven days a week
Makers of unique Caribou Road mountain bikes, folding bike experts, recumbents, hire and big workshop.

Bath
John's Bikes
80-84 Walcot Street, Bath, Avon BA1 5BD.
Tel 01225 334633 Fax 01225 480132
Hrs 9-5.30 six days a week
Specialists in touring cycling since 1972.
Shimano service centre.
Main stockists for Marin and Trek. Bike hire available April through September.

Basingstoke
Basingstoke Cycle Works
Unit 1 Station Approach, Basingstoke Railway Station, Basingstoke, Hants. RG21 5NB. Tel 01256 814 138
Fax 01256 355 655
Shimano Service Centre, upgrades our speciality. Re-cycles our forte!

Berwick-upon-Tweed
Brilliant Bicycles
17a Bridge Street, Berwick-upon-Tweed, Northumberland, TD15 1ES.
Tel 01289 331 476 Fax 01289 302 345
Email enquiries@brilliantbicycles.co.uk
Website www.brilliantbicycles.co.uk Hrs 9-5:30
A brilliant range of cycles, tricycles, special needs products and cycle hire.

Birmingham
Feet First
170 Widney Manor Road, Solihull, W Midlands. Tel 0121 704 4412 Fax 0121 233 9928 garyh@compuserve.com or gary7@dial.pipex.com
Hrs 6 days per week – please phone first
Specialist offering demonstrations, hire and sales of a wide range of UK and European recumbents, folding bikes and special needs.

Birmingham
On Your Bike
10 Priory Queensway, Birmingham B4 6BS.
Tel 0121 627 1590
Hrs Mon-Fri 10-6 Sat 9.30-6
Situated in the centre of the city and staffed by enthusiastic knowledgeable staff, the store is a mecca for cyclists in the Midlands.

Bodmin (Cornwall)
The Bike Shop
25 Honey Street, Church Square, Bodmin, Cornwall PL31 2DP. Tel 01208 72552 Fax 01208 78476
Hrs: Summer 9-6 Mon - Sat 10-4 Sun, Winter 9.30 – 5.30 Mon -Sat
Servicing and bicycle repairs, hire, bicycle sales, clothing, Gore bike wear, Pace clothing and accessories, Giant bicycles, and Shimano stockist.

Cambridge
Ben Hayward Cycles
69 Trumpington Street, Cambridge CB2 1RJ. Tel 01223 352294 (workshop 301118) Fax 01223 573989
robturner@dial.pipex.com
Hrs Mon-Sat 8.30-5.30
All types of quality cycles, clothing and accessories.

Cambridgeshire (Thetford, nr. Ely)
D. Tek HPVs
Main Street, Little Thetford, Nr. Ely, Cambridgeshire CB6 1BR. Tel 01353 648177 Fax 01353 648777 BT One Number 07071 CYCLES
March-Oct. 7 days a week 9.30 to 5, Winter Mon-Fri 10-4. Bookings essential – other hours by arrangement.
Outstanding range of recumbents for hire or sale.
Unique 'one-stop trailer shop'. Solutions for the disabled 'We won't say 'can't'!

Chester (Cheshire)
The Bike Factory
153-161 Boughton, Chester, CH3 5BH. Tel 01244 317893/320173 Fax 01244 317916
Hrs 9.30 - 5.30 Mon to Sat, 10.00 - 4.00 Sun.
We pride ourselves on good advice and quality service. Try us, you won't be disappointed.

Chester (Cheshire)
Davies Brothers Cycles Limited
5 Delamere Street, Chester CH1 4DF.
Tel 01244 371341/381177 Fax 01244 381175
Hrs 9.30 - 5.30 Mon to Sat, 10.00 - 4.00 Sun
We pride ourselves on good advice and quality service. Try us, you won't be disappointed.

Diss (Norfolk)
Madgetts Cycles
8 Shelfanger Rd, Diss, Norfolk IP22 3EH.
Tel 01379 650 419 Fax 01379 642 735
Hrs 9-5:30, closed Tuesdays PM and Sundays
Long-established, family-owned shop for the complete cycling experience.

Dorset (Dorchester)
Dorchester Cycles
31B Gt Western Road, Dorchester, Dorset DT1 1UF.
Tel 01305 268787 Fax 01305 268784
Hrs Mon-Sat 9-5.30
Tourers, tandems, unicycles, folders, hybrids & ATBs, adult tricycles, electric bikes and add-on power kits, plus servicing and repairs. Enormous selection of accessories, clothing and spare parts. Cycle hire always available.

East Sussex (Forest Row)
FutureCycles
Friends Yard, London Road, Forest Row, Sussex RH18 5EE.
Tel 01342 822 847 Fax 01342 826 726
Email bikes@futurecycles.prestel.co.uk Website http://there.is/futurecycles
Hrs Mon-Sat 9.30-5.30. Half day Wed.
Specialising in recumbents, we offer a complete range of conventional bikes including folders. Traffic-free test ride area in rural location

Ilkley (West Yorkshire)
JD's Bicycle Workshop
42A Nelson Road, Ilkley, West Yorkshire LS29 8HN. Tel 01943 816101 Fax 01943 601829 Email jd@ilkley.com
Hrs 9.00 - 6.00pm Mon - Sat.
An established cycle shop, extensive showroom with on-site workshop. A proper bike for proper cyclists.

Kent (Rochester)
Geoff Wiles Cycles
45-47 Caxton Road, Strood, Rochester, Kent ME2 2BU.
Tel 01634 722586 Fax 01634 727416
A friendly shop with a wide range of cycles. Also made-to-measure, and a knowledgeable custom service for the disabled.

Kielder (Northumberland)
Kielder Bikes
Castle Hill, Kielder, NE48 1ER. Tel 01434 250392
Open 10.00-6.00 April - September. Otherwise by appointment
Hire bikes, cycle sales, parts, repair. Rescue service for touring cyclists. Scenic situation by castle. Owner Ken Bone lives on site.

Liverpool
Liverpool Cycle Centre
9-13 Berry St., Liverpool L1 9DF. Tel/Fax 0151 708 8819
Hrs 10-6.
Providing a helpful service to everyone from the first-time buyer to the seasoned professional, regardless of age or gender.

London SE1
On Your Bike
52/54 Tooley Street, London Bridge, London SE1 2SZ.
Tel 0171 378 6669 Fax 0171 3577600
Hrs Mon - Fri 9 - 6 Sat 9.30 - 5.30 Sun (summer only) 11 - 4.
Since 1983, OYB have catered for the city cyclist, also keeping the latest components & clothing in stock for the avid mountainbiker and enthusiast.

London SE24
London Recumbents
Rangers Yard, Dulwich Park, College Road, London SE21 7BQ. Tel/Fax 0181 299 6636 Email recumbents@aol.com
Hire/sales for family/disability cycling, work bikes and recumbents.

London SW11
Phoenix Cycles
59a Battersea Bridge Road, London SW11 3AV.
Tel/Fax 0171 7382766
Email info@phoenix-folders.demon.co.uk
Hrs Tue-Fri 10-6.30 Sat 10-5
Lots of folding bikes and accessories, also Pashley cycles and friendly expert advice in central London.

London SW9
Brixton Cycles
435-437 Coldharbour Lane, Brixton, London SW9 8LN.
Tel 0171 733 6055 Fax 0171 733 5595
brixcyke@dircon.co.uk
Hrs Mon-Sat 9-6 Thrs 9-7(closed for lunch every day 2.30-3.15)
Sale and repair of all types of bicycle. Hub gears, commuter support, advice, trailers. London's only bicycle co-op.

London W11
Bicycle Workshop
27 All Saints Road, Westbourne Park, London W11 1HE.
Tel 0171 229 4850 Email ninon@copuserve.com
Hrs Tue-Sat 10-6 (closed 2-3)
Specialises in repairs, including jobs many shops don't like, supplier of Sturmey-Archer hubs. Sells spares and accessories. Has a strong base in the local community and a wider catchment area.

London W14
Cyclecare-Olympia
30 Blythe Road, London W14 0HA. Tel 0171 602 9757
Fax 0171 602 9757
Hrs Mon-Fri 10-6,30 Sat 10-5
Brompton since 1988, Dawes, Pendle, Polaris, Raleigh, Respro, commuting-oriented.

London W3
Stuart Bikes
309/311 Horn Lane, London W3 0BU. Tel 0181 993 3484
Fax 0181 993 1891 Email sales@bikebook.demon.co.uk
Hrs Mon-Sat 9.30-6 Sun 11-4 Closed Weds
Sister company to Bicycling Books, specialising in cycling books, videos, jewellery novelties and also sells cycles, helmets, clothing and shoes.

London WC1
Bikefix
48 Lamb's Conduit Street, London WC1N 3LJ.
Tel 0171 4054639 Email bikefix@bikefix.co.uk
Website http://www.bikefix.co.uk/humanpower/
Hrs Mon-Fri 8.30 - 7pm Sat 10 - 5pm.
The complete Encycleopedia shop, with recumbents, trailers and folding bikes.

Loughborough (Leicestershire)
Beacon Cycles
88 Derby Road, Loughborough, Leicestershire, LE11 5AG.
Tel 01509 215448
Hrs 9.00 - 5.30pm
Bike and bits, everything for happy cycling.

Malden (Essex)
Pedal Parteners
12 East Street, Tollesbury, Malden, Essex, CM9 8QD.
Tel/Fax 01621 869974
Hrs Tues - Sat 9.00 - 6.00 Sun 10.00 - 4.00 Closed Mon.
Everything cyclable & associated, Special needs/able bodied. Sales, hire and information.

Manchester
Bicycle Doctor
68-70 Dickenson Road, Rusholme, Manchester M14 5HF.
Tel 0161 2241303 Fax 0161 257 3102
Hrs Mon-Fri 10 - 6 Sat 10 - 5.30
Email sales@bikedoc.demon.co.uk
Mon-Fri 10.00 – 18.00 Sat 10.00 – 17.30
High quality tourers, mountain, city bikes, folders, top class workshop.

Manchester
Bikehouse
177 School Lane, Manchester, M19 1GN. Tel 0161 4431235 Fax 0161 442 5568
Hrs 9.00 - 6.00 Mon - Sat
Independent bicycle dealer with total commitment to the pleasure and practicality of cycling.

Manchester
The Bike Factory at Manchester Velodrome
Manchester Velodrome, Stuart Street, Manchester M11 4DQ Tel 0161 230 7100
Hrs 9.30 - 5.30 Mon to Sat, 10.00 - 4.00 Sun.
We pride ourselves on good advice and quality service. Try us, you won't be disappointed.

Newark (Nottinghamshire)
Castle Cycles
16 Boar Lane, Newark, Nottinghamshire,NG24 1AJ.
Tel 01636 681168 Fax 01636 681169
Hrs 9.00 - 5.00pm Closed Thurs/Sun
We aim to meet all your cycling needs, all year round!

Norwich (Norfolk)
Specialised Cycles
80 Connaught Road, Norwich, Norfolk, NR2 3BS
Tel/Fax 01603 665668 Email specycle@globalnet.co.uk
Hrs 08,30 - 18,00
Lightweight sales, spares, repairs, wheelbuilding, refinishing, clothing, shoes, Dawes, Bromptons.

Nottingham
Bunneys Bikes
97 Carrington Street, Nottingham NG1 7FE. Tel 0115 947 2713 Fax 0115 956 9525 Email snequest@lineone.co
Hrs 9.00 - 5.30 Mon - Fri 9.00 - 5.00 Sat 11.00 - 3.00 Sun
Good range of bikes for all types of rider. Repair service (we loan out a bike while yours is being repaired). Cycle hire, used bikes, spares and accessories. Collection and delivery service available.

Somerset (Bridgwater)
St John Street Cycles
91/93 St John Street, Bridgwater, Somerset TA6 5HX.
Tel 01278 423 632 Fax 01278 431107
Email sjscycles@dial.pipex.com
Website http://www.sjscycles.com
Hrs Mon-Sat 9-6 Sun 10-4
Probably Europe's largest retail supplier of tandems and audax bikes. Free UK delivery.

Stockport (Cheshire)
L H Brookes Cycles
3 The Boulevard, Hazel Grove, Stockport, Cheshire SK7 5PA Tel 0161 483 2261
Hrs 10-5.30
Well-established dealership, run by enthusiasts. Dedicated to good service.

Stratford upon Avon(Warwickshire)
Pashley
6A Union Street, Stratford upon Avon, CV37 9NL
Tel 01789 297214 Fax 01789 204654
Hrs 9.00 - 6.00 Mon - Sat.
Different by design. Distinctive by nature. Cycles, clothing and lifestyle accessories for all the family.

Surrey (Dorking)
Action Packs
The Booking Hall, Boxhill Station, Westhumble, Surrey RH5 6BT. Tel 01306 886944 Fax 01306 886944
Hrs Thrs - Mon 9.30 - 5.30 Wed 9.30 - 1
Cycle hire, sales, service and accessories. Accessible from London Victoria & M25. Based in the Surrey Hills on A24 near Dorking.

Worcester
Peddlers
46-48 Barbourne Road. Worcester, Worcestershire, WR1 1HV. Tel 01905 24238
Hrs Mon-Sat 09,30 - 18,00 Sun 09,30 - 16,30
Dedicated to enhancing cycling: Moulton and Brompton sales & servicing.

York
Cycle Heaven
2 Bishopthorpe Road, York YO23 1JJ. Tel 01904 651 870
Fax 01904 672 059 Email cycleheaven@enterprise.net
Hrs MTuWF 9-6, Th 10-6, Sat 9-5, Sun 12-5
Featuring Dawes, Scott, Kona, Brompton, and Gazelle. Cycle Heaven is also a Shimano Service Centre.

York
York Cycleworks
14-16 Lawrence Street, York YO1 3BN.
Tel 01904 626 664 Fax 01904 612 356
Hrs Mon-Sat 9-6
York Cycleworks is a worker co-operative. We actively encourage all kinds of cyclists and stock an eclectic cornucopia of cycles.

SCOTLAND

Edinburgh
Bike Trax
13 Lochrin Place, Edinburgh EH3 9QX.
Tel 0131 228 6633 Fax 0131 228 6333
Email 101520,2274@compuserve.com
Hrs 10 - 5.30
A new shop aimed at the leisure and touring cyclist (not racers). Stocking hybrids, tourers, budget mountain bikes, trailers, kids seats, kiddy trailers, and a full repair service.

Glasgow
Gear of Glasgow
19 Gibson Street, Hillhead, Glasgow G12 8NU. Tel/Fax 0141 339 1179 Email j.allan@btinternet.com
Hrs Mon-Sat 10-6
We specialise in mountain bikes and recumbents, now a Shimano Service centre, we have started mountain bike and recumbent tours.

Glasgow
Kinetics
15 Rannoch Drive, Bearsden, Glasgow G61 2JW. Tel/Fax 0141 946 3739 Email ukkinetics@aol.com
Hrs 10.00 - 6.00 Tue - Sun
Folders, recumbents, and trailers. Specialist framebuilding and S & S Torque Couplings.

WALES
Machynlleth (Powys)
Centre for Alternative Technology
CAT Shop, Centre for Alternative Technology, Pantperthog, Machynlleth, Powys, Wales, SY20 9AZ.
Tel 01654 702948 Fax 01654 703409
Email orders@catmailorder.demon.co.uk
Hrs 10am - 5.30 pm Dusk in Winter.
Working demonstrations of alternative technology, 50% Discount off entry to the Centre for cyclists. Selection of books on transport in the shop.

USA
Alaska
The Bicycle Department
Anchorage, Alaska Tel 907 561 1131
This shop sells custom bicycles and alternative forms of transportation, and supports commuter cyclists.

Arizona
Mountain Sports
1800 South Milton St E. 100, Flagstaff, AZ 86001.
Tel 520 779 5156 Toll Free 800 286 5156
Fax 520 774 5509 Email mountain@infomagic.com
Website http://www.mountainsport.com

California
American Cyclery
510 Frederick St., San Francisco, CA 94117.
Tel 415 664 4545 Fax 415 876 4507
Email KimoToguchi@americancyclery.com
Website http://www.americancyclery.com
An historic landmark of San Francisco and West Coast Cycling, specializing in custom, classic and high quality commuting bikes, and offering a unique array of European and American bicycles.

California
Aquarian Bicycles
486 Washington St., Monterey, CA 93940.
Tel 408 375 2144 Fax 408 375 2843
Voted the best bike shop eight years in a row by the county paper, Aquarian specializes in mid- to high-end bicycles, recumbents and tender loving care.

California
Open Air Bicycles
437 W. Channel Islands Blvd., Port Hueneme, CA 93041.
Tel 805 985 5045 Fax 805 984 7123
Email openair12@aol.com
A local store dedicated to keeping cycling fun and carefree on the beautiful south central coast of California

California
Pacific Coast Cycles
2801 Roosevelt, Carlsbad, CA 92008. Tel 760 729 7671
Road, mountain, classic-to-modern, certified wheel building (special purpose and problem solving), ATB experts, knowledge and parts for older bikes, sealed bearings, mountain bike drop bars.

California
People Movers
980 North Main St., Orange, CA 92667. Tel 714 633 3663
Fax 714 633 7890 Email peplemovrs@aol.com
People Movers has been open for five years and regularly adds new and unusual products to their line to meet the unique requirements of their recumbent customers.

California
The Chain Gang Bike Shop
1180 Industrial Street #A, Redding, CA 96002.
Tel 916 223 3400 Fax 916 223 3783
Instrumental in making bicycling a part of its community's history and a recent convert to and advocate of recumbent bicycles.

California
The Missing Link Bicycle Co-op
1988 Shattuck Ave., Berkeley, CA 94704. Tel 510 843 7471 Fax 510 848 5322 Website www.missinglink.org
Set up as workers' co-op. Radical ideas for promoting pedal power. Free repair classes, facilities for doing your own repairs. We both rent and sell bicycles.

California
Wheelsmith
201 Hamilton Ave., Palo Alto, CA 94301. Tel 650 493 8776 ext 12 Fax 650 324 2247 Email ric@wheelsmith.com
Website http://www.wheelsmith.com
Founded by Eric and Jon Hjertberg, Wheelsmith is a different kind of bicycle business. 'Store, workshop, museum' is still our motto 22 years later.

Colorado
American Cyclery
2140 S. Albion, Denver, CO 80222. Tel 303 756 1023
Toll Free 888 236 1941
Started in 1959, everyone in Denver knows Pat, the owner: mountain bikes, road bikes, family-oriented shop. Sales, service.

Colorado
AngleTech Cyclery
318 N. Hwy 67, PO Box 1893 Woodland Park, CO 80863.
Tel 719 687 7475 Toll Free 800 793 3038
Fax 719 687 7475 Email anglezoom@aol.com
Website http://www.bikeroute.com/AngleTech
An alternative cyclist's dream. A full line of recumbents, folding bikes and cycles for special needs. Two hours browse time recommended.

Colorado
The Alpha Bicycle Co
6838 S. Yosemite, Englewood, CO 80112.
Tel 303 220 9799 Fax 303 220 9799
Email elleny@alphabicycle.com
Website http://www.alphabicycle.com

Florida
Fools Crow Cycles & Tours
1046 Commercial Dr., Tallahassee, FL 32310.
Tel 1 805 224 4767 Email edde@freenet.tlh.fl.us
Website http://www.bikeroute.com/FoolsCrowHPV.htm
A user-friendly shop specilizing in recumbents and cool bikes the other guys don't carry.

Florida
Lakeshore Schwinn
2108 Blanding Blvd., Jacksonville, FL 32210.
Tel 904 388 0612 Fax 904 384 7945
An old-style family bike shop. We want to sell you what you want, not what we think you need. If we don't have it, we'll get it.

Georgia
Free Flite
2949 Canton Road., Marietta, GA 30066.
Tel 770 422 5237 Fax 770 422 0912 Email freeflite.com
Operating since 1978, Free Flite has grown to become the area's premier bicycle shop. Dedicated to cycling enthusiasts at your service.

Hawaii
Island Triathlon & Bike
569 Kapahulu Ave., Honolulu, HI 96815.
Tel 808 737 7433 Sales 808 732 7227 Fax 808 737 2399
Email itb@aloha.net
Website http://haleakala.aloha.net/~itb/
A multisport shop staffed by experienced, knowledgeable athletes and sales professionals, serving beginners and pros alike!

Illinois
Rapid Transit
1900 W.North Ave., Chicago, IL 60622.
Tel 773 227 2288 Fax 773 227 2328
Bikes for the year-round urban cyclist. Run by commuter cyclists. Also recumbents (including the ATP Vision) available for test rides.

Maine
Back Bay Bicycle, Inc.
333 Forest Ave., Portland, ME 04101.
Tel 207 773 6906 Fax 207 773 5404

Maryland
Mt Airy Bicycle
4540 Old National Pike, Mt. Airy, MD 21771,
Tel 410 795 2929 Fax 301 831 5877
Website http://www.bike123.com/
Earth's most interesting collection. Virtual museum. All for sale. Vintage/modern. 100 tandems. 50 Recumbents. Rentals. Trades. Long test rides.

Maryland
College Park Bicycle
4360 Knox Rd, College Park, MD 20740. Tel 301 864 2211
Fax 301 831 5877 Website http://www.bike123.com/
Over 800 used bikes for sale, rapid frame repair, same-day wheel building and six types of trailers. Extensive hire service includes recumbents, tandems and folders.

Massachusetts
Lincoln Guide Service
152 Lincoln Rd., Lincoln, MA 01773-0100.
Tel 617 259 1111 Fax 617 259 1722
Everything for the self-propelled: bikes, cross country skis, snow shoes and in-line skates. Ryan and Lightning recumbents. Cycle repair classes.

Michigan
Recumbent Sea
1334 Logan S.E., Grand Rapids, MI 49506.
Tel 616 866 2226 or 616 877 2050 Fax 616 454 4718
Email bikewalla@juno.com
Specializing in affordable recumbents, special needs and other unusual bikes. We are a seasonal shop so call for an appointment.

Minnesota
Calhoun Cycle
1622 West Lake St., Minneapolis, MN 55408. Tel 612 827 8231 Fax 612 926 0719 Email bent4good@aol.com
Calhoun Cycle is Minnesota's premier recumbent dealer. Featuring the largest selction of recumbent bikes and trikes for sale and rent. They are also the worlds largest source for recumbent - specific cycling apparel. Free clothing catalog available on request.

Minnesota
Freewheel Bicycle Co - op
1812 South Sixth St., Minneapolis, MN 55454.
Tel 612 339 2219 Fax 612 339 8268
Email freewheel@freewheelbicycle.com
Website http://www.freewheelbicycle.com
Centrally located within Minnesota's twin cities, we sell new bikes, service any brand, and offer a do-it-yourself workshop for our customers. Repair classes and a thorough parts, accessories and small parts selection.

New Jersey
North East Recumbents
9 Wayland Dr., Verona, NJ 07044. Tel 609 298 6957
Over a dozen different recumbents for sale and rent. Good advice for novices, excellent service and facilities, custom modifications.

Oregon
Citybikes Workers' Cooperative
734 S E Ankeny, Portland, OR 97214. Tel 503 239 6951 or 503 239 0553
A worker-owned cooperative aimed at making bike-riding and commuting easily accessible. Specializing in 3-speeds, trailers and upright commuter bikes.

Oregon
Eugene Bicycle Works / C A T
455 West 1st Ave, Eugene, OR 97401. Tel 541 683 3397
Fax 541 686 1015 Email cat@efn.org
The CAT believes that bicycles are essential tools for modern civilization and builds, sells and rents utilitarian bicycles, cargo bikes, heavy-duty work trailers, recumbents and adult tricycles.

Pennsylvania
Jay's Pedal Power Bikes
512 E. Girard Ave., Philadelphia, PA 19125.
Tel 215 425 5111 Fax 215 426 2653
Jay's is a professional shop with 20 years experience and a large selection of components and parts. Electric bikes, tandems, recumbents and folding bikes. Largest selection of bikes in Philadelphia. Will ship globally.

Tennessee
Mt. Moriah Bicycle Co, Inc.
5715 Mt. Moriah, Memphis, TN 38115. Tel 901 795 4343
Fax 901 795 4310 Email mtmoriah1@aol.com
Oldest continuous Schwinn dealership in the world. Triathlon and other high-end cycles. Many 'alternative' bikes, including recumbents and portables.

Texas
Freewheeling Bicycles
2401 San Gabriel, Austin TX 78705.
Tel 512 477 6846 Fax 512 478 3733
A caring, professional service, and a fine choice of cycles and accessories. Good advice for novices.

Utah
Avalon Recumbents
465 S. 1250 East Pleasant Grove, UT 84062.
Tel 801 785 1461 Fax 801 785 2994
Specializing in recumbents and hard-to-find bikes, handcycles, special needs bikes and trikes, trailers and folding bikes. Bikes for hire, too.

Washington
Elliott Bay Bicycles
2116 Western Ave., Seattle, WA 98121.
Tel 206 441 8144 Fax 206 441 1815
Home of the Davidson line of handbuilt bicycles. A wealth of experience in racing, international touring and custom design.

Washington
The Bikesmith
2309 N. 45th, Seattle, WA 98103. Tel 206 632 3102
Speciality: whatever no one else does. Bike and parts – vintage to modern, new, used and reconditioned. Custom jobs welcomed.

Washington, D.C.
City Bikes
2501 Champlain St., N W Washington, D.C. 20009. Tel 202 265 1564 Fax 202 462 7020 Website www.citybikes.com
Supports bicycling as THE transportation alternative. Bikes, gear, parking, etc. Everything you need to ride. Declare your auto-nomy – ride a bike!

Wisconsin
Yellow Jersey
419 State St., Madison, WI 53703. Tel 608 257 4737
Office 608 257 4818 Fax 608 257 5161
Email yellowje@execpc.com
Website http://www.execpc.com/yellowje
Full service since 1971. Machining, frame service, eclectic bits, custom fabrication/modification. Real touring bikes, internal gearboxes, roadsters, Dynohubs, too!

Wyoming
Dr. Spokes Cyclery & Museum
240 South Center, Casper, WY 82601-2524.
Tel 307 265 7740 Fax 307 265 7740
Buy-Sell-Trade antique bicycles, tricycles, pedal cars, related advertising samples and curios. Restoration work done. Carries new line of Harley Davidson Bicycles.

Manufacturers and agents

Alex Moulton Ltd: *Moulton New Series*
Holt Road, Bradford on Avon, Wiltshire, BA15 1AH, UK Tel +44 1225 865895 Fax +44 1225 864742
ambikes@alexmoulton.co.uk
www.alexmoulton.co.uk

Alligt Ligfietsen: *Kleine Fiets*
Vogelplein 46, 5212 VK Den Bosch, Netherlands
Tel +31 3173 6911 388 Fax +31 3173 6911 387

Animal Bikes: *Swift*
Redlands Farm, Station Road, Longstanton, Cambridge, CB4 5DS, UK
Tel +44 1954 261557
richard.loke@analysys.co.uk
www.animalbikes.com

ARES Group: *Karbyk*
via Guglielmo Marconi n. 18, 33010 Reana del Royale (UD), Italy
Tel +39 0338 290 6629 Fax +39 0432 857 504
www.karbyk.com
Germany: Extreme Sign Sportmarketing, Poststr. 1, 38440 Wolfsburg. Tel 05361 24546
Fax 05361 25421

Arved Klütz Spezialräder: *Toxy*
Stubbenhuk 4, 25225 Elmshorn, Germany
Tel +49 4127 92284 Fax +49 4127 92283

Babybike Nederland bv: *Babybike*
Postbus 372, 1400 AJ Bussum, Netherlands
Tel +31 35 695 1908 Fax +31 35 695 1908
babybike@tip.nl

Bike Hod All Terrain Trailers: *Bike-Hod*
2 Middle Way, Lewes, Sussex, BN7 1NH, UK
Tel +44 1273 480479 Fax +44 1273 480479
bike-hod@pavilion.co.uk
Europe: Zwei plus zwei, see separate entry

BikeE Corp: *BikeE AT*
5460 SW Philomath Blvd, Corvallis, OR 97333-1039, USA
Tel +1 541 7539 747 Fax +1 541 7538 004
bikeevol@aol.com www.bikee.com
Austria: B.I.E.R. Fahrrad-Studio, A-2500 Baden. Tel 02252 47690
Australia: Reynard Enterprises, Victoria.
Tel 03 542 61633
Canada: Call BikeE for details of 15 dealers
UK: UK Recumbent Distribution, PO Box 192, Patchway, Bristol BS32 0YG. Tel 0870 7878 736
Fax 0870 7878 739
Email 101520.1005@compuserve.com
BikeFix, London. Tel 01432 2524 7690;
Valley Cycles, Wellingborough, England.
Tel 01933 271 030
Germany: Velopedes OHG, D-4939 Flensburg
Japan: BikeE Japan, Aomori 035. Tel 0175-24-4636
Switzerland: Haso's Velo Laden. Tel 411 937 4330

Bishopthorpe Bikes: *Dwarf Safety*
Mike West, 35 Keble Park North, Bishopthorpe, York, YO23 2SX, UK
Tel +44 1904 703 413

BKTech AG: *Flyer*
Industrie Neuhof 9, 3422 Kirchberg, Switzerland.
Tel +41 34 448 60 60 Fax +41 34 448 60 61
bktech@bluewin.ch www.bktech.ch

Blømson International bv: *Maurizio*
A. Hofmannweg 28, 2031 BL, Haarlem, Netherlands
Tel +31 23542 2044 Fax +31 23542 2044
blomson@wxs.nl

BOB Trailers: *YAK 16 & Coz*
3641 Sacramento Dr. #3, San Luis Obispo, CA 93401, USA
Tel +1 805 541 2554 Fax +1 805 543 8464
bob@bobtrailers.com www.bobtrailers.com
Australia: St. Kilda Cycles, 11 Carlise Street, St. Kilda 3182. Tel +61 3 534 3074 Fax +61 3 534 3045
Austria: Zwei plus zwei (see Germany) or B.I.E.R. Fahrradstudio, Jägerhausgasse 20, A-2500 Baden.
Tel +43 2252 47690 Fax +43 2252 47690
Email fahrradstudio@gmx.net
www.spinnst.co.at/fahrradstudio/
Holland / Benelux: Vertex Cycle Systems, Flemingstraat 100A, 2041 VL Zandvoort.
Tel +31 23 571 81 84 Fax +31 23 571 86 06
Email vertex@wxs.nl
Canada: BELL Sports Canada, Inc., Cycletech Division, 700 Chemin Bernard, C.P. 11000, Granby, Quebec, Calgary J2G 9H7. Tel +1 800 661 1662
Fax +1 513 378 9934
Denmark: A. Winther A/S, Rygesmindevej 2, DK 8653 Them.
Tel +45 86 84 7288 Fax +45 86 84 8528
Finland: Monark Stiga OY, PO Box 116, 01721 Vantaa. Tel +358 9 849 40 20
Fax + 358 9 853 23 97
France: Riteway Products France, Avenue du Gal de Gaulle, 54280 Seichamps.
Tel +33 3 83 33 81 50 Fax +33 3 83 20 61 61
Germany: Zwei plus zwei Marketing GmbH, Bismarckstrasse 56-62, 50672 Cologne.
Tel +49 221 95 14 70 0 Fax +49 221 95 14 70 20
Email zweiplus@aol.com
Italy: RaceWare Srl, Piazza GAribaldi 18, 17024 Finale Ligure (SV). Tel +39 19 680639
Fax +39 19 680638
Email raceware@sv.infocomm.it
Japan: Fun Fancy Co., 1551 Kishiwada, Kadoma-shi, Osaka-fu 571. Tel +81 720 85 6562
Fax +81 720 85 6556
New Zealand: Cycle Works, P.O. Box 33051, Christchurch. Tel +643 338 6803
Fax +643 338 6231
Email d_whit00@tpnet.co.nz
Norway: DBS Racing Depot, Elvegt 11, N-4300 Sandnes. Tel +47 51 66 35 81 Fax +47 51 66 03 38
Portugal: tn tao natural, Murtais, 8700 Moncarapacho. Tel +351 89 79 29 67
Fax +351 89 79 29 09
Sweden: Monark Crescent AB, Birger Svenssonvag 28, S-43282 Varberg. Tel +46 34 08 60 00
Fax +46 34 08 74 63
Switzerland: Vitelli Velo-Bedarf AG, Dornacherstr. 101, CH-4053 Basel. Tel + 61 361 57 70
United Kingdom: Caratti Sport Limited, 1180 Aztec West, Bristol BS12 4SJ. Tel +44 1454 201 700 x 24
Fax +44 1454 202 577

Brilliant Bicycles/Pashley Cycles: *Two's Company, U+1, U+2*
17a Bridge Street, Berwick-upon-Tweed, Northumberland, TD15 1ES, UK
Tel +44 1289 331 476 Fax +44 1289 302 345
enquiries@brilliantbicycles.co.uk
www.brilliantbicycles.co.uk

Brompton Bicycle Ltd: *Brompton*
Kew Bridge Distribution Centre, Lionel Rd, Brentford, Middlesex, TW8 9QR, UK
Tel +44 181 232 8484 Fax +44 181 232 8181
Australia: Stratum, PO Box 7933, Cairns, QLD 4870, Tel +61 41 241 6607, Fax +61 41 221 6628
Canada: City Bikes, 28 Oakwood N. Unit 2, Mississauga, Ontario, L5G 3L7,
Tel +1 905 274 3387, Fax +1 416 251 1841
Denmark: Preben Pedersen, Sminge Cykler, Sortenborgvej 7, DK-8600 Silkeborg. Tel 8680 0411
Fax 8682 8622
Eire: Cycle Ways, 185-186 Parnell Street, Dublin 1, Tel +3531 873 4748, Fax +3531 872 9462
Finland: OY Mollhausen AB, Gustav Wasas gata 4, Fin-10600 Ekenas, Tel +358 19 2411 394,
Fax +358 19 2411 391
France: Ste Antema, 17 Place Jean Jaures, 37110 Chateau Renault, Tel +334 7605 3535,
Fax +334 7605 6000
Germany: Voss Spezial-Rad GmbH, D-25524 Itzehoe-Ebendorf, Tulpenweg 2. Tel 04821 78023
Fax 04821 41014
Netherlands & Belgium: Fiets A Parts, Gantel 2, 8032 BR Zwolle, Holland, Tel +31 38 455 1580,
Fax +31 38 455 1685
Norway: Bjerva Marketing, Grefsen alle 10, 0488 Oslo, Tel +47 2215 9924, Fax +47 2272 3011
Sweden: Awimex International AB, Box 11, S-27221 Simrishamn, Tel +46 4141 6050,
Fax +46 4141 6555
Switzerland: Diverso, Grossitz, 6372 Ennetmoos, Tel +41 4161 07126, Fax +41 4161 21170
USA: CM Wasson Co, 423 Chaucer St., Palo Alto, CA 94301-2202. Tel 415 321 0808 Fax 415 321 8375

Brüggli: *Leggero Classico*
Hofstr. 3+5, CH-8590 Romanshorn 1, Switzerland
Tel +41 71 466 9494 Fax +41 71 466 9495
info@brueggli.ch www.brueggli.ch
Europe: Zwei plus zwei, see separate entry.

Bürkle: *Die Radfabrik: Rikscha*
Rösleinweg 10, 75334 Straubenhardt, Germany
Tel +49 7082 50106 Fax +49 7082 50106

Burley Design Cooperative: *Burley-Cub*
4020 Stewart Road, Eugene, OR 97402, USA
Tel +1 541 687 1644 Fax +1 541 687 0436
burley@burleybike.com www.burley.com
Chile: Echard Bike Centre, Santiago. Tel 2 219 1477
Colombia: Dicode, Ltd, Medellin. Tel 3054 7762
Denmark: DCF, Copenhagen Tel +45 33 32 0121
Finland: Mt-bike, Joensun. Tel 73 224 891 or Velosport ky, Helsinki Tel 9 757 1377
Germany: Centurion Renner KG, Magstadt.
Tel 07159 9459 30
Holland: Better Bikes Holland, Utrecht.
Tel 302 315 780
Italy: Sebastiano Rech Morassutti, Milano.
Tel 02 349 5783
Norway: G-Sport Futura, Kristiansund
Tel 7167 1792 or Sykkeldelisk, Oslo, Tel 2241 5080 or Syklistenes Landsforening, Oslo, Tel 2241 5080
Switzerland: Haso's Velo-Laden, Hinwil, Zurich
Tel 1937 4330
UK & Eire: UK Trailer, Wadebridge, Cornwall
Tel 01208 815 715
USA/Canada: Call Burley 800 311 5294 for details of Burley dealers nationwide.

Bykaboose International: *Bykaboose*
466 Central Avenue, Suite 37, Northfield, IL 60093, USA
Tel +1 847 441 9163 Fax +1 847 441 9167
chip@bykaboose.com www.bykaboose.com
Contact Bykaboose in the USA for details of agents. Latest details also appear on their website.

Carradice of Nelson Ltd: *Bike Bureau*
Westmoreland Works, St Mary's Street, Nelson, BB9 7BA, UK
Tel +44 1282 615886 Fax +44 1282 602329
Denmark: DCF, Copenhagen Tel +45 33 32 0121
Germany: Rasko, Tel 0241 533 006
Fax 0241 557 350

Challenge b.v. Ligfietsen: *Hurricane Luxe & Wizard*
Anklaarseweg 35-37, Apeldoorn, 7316 MB, Netherlands
Tel +31 55 521 2405 Fax +31 55 521 3173
www.ligfiets.net/challenge
Belgium: de ligfiets, Lange Violettestraat 217, 9000 Gent. Tel +32 9 223 44 96
Fax +32 9 223 44 96
Denmark: Hurricane Denmark, Ribergaardsvej 1, 4894 Xster Ulslev. Tel +45 5386 53 29 Fax +45 5487 66 26 email vodder@image.dk
Germany: Mikus Fahrradladen, Am Stein 5, 65391 Lorch. Tel +49 6775 1763 Fax +49 6775 1763
UK: UK Recumbent Distribution, PO Box 192, Patchway, Bristol BS32 0YG. Tel 0870 7878 736
Fax 0870 7878 739 Email
101520.1005@compuserve.com

Chariot Carriers Inc: *Chauffeur CTS*
Bay F, 6810-6th St. SE, Calgary, Alberta T2H, Canada
Tel +1 403 640 0822 Fax +1 403 640 0749
www.chariotcarriers.com
Europe: Zwei plus zwei, see separate entry

Christiania Bikes: *Christiania Trike*
Dammegardsvej 22, DK-3782 Klemensker, Denmark
Tel +45 56966700 Fax +45 56966708
Germany: Christiania Bikes, Köpernicker Str 8b, D-1000 Berlin 36. Tel 030 6188015 Fax 6113697 or Räderwerk, Calenberger Str. 50, D-30169 Hannover.
Tel 0511 717174 Fax 0511 715151 or Zwei plus zwei: Bismarkstr. 56-62, D-50672 Köln.
Tel 0221 9514700 Fax 0221 95147020.
Holland: Christiania Bikes, Christiania Import, Boslaan 10, 7875 AR Exloo. Tel/Fax 0591 549539
Sweden: Bra Indredningar, Fältvägen 1a, 44331 Lerum, Sweden
UK: Andrea Casalotti, ZERO, 66 Rossmore Court, Park Road, London, NW1 6XY. Tel 0171 723 2409

Comfort Cycle: *Chaise 3*
1422 Euclid Ave, Suite 872, Cleveland, OH 44115, USA
Tel +1 216 475 6100 Fax +1 216 475 1033
Website www.comfortcycle.com

Cool Breeze UK Ltd: *Prone Low-profile*
194 Upper Street, Islington, London, N1 1RQ, UK
Tel +44 171 704 9273 Fax +44 171 354 9641

Dahon: *Speed*
833 Meridian Street, Irwindale, CA 91010, USA
Tel +1 626 305 5264 Fax +1 626 305 9153
dahon@ficnet.net www.dahon.com
For details of agents in other countries, contact Dahon in the USA.

De Vogel: *Kid Car Komfort & Cocoon*
Postbus 567, Drachten 9200 AN, Netherlands
Tel +31 561 441615 Fax +31 561 441 731
Europe: Zwei plus zwei: see separate entry.

Deuxjon Trailers: *Deuxjon*
78 Craven Avenue, Plymouth, PL4 8SW, UK
Tel +44 1752 253638

Dynosys AG: *LightSPIN*
Haupstr. 104, CH-9422 Staad, Switzerland
Tel +41 62 827 4828 Fax +41 62 827 4829
info@dynosys-ag.ch www.dynosys-ag.ch

EGS: *Synchro-Shift*
1 Rue Nungesser et Coli, BP 476, Chatellerault cedex, F-86104, France
Tel +33 549 20 22 10 Fax +33 549 85 35 42
info@e-g-s.com www.e-g-s.com
Australia: Narrow Margin, 39 Harris St, Peddington, NSW 202. gfrancal@club-internet.fr
Belgium: Codagex, Meistraat 3, B-2480 Dessel.
jeffrey@e-g-s.com
Canada: Cycles Lambert, 100 rues des Riveurs, Levis, Quebec, G6V 7H5. caro@e-g-s.com
France: Philamy, 1384 Parc Ind, St Maurice, 04100 Manosque. renaud@e-g-s.com
Germany: Sport Import, 26188 Edexecht.
jeffrey@e-g-s.com
Holland: Codagex, Meistraat 3, b-2480 Dessel.
jeffrey@e-g-s.com
Hong Kong, Philippines, Thailand: Sports Connexion, 1505 Car Po Building, 18-20 Lyndhurst Terrace Central, Hong Kong.
gfrancal@club-internet.fr
Italy: Motorquality, Via Venezia 2, 20099 Sesto, S.Giovanni (Mi). renaud@e-g-s.com
Japan: Link Inc, 8-2-37 Kitamikunigaoka-cho, Sakai Shi, Osaka-fu 590. gfrancal@club-internet.fr
South Africa: Supersport Cycle (Pty) Ltd, PO Box 1811, Houghton, 2041, Johannesburg.
renaud@e-g-s.com
UK: Raleigh Industries Limited, Triumph Road, Nottingham, NG2 2DD. jeffrey@e-g-s.com

Flevobike: *Fifty Fifty*
De Morinel 55, 8251 HT Dronten, Netherlands
Tel +31 321 337 200 Fax +31 321 337 201
flevobike@wxs.nl www.ligfiets.net/flevobike/

Florian Schlumpf Spezialmaschinenbau: *Mountain Drive*
Dorfstr. 10, CH-7324 Vilters, Switzerland
Tel +41 817238009 Fax +41 817238364
schlumpf_ing@bluewin.ch www.schlumpf.ch

Flux: *V-200*
Kreutzbreitlstr. 8, D-82194 Gröbenzell, Germany
Tel +49 8142 53180 Fax +49 8142 53180

Gazelle: *see Koninklijke Gazelle BV*

Greenspeed: *Greenspeed Suitcase Trike*
69 Mountain Gate Drive, Ferntree Gully, Vic 3156, Australia
Tel +61 3 9758 5541 Fax +61 3 9752 4115
ian@greenspeed.com.au
www.greenspeed.com.au
Europe: HP Velotechnik, Goethestr. 5, 65830 Kriftel, Germany.
Tel +49 6192 410 10 Fax +49 6192 910 218

H Power Corp.: *Hydrogen fuel cell*
60 Montgomery Street Belleville, NJ 07109, USA
Tel +1 973 450 4400 Fax +1 973 450 9850
moreinfo@hpower.com www.hpower.com

Hase Spezialräder: *KettWiesel*
Karl-Friedrich-Str. 88, 44795 Bochum, Germany
Tel +49 234 9469050 Fax +49 234 9469099
www.t-online.de/home/Hase.Bochum

Heydenreich Präzisionstechnik: *Heylight Atlas*
Glonnerstr. 8, 85667 Oberpframmern, Germany
Tel +49 8093 1077 Fax +49 8093 2589

Hjordt Specialcykler: *Banana Trike*
Granstein 4, 5700 Svendborg, Denmark
Tel +45 62 226231 Fax +45 62 226239

Hubert Meyer GmbH: *Culty*
Herderstr. 29, D-72762 Reutlingen, Germany
Tel +49 177 277 7592 Fax +49 7121 204 085
culty@liegerad.com

Hydro-Bike, Inc.: *Hydro-Bike Explorer*
PO Box 889, Wyoming 55092, USA
Tel 001 612 462 2212 Fax 001 612 462 1752
http://www.hydrobikes.com/

Germany: Victor GmbH, Halbmond 8, 21481 Lauenburg, Germany. Tel 0049 4153 52 323 Fax 0049 4153 51048
There are agents in many other countries: contact Hydro-Bike in the USA for details.

Invacare Top End: *Excelerator XLT*
Action Top End, 4501 63rd Circle North, Pinellas Park, Florida 33781, USA
Tel +1 727 522 8677 Fax +1 727 522 1007
info@invacare.com http://www.invacare.com
Australia: Invacare Australia Pty. Ltd., 126 Greville Street, Chatswood, N.S.W. 2067, Tel +61 2 9904 8011 Fax +61 2 9904 8022
Canada: Invacare Canada Inc, 5970 Chedworth Way, Mississauga, Ontario, L5R 3T9. Tel +1 905 890 8838 Fax +1 905 890 5244
France/European HQ: Invacare International, Les Roches, 37230 Fondettes, France. Tel +33 2 4762 6491 Fax +33 2 4762 6488
Germany: Invacare Deutschland GmbH, Dehmer Strasse 66, 32549 Bad Oeynhausen. Tel +49 5731 754 0 Fax +49 5731 754 150
Netherlands: Invacare Nederland, Fokkerstraat 36, 3905KV Veenendaal. Tel +31 318 550 056 Fax +31 318 555 054
New Zealand: Invacare New Zealand, 7 Wagener Place, St Lukes, Auckland. Tel +64 9 849 5141 Fax +64 9 849 8236
Portugal: Invacare Portugal LDA, R. Senhora de Campanaha, 105, 4300 Porto. Tel +351 2 510 59 46/47 Fax +351 2 510 57 39
Spain: Rehadap SA, c/ Areny s/n, Poligon Industrial de Celrà, 17460 Celrà (Girona). Tel +34 972 493200 Fax +34 972 493220
Sweden: Invacare AB, Slalgatan 20, 163 53 Spaanga. Tel +46 8 621 1267 Fax +46 8 761 2041
Switzerland: Küschall Design AG, Ringstrasse 15, 4123 Allschwil. Tel +41 61 481 5666 Fax +41 61 481 5240
UK: Invacare UK Ltd, South Road, Bridgend Industrial Estate, Bridgend, Mid Glamorgan, CF31 3PY. Tel +44 1656 664 321 Fax +44 1656 667 532

Kemper Fahrradtechnik: *Filibus*
Rheinweg 70A, 41812 Erkelinz Grambusch, Germany
Tel +49 2431 77017 Fax +49 2431 980 672
Netherlands: 't mannetje, Frans Halsstraat 26A, 1072 BR Amsterdam. Tel +31 20 6792 139 Fax +31 20 471 5217

Koninklijke Gazelle BV: *Furore*
Postbus 1, 6950 AA Dieren, Netherlands
Tel +31 313 429 911 Fax +31 313 422 558
info@gazelle.nl www.gazelle.nl

Kool Stop International Inc: *Koolite Trailer & Stroller Pack*
1061 S. Cypress Street, La Habra, CA 90632, USA
Tel +1 714 738 4971 Fax +1 714 992 6191
www.koolstop.com
Holland: Third Wave Carriers bv, Zuidermolenweg 20, 1069 CG Amsterdam. Tel +31 2 0610 7033 Fax +31 2 0610 7099

Kunst & Leder: *Toony Saddles*
Galerie "Allerhand", Turnitzstr. 29, D-91522 Ansbach, Germany
Tel +49 981 957 67 Fax T/F +49 9826 9446
Alternative contact: Stephanie Rothemund, Esbacherstr.2, D-91746 Weidenbach. Tel/Fax +49 9826 9446

Liegerad Münster GmbH: *Radius Hornet II*
Borkstr. 20, D-45163 Münster, Germany
Tel +49 251 747 5146 Fax +49 251 747 5149
mail@radius-liegeraeder.de
www.radius-liegeraeder.de

LW Composite GmbH: *Tripendo*
Industriestraße, 35683 Dillenburg, Germany
Tel +49 2771 392 492 Fax +49 2771 392 489
LW-Composite@tripendo.com www.tripendo.com

Nicator s.c.: *Picnic*
Biuro Handlowe, Lokal Nr 308, ul. Ostrobramska 101, 04041 Warszawa, Poland.
Tel. +48 22 673 6043 Fax +48 22 673 6069
nicator@supermedia.pl
www.nicator.supermedia.pl
Germany: UBA GmbH, Eilter Dorstrasse 47, 29693 Ahlden Tel/Fax +5164 909647
UK & Eire: AIM Plastics Group Ltd, North Farm Rd, Tunbridge Wells, Kent, TN2 3DY Tel +44 1892 515544 Fax +44 1892 514354

Ortlieb Sportartikel GmbH: *Ortlieb Panniers*
Rainstr. 6, 91560 Heilsbronn, Germany
Tel +49 9872 8000 Fax +49 9872 800266
info@ortlieb.de www.ortlieb.de
Australia: Nomad Travel Equipment, P.O.Box 859, Leichhardt, NSW, 2040. Tel +61 2 9564 6988 Fax +61 2 9564 0935
Austria: Techno-Trade Guni GmbH, Wiesenstr. 71, A-4601 Wels. Tel +43 7242 60407 Fax +43 7242 60407 7
Belgium: Singing Rock N.V. Outdoor Equipment, Lodistraat 123, B-8020 Hertsberge. Tel +32 508 27101 Fax +32 508 27 089
Canada: NRG Enterprises Ltd, 715 Vernon St., CAN-Nelson, B.C V1L 4G3. Tel +1 604 352 2099 Fax +1 604 352 2038
Finland: North-West Import, Särkikuja 4, FIN-02170 Espoo. Tel +358 9 4523226 Fax +358 9 426714
France: V.M. Sports s.a.r.l., 3, Route de Vovray, F-74005 Annecy Cedex. Tel: +33 450 45 0095 Fax +33 450 45 5713
Germany: dealer hotline: +49 9872 8000
Italy: V.M. Sports, Ferrino & C.S.p.A.L, C.SO Lombardia 73-Autoporto Pesc, I-10099 San Mauro (To). Tel +39 11 2230 711 Fax +39 11 2230 700
Japan: (outdoor range): MT.Dax Co. Inc., 22-15, Nishimizumoto, 6-chome, J-Katsushika-ku, Tokyo. Tel +81 3 3608 8441 Fax +81 3 3600 7371
Japan: (bike range): PR International Inc., EBS Bldg. 8F, 6-27, Marunouchi 3-chome, J-Naga-ku, Nagoya, 460. Tel: +81 52 774 8756 Fax +81 52 774 6726
Netherlands: Singing Rock N.V. Outdoor Equipment, Lodistraat 123, B-8020 Hertsberge. Tel +32 508 27101 Fax +32 508 27 089
New Zealand: Outsider, 946 Lower Styx Road, NZL - Christchurch. Tel +64 3 329 8604 Fax +64 3329 8605
Norway: Ute Depot a.s., Ute Telwest, Kvennhusvn 1, Tjurrufabrikken, N-7460 Røros. Tel +47 7241 1255 Fax +47 7241 1257 Mobile +47 918 10344
Sweden: Svima-Sport, Box 30034, S-10425 Stockholm. Tel +46 8 730 1310 Fax +46 8 276 992
Switzerland: Exped AG, Hardstr. 81, CH-8004 Zürich. Tel +41 1 497 1010 Fax +41 1 497 1011
Spain: Vertical Sports, Pere IV, 29-35, 3er 1a, E-08018 Barcelona. Tel +34 3 309 1091 Fax +34 3 485 0949
UK and Ireland: Lyon Equipment Ltd., Rise Hill Mill, Dent Sedbergh, LA10 5QL Cumbria. Tel +44 1539 625 493 Fax +44 1539 625 454
USA: Ortlieb-USA, 140220th. St. N.W. Suite 7, Auburn, WA 98001 Tel +1 253 833 3939 Fax +1 253 833 4559

Paris Maderna GmbH: *Maderna City Scooter*
Zeltgasse 12, A-1080 Vienna, Austria
Tel +43 140 30158 Fax +43 140 301584
maderna-city-scooter@netway.at

Pashley Cycles: *PDQ*
Masons Road, Stratford-Upon-Avon, Warwickshire, CV37 9NL, UK
Tel +44 1789 292263 Fax +44 1789 414201
info@pashley.co.uk www.pashley.co.uk

Radical Design: *Radical bags & Cyclone trailer*
Hoofdstraat 8, 9514 BE Gasselternijveen, Netherlands
Tel +31 599 513 482 Fax +31 599 513 482
http://www.ligfiets.net/radicaldesign/
UK: UK Recumbent Distribution, PO Box 192, Patchway, Bristol BS32 0YG. Tel 0870 7878 736 Fax 0870 7878 739
Email 101520.1005@compuserve.com
Germany: Mikus Fahrradladen, Am Stein 5, D-65391 Lorch. Tel/Fax 06775-1763

Reiko: *Transport Bike*
Postfach 2112, 33251 Gütersloh, Germany
Tel +49 5241 33 77 77 Fax +49 5241 33 77 99

Rideable Bicycle Replicas: *Mobilis*
2329 Eagle Avenue, Alameda, California 94501, USA
Tel +1 925 769 0980 Fax +1 925 521 7145
mbarron@barrongroup.com www.hiwheel.com

riese & müller: *Birdy, Culture/Avenue/Delite*
Erbacher Str. 123, D-64287 Darmstadt, Germany
Tel +49 6151 424034 Fax +49 6151 424036
team@r-m.de www.r-m.de
Switzerland: Cortebike, Sur le Crêt 6, CH-2606 Corgémont. Tel 032 972 414 Fax 032 972 428
USA: Burley Design Cooperative, 4020 Steward Rd, Eugene, OR 97402, USA. Tel +1 541 687 1644 Fax +1 541 687 0436 Email burley@burley.com Website http://www.burley.com

Robert Hoening Spezialfahrzeuge: *Rollfiets, Copilot, T-Bikes*
Ulmer Straße 16/2, D-71229 Leonberg, Germany
Tel +49 7152 43046 Fax +49 7152 73589
Denmark: H. Meyland-Smith APS, Käthe Brondum, Industrievej 27, DK-9830 Tars. Tel +45 98 961 985 Fax +45 98 961 986
Holland: Freewiel Techniek BV, Sander van Dooren, Koperslager 3, NL-5521 DE Eersel. Tel +31 497 514757 Fax +31 497515124
Norway: MEDEMA, Peter Nelson, Sven Oftedalsvei 2-8, N-0903 Oslo. Tel +47 22 168190 Fax +47 22 168100
Switzerland: B&M Mobility Systems GmbH, Fischermättelistr. 18, CH-3008 Bern. Tel +47 31 376 0001 Fax +47 31 376 0005
UK & Eire: Pashley Cycles, Mason's Road, Stratford-upon-Avon, Warwickshire, CV37 9NL, UK Tel: +44 1789 292 263 Fax: +44 1789 414 201
USA, Canada: Frank Mobility Systems Tel 412 695 2122 Fax 412 695 2922

Rohloff GmbH: *Speedhub 500/14*
Mönchebergstr. 30, 34125 Kassel, Germany
Tel +49 561 87 5615 Fax +49 561 87 5338
service@rohloff.de http://www.rohloff.de
Austria: Fun Bike, Norbert Katsch, Salzachweg 1, A-5061 Salzburg-Elsbethen, Tel +43 662-636 2450 Fax +43 662 636 2455
Canada: Cycles Lambert, Inc., 1000, Rue des Riveurs, CDN-Lévis, Québec, G6V 7M5, Tel +1 418 835 1685 Fax +1 418 835 5322
Canada: NRG Enterprises, Bruce Gardave, 715 Vernon Street, Nelson BC, Canada VIL 4G3, Tel +1 250 352 2099 Fax +1 250 352 2038
Denmark: bike toyz, Alan Wolk, Hjortensgade 3A, DK-8000 Arhus C. Tel +45 86 12 59 31 Fax +45 86 12 59 32
Finland: MT Bike, Ulla Miettinnen, Koulukatu 40, SF-80100 Joensuu, Tel +358 13 22 48 91 Fax +358 13 22 48 92
France: Philamy SA, Derrick Coetzer, 1384 Pl. St. Maurice, F-04100 Manosque, Tel +33 4 92 70 97 00 Fax +33 4 92 72 60 70
Great Britain: Ison Distribution, Lloyd Townsend, 307 Millroad, GB-Cambridge CB1 3DF, Tel +44 1223 21 3800 Fax +44 1223 56 8361
Hungary: Lenkei Bike Components Bl., Peter Lenkei, Kevehàza u. 11, H-1119 Budapest, Tel +36 1 204 2045 Fax +36 1 204 2045
Italy: LARM SpA, Via Cadell'Orbo, 36(BO), I-40055 Villanova di Castenaso, Tel +39 51 605 3460 Fax +39 51 605 3411
Netherlands: Vertex Cycle Systems BV, Flemingstraat 100 A, NL-2041 VL Zandvoort, Tel +31 2357 18 184 Fax +31 2357 18 606
New Zealand: Composite Cycles NZ Ltd, Graham & Lynda Sisson, 42 Quarantine Rd., Nelson, NZ, Tel +64 3 547 8386 Fax +64 3 547 8388
Norway: Sportscompagniet AS, Ole-Andreas Petersen, Tollbugata 14, N-3044 Drammen, Tel +47 32 89 2250 Fax +47 32 89 2272
Poland: Bike-Program, Radek Wozniak, ul. Dabrowskiego 1B/3, PL-66300 Miedzyrzecz, Tel +48 61 47 3265 Fax +48 61 51 8612
South Africa: Bruce Reyneke Cycles C.C., Bruce Reyneke, 275 Lynnwood Road, RSA-Pretoria, Tel +27 12 362 1628 Fax +27 12 362 1630
Switzerland: Intercycle, Stefan Küng, Industriegebiet, CH-6210 Sursee (Switzerland), Tel +41 41 926 6511 Fax +41 41 926 6352
USA: ROHLOFF Inc., USA, Thomas Siemann, 1327 Richmond Street, USA - El Cerrito, CA 94530, Tel +1 510 232 4833 Fax +1 510 527 6650

Roland Plastics Ltd: *Strida 2*
Wickham Market, Suffolk, IP12 0QZ, UK
Tel +44 1728 747 777 Fax +44 1728 748222
strida@rolandplastics.co.uk
www.rolandplastics.co.uk/plastics/strida.htm

Schauff GmbH: *Andalusia Disc*
Postfach 1669, D-53406 Remagen/Rhein, Germany
Tel +49 2642 93640 Fax +49 2642 3358
schauff@aol.com www.schauff.com

SIC: *Cloud 9 Stems*
811 Russell Avenue, Suite J, Gaithersburg, MD 20879, USA
Tel +1 301 527 2337 Fax +1 301 527 6370
sicdesign@aol.com

Sinner Ligfietsen: *Comfort*
Walkumaweg 6, 9923 PK Garsthuizen, Netherlands
Tel +31 595 464 318 Fax +31 595 464 271
sinner@sinner.demon.nl www.sinner.demon.nl

Spinskins: *Spinskins*
Warwick Mills, 301Turnpike Road, New Ipswich, NH 03071, USA
Tel +1 603 878 1565 Fax +1 603 878 4306
spinskins@aol.com www.SpinSkins.com

SMARTWHEELS Corp.: *Smartwheels*
60 Prescott St., Worcester, MA. 01605, USA
Tel +1 508 7913200 Fax +1 508 791 6886
smartwheels@earthlink.net
www.smartwheel.com

SRAM: *Gripshift*
Try your local bike shop.
Website www.sram.com
Global headquarters: Tel +1 312 664 8800 Fax +1 312 664 8826.
European headquarters: Tel +31 33 450 6060 Fax +31 33 457 0200

St John Street Cycles: *Me'n'u2*
91/93 St John Street, Bridgwater, Somerset, TA6 5HX, UK
Tel +44 1278 423632 Fax +44 1278 431107
sjscycles@dial.pipex.com www.sjscycles.com

Staller Studio: *Octos*
Herengracht 100, 1015 BS Amsterdam, Netherlands
Tel +31 20 624 9198 Fax +31 20 624 9198
urbanufo@euronet.nl

sTRAKa sPORTs: *Ciro*
Niebuhrstrasse 62, D-10629 Berlin, Germany
Tel +49 30 3270 1616 Fax +49 30 3270 1617
strx@berlin.snafu.de
http://ourworld.compuserve.com/homepages/ciro_roller

Tactic Bike Company: *Panache*
263 Goldhurst Terrace, London, NW6 3EP, UK
Tel +44 171 624 6268 Fax +44 171 813 2890
www.tacticbike.com
Contact Tactic for details of distributors.

The Seat of the Pants Company: *Pickup & Burrows Windcheetah*
L&M Business Park, Norman Road, Altrincham, WA14 4ES, UK
Tel +44 161 928 5575 Fax +44 161 928 5585
bobdixon@seatofpants.u-net.com
www.windcheetah.co.uk

tm-design GmbH: *CMK*
Itterstr. 35, 42719 Solingen, Germany
Tel +49 212 2331447 Fax +49 212 2331448
tm-design@t-online.de

Treadle Cycles Inc: *Step 'n Go Cycles*
6 Linden Terrace, Burlington, VT 05401 4928, USA
Tel +1 800 648 7335 Fax +1 802 864 6156
stepngo@together.net www.stepngo.com

Tretauto GmbH: *Zampano*
Westenriederstr. 41, D-80331 München, Germany.
Tel +49 89 2904121 Fax +49 89 22802773

Utopia: *Nirorad*
Kreisstr. 134f, 66128 Saarbrücken, Germany
Tel +49 681 970 360 Fax +49 681 970 3611
utopia@saarmail.de www.utopia-fahrrad.de

Velocity Engineering AG: *Dolphin*
Burgweg 15, CH-4058 Basel, Switzerland
Tel +41 61 693 4358 Fax +41 61 693 4332
velocity@swissonline.ch www.velocity.ch

Veloladen Liegeräder: *Velvet Scooterbike & Velvet Quix*
Dolman Strasse 20, 51427 Bergisch-Gladbach, Germany
Tel +49 2204 61075 Fax +49 2204 61076
velvet@veloladen.com www.veloladen.com

Vitelli: *Touring*
Dornacherstr. 101, CH-4053 Basel, Switzerland
Tel +41 61 361 7070 Fax +41 61 361 5770
Europe: Zwei plus zwei, see separate entry.

VK International: *VK Strongbox*
Vliegerstraat 2, 6005 PR Weert NL, Netherlands
Tel +31 495 545 050 Fax +31 495 546 017

Voss Spezial-Rad GmbH: *Turnaround*
Tulpenweg 2, D-25524 Itzehoe-Eden, Germany
Tel +49 4821 41409 Fax +49 4821 41014
Voss-Spezialrad@t-online.de

Waterford Precision Cycles: *2200*
814 W Bakke Ave, Waterford, WI 53185, USA
Tel +1 414 534 4190 Fax +1 414 534 4194
www.waterfordbikes.com

Weber Werkzeugbau: *Ritchie*
Königstr. 25, D-83254 Breitbrunn, Germany
Tel +49 8054 7544 Fax +49 8054 1234
Europe: Zwei plus zwei, see separate entry

ZAP Power Systems: *Z Bike and Zappy*
117 Morris St., Sebastopol, CA 95472, USA
Tel +1 707 824 4150 Fax +1 707 824 4159
zap@zapbikes.com www.zapbikes.com
Europe: ZAP Europe, XtraMOBIL AG, Schlössli im Laubi, CH-8193 Eglisau, Switzerland. Tel +41 1867 1525 Fax +41 1867 1406

Zwei plus zwei: *Bernds folder & Blacky trailer*
Bismarckstr. 56-62, 50672 Köln, Germany
Tel +49 221 9514700 Fax +49 221 95147020
zweiplus@aol.com
UK: Two plus two UK, PO Box 2607, Lewes, E Sussex BN7 1DH, UK. Tel/Fax +44 1273 480479 Mobile +44 403 649 408
Email bike-hod@pavilion.co.uk

Zweirad und Zukunft: *Horizont-top*
Fahrradkulturwerkstatt in Altona e.V, Gaußstraße 19, 22765 Hamburg, Germany
Tel +49 40 395 285 Fax +49 40 390 3221

Index